Assembly
by Design

Buell Center Books in the History and Theory of American Architecture

Reinhold Martin, Series Editor

The Temple Hoyne Buell Center for the Study of American Architecture at Columbia University was founded in 1982. Its mission is to advance the interdisciplinary study of American architecture, urbanism, and landscape.

The Temple Hoyne
Buell Center
for the Study of
American Architecture

Assembly by Design

The United Nations and Its Global Interior

Olga Touloumi

University of Minnesota Press
Minneapolis
London

Open access edition funded by the National Endowment for the Humanities.

Published by the University of Minnesota Press
111 Third Avenue South, Suite 290
Minneapolis, MN 55401–2520
http://www.upress.umn.edu

ISBN 978-1-5179-1332-8 (hc)
ISBN 978-1-5179-1333-5 (pb)

Available as a Manifold edition at manifold.umn.edu

A Cataloging-in-Publication record for this book is available from the Library of Congress.

Printed in the United States of America on acid-free paper

The University of Minnesota is an equal-opportunity educator and employer.

33 32 31 30 29 28 27 26 25 24   10 9 8 7 6 5 4 3 2 1

For Konstantinos Touloumis and Effrosini Touloumi,
my parents

Contents

Abbreviations

ABC	American Broadcasting Company
AIA	The American Institute of Architects
BBC	British Broadcasting Corporation
BBN	Bolt, Beranek, and Newman
CBC	Canadian Broadcasting Corporation
CBS	Columbia Broadcasting System
CIAM	Congrès Internationaux d'Architecture Moderne (International Congresses of Modern Architecture)
CPA	Community Projects Administration
DPI	Department of Public Information
EAL	Electro-Acoustic Laboratory, Harvard University
ECA	Economic Commission for Africa
ECAFE	Economic and Social Commission for Asia and the Far East
ECE	Economic Commission for Europe
ECLA	Economic Commission for Latin America
ECLAC	Economic Commission for Latin America and the Caribbean
ECOSOC	Economic and Social Council
ESCWA	Economic and Social Commission for Western Asia
FAO	Food and Agriculture Organization
HTCP	Housing and Town and Country Planning
ICTY	International Criminal Tribunal for the former Yugoslavia
IFTCP	International Federation for Town and Country Planning
ILO	International Labor Organization
MoMA	Museum of Modern Art, New York
NBC	National Broadcasting Company
NDRC	National Defense Research Committee
OSRD	Office of Scientific Research and Development
OSS	Office of Strategic Services
PAL	Psycho-Acoustic Laboratory, Harvard University

RKO	Radio-Keith-Orpheum Pictures
SOM	Skidmore, Owings & Merrill
TAA	Technical Assistance Administration
UN	United Nations
UNESCO	United Nations Educational, Scientific, and Cultural Organization
UNIO	United Nations Information Organization
UNRRA	United Nations Relief and Rehabilitation Administration
UNWCC	United Nations War Crimes Commission
WHO	World Health Organization

Introduction
The Global Interior

On November 29, 2017, Slobodan Praljak, a Bosnian Croat general who served in the Croatian army, stood in Courtroom One before the United Nations judges for his adjudication on war crimes during the Yugoslav Wars. His verdict was the fourth in the collective appeal that concluded the International Criminal Tribunal for the former Yugoslavia (ICTY), a criminal court established by the United Nations Security Council twenty-four years earlier. Rising from the defense side, against juridical protocol, Praljak uttered in Croatian: "Slobodan Praljak is not a war criminal! I reject your judgment with contempt."[1] He then gulped down a potion in what seemed to be a suicide attempt. Considering it dramatics, the judge continued with the process, but a voice interrupted to confirm that Praljak had indeed taken poison. In the highly mediated environment of the Tribunal courtroom, where interpreters and screens organized the judicial landscape, judges and clerks froze in bewilderment. Confusion ensued, aggravated by surprise and bureaucracy, until the judge brought an end to the commotion, dropping the proverbial (and literal) curtain on the unfolding drama. Praljak was rushed to the hospital, where he died. We know what happened because recording cameras and broadcast infrastructure made us privy to this unscripted spectacle of malfunctioning judicial process.

A freelance theater, television, and film director, Praljak had courtroom theatrics figured out.[2] ICTY, admittedly with some hesitation, had agreed to televise (and later stream) the hearings for an international audience, turning the courtroom into a stage and classroom at the same time. The architecture of the courtroom itself arranged clerks, judges, attorneys, and witnesses in a tight judicial scheme, with a raised bench for the judges at the top; defense and prosecution facing each other in a symmetrical yet antagonistic configuration; and, behind glass galleries, the public and press wired into the interpretation system of the courtroom.[3] All constituents had clearly demarcated places in the judicial social landscape, and audiences around the world would see that. Laura Kurgan calls Courtroom One a recording, legal, and broadcasting architecture for good reasons.[4] This was a new breed of governing space—at once international, open, and public but also closed off, controlled, and insulated. Monitors and cameras transmitted the court's sanctions to global audiences watching from the comfort of their homes. Addressing the cameras meant addressing a global polity residing both inside and outside the courtroom.

I call this new public space the "global interior." This type of space emerges from early twentieth-century efforts to house multilateral organizations of institutional internationalism that solidified in form and structure during the construction of the United Nations Headquarters. Global interiors invited architects, diplomats, and engineers to reimagine the site of politics and representation beyond national narratives. At the same time, these spaces differ from other forms of public interiors in that they aim to place issues of global concern in front of an international polity. As interiors that purport to include all, these spaces actively construe multilateral organizations as "home" to member states. Echoing turn-of-the-century metaphors that the U.S. Department of the Interior had pioneered to consolidate control over occupied territories and their peoples, namely addressing its interior as "home" and domestic affairs as "housekeeping," the UN presented these global interiors as a new home, this time for the world that they would bring and keep in order, albeit through international relations.[5]

In this book I investigate the emergence of global interiors in the series of platforms and forums that the United Nations launched, initially for its constitutive conferences and events, and later for its subsidiaries. These forums stand in for a much larger system of global management, a vast bureaucratic organization hard to comprehend in its entirety. Only its stages—the General Assembly, the Councils, and occasionally the worm's-eye views of the Secretariat Tower—make it to the screens, print media, and imaginations of audiences around the world. There, architects organize and structure in space the global polity, instilling hierarchies and coordinating the place of the general public.

These global interiors circulate around the world as meaningful representations of international relations, ultimately becoming the message and medium of liberal internationalism—roughly defined as the effort to anchor the ideological core of the post-1945 world order in liberal values that also guide institutional, military, or humanitarian interventions around the world. Architecture framed the experience of internationalism but also defined the symbolic order of globality. In this sense, architects shaped ideas about the nature of international organizations and the new global democratic world order while establishing models of public space that international institutions would later follow.

Historians and scholars of internationalism have decidedly situated the UN within a historical shift from an imperial to an institutional organization of the world. Anti-colonial visions of self-determination and global society notwithstanding, they demonstrate that the UN posited the nation-state as the organizing unit for global diplomacy and political representation.[6] Yet this fragmentation of the world into nation-states came hand in hand with the emergence of new global institutions to manage international affairs and commerce, as well as a new understanding of communications (formerly a colonial enterprise) as the structural component of a liberal world order. Communication was the metaphorical and concrete architecture on which the UN's multilateralism depended and that allowed the organization to function as an organism.

The networked structure of institutional internationalism, I claim, rested on the tactical use of global interiors that created an idealized fiction of egalitarian and collaborative diplomatic practices at the United Nations, even when the operational reality on the ground pointed to power asymmetries. These public interiors served as teaching tools for people around the world who were too far away to visit and see the UN at work for themselves. Media carried the public mission of the international institution beyond its physical headquarters and offered metaphorical windows onto the organization. Historical studies have unearthed the discussions and ideas that framed this institution, but we have yet to comprehend how the material culture of the UN and its sister institutions set the stage of appearances. Architecture organized publics and bodies, but also media, making the UN legible to the remote publics outside its Headquarters. We can think of the UN's architecture as another tool of legibility that nation-states and international organizations put to work.

Moving beyond establishing and analyzing the architectural value of the UN Headquarters, my goal here is to place the emergence of global interiors within a conversation of the "imaginary institution" of a world community.[7] Cornelius Castoriadis argues that societies come into being and exist in relationship to the "world of signification" they establish. Unlike the Foucauldian institution that governs through exercising power, Castoriadis's institution organizes the systems of interpretation that define and legitimize each society: language, history, government, and techniques. These acts of signification make societies legible. "Society as such is a form, and each given society is a particular, even a singular, form. Form entails organization, in other words, order (or, if you wish, order/disorder)," he declares. To Castoriadis, the forms through which a society manifests embody a "social imaginary," a "creation," a new "type" of social organization that internally decides what constitutes "old," "disorder," and "noise" within its system of interpretation. He proclaims that society-making is fundamentally an act of form-creation and explains that within this world of forms, myths and imagination "vest meaning" both to the world of signification that a society institutes and to its life within that world.[8] Castoriadis's claims allow us to examine within these new public forms the social imaginary and the world of signification that architects and diplomats mobilized to produce the myth that bestowed meaning on the new world order and its practices. A thorough examination of the lines of labor and expertise behind global interiors connects the UN Headquarters with sites of management, military research, and communications theories. When analyzed as a set of meaningful forms through which global institutions sought to make legible the new world order, the UN Headquarters opens windows onto the mode of production of liberal internationalism and its material reality, but also onto how architecture globalized new systems of management and organization.

The United Nations in the History of Architecture

The UN Headquarters is a building that we think we know intimately, although we do not. Looking over the East River, the UN Headquarters spans from Forty-Second to Forty-Eighth Streets in eastern Manhattan, right on Turtle Bay—a site that used to house slaughterhouses, cattle pens, and coal yards. It was a "dead end in the traffic sense, and a dead end to life itself," as a journalist described the area in 1947.[9] Organized along the north-south axis, the complex presents Manhattan with the Secretariat glass slab towering over the General Assembly that bends under the weight of its own dome, an image highly circulated via postcards, stamps, films, and other UN paraphernalia (Figure I.1). Inside, council chambers, meeting halls, and lobbies anchor the ever-busy floors of the Headquarters and center the institution's multilateralism on round tables and podiums in front of UN emblems, modernist design, and the abstract materiality of wood, marble, and glass. Every fall we get glimpses of the General Assembly when footage of speakers or delegates in the auditorium circulates on broadcast news. At times, heated debates garner the Assembly more airtime, or a particularly contested Security Council meeting might give us a bird's-eye view of the room, but this is where our imagination ends (Figure I.2). We never get to see the full room, with its architecture of subject positioning, or the connections the design forges among its constituents in its off-camera sites of active diplomatic work. Our view of the Headquarters, although seemingly intimate, is decidedly fragmented and partial.

There are reasons for this misconception of the building as a familiar object. A series of well-illustrated publications during its fiftieth anniversary celebrated the UN Headquarters as an iconic example of modern architecture produced in the intersection of a real estate transaction between William Zeckendorf and Nelson Rockefeller, and Le Corbusier's architectural rivalry with Oscar Niemeyer.[10] Around the same time, Wallace K. Harrison's right hand, George A. Dudley, published his own detailed record of the architectural conversations, accompanied by drawings, minutes, and other print matter—a historical record that nonetheless puts the weight of the discussion on the four months of architectural debate that took place in 1947.[11] In monographs, architectural historians have carefully articulated the individual contributions of member architects, focusing on the role

Figure I.1. Exterior view of the Secretariat and the General Assembly Building, 1952. Courtesy of the United Nations Photo Library.

that the UN Headquarters played in the development of architectural modernism.[12] Still, those accounts hesitate to contextualize the building within a social and political framework that critically encounters the institution vis-à-vis the era of decolonization and multilateralism.

Architectural historians, initially in response to feminist critiques, have been moving beyond a focus on professionalized actors, widening the scope of who counts as architect.[13] Building on these criticisms, *Assembly by Design* examines the interdisciplinary nature of the enterprise, thus challenging the artificial construction of the UN Headquarters' history around a handful of architect-protagonists.

Figure I.2. Interior view of the Assembly Hall during the first meeting of the United Nations General Assembly in the organization's permanent headquarters, 1952. Courtesy of the United Nations Photo Library.

I approach architecture as a discursively formed field and the territory of political contestation. Apart from designers, the architects of the UN include engineers, diplomats, midlevel bureaucrats, administrative assistants, librarians, and manufacturers. I understand those professionals as constituting interacting ecologies of expertise, architects in their own right who determined the cultures of assembly, the place of media, and the overall material culture of international relations.

The UN Headquarters has often been incorporated in theories of modernist evolution articulated in exhibitions and books. In the 1952 edition of *Built in USA,* for instance, Philip Johnson and Henry-Russell Hitchcock added the UN Secretariat to their list of prime examples of American corporate architecture.[14] In 1968, Reyner Banham used the UN Headquarters to theorize architecture as systems of environmental control, a conversation that Alexandra Quantrill and Joseph Siry have critically revisited since.[15] And again in 1978, Rem Koolhaas called for us to think of the complex as a "utopian fragment" that concludes what, he argued, was an era of urban development and experiment unique to

Manhattan.[16] An exception here is Ada Louise Huxtable, who treated the Headquarters as an imperfect variant of modern architecture, declaring it a work-in-progress with its unfinished ceilings and colliding aesthetics of infrastructures, sculptural balconies, and dramatic staircases.[17] But what happens when we situate and examine the UN Headquarters from the perspective of the network of global institutions and the fields of power that produced it, as well as the aspirations and resistances that shaped the project of liberal internationalism? How does this shift in perspective change the stories we tell about the building and the lineages of architectures of internationalism?

Architectural history survey books place the UN Headquarters firmly within a canon of modern architecture in North America and Western Europe, but not without criticism.[18] Either to illustrate corporate architecture in the United States or to exemplify the failures of architectural modernism in the post-1945 period, these accounts reiterate two major critiques issued against the building at the time of its completion: the first, by Lewis Mumford, declared the complex a "disoriented symbol" of "corporate America,"[19] and the second, by Sigfried Giedion, dismissed the complex as altogether unoriginal.[20] It is true that the United Nations was conceived as a bureaucracy on a global scale, and the diplomats and functionaries involved in its making rarely shied away from this managerial reality. Along the same lines, originality was never part of the vocabulary essential to the building and the organization. In fact, skepticism toward avant-gardism and its associations with political radicalism drove many of the decisions that handed Wallace K. Harrison supervisory control of the project. Building on those criticisms, architectural discourse has systematically interrogated the Secretariat Tower, at times conflating it with the entirety of the UN Headquarters. Here I am attempting a revision of the disciplinary framework, contextualizing those criticisms rather than building on them, and recovering the rest of the built reality of the UN Headquarters and its significance for the liberal order it came to serve.

Urban historians have interrogated the impact that the United Nations Headquarters had on New York City, displacing industries and reorganizing the waterfront while opening the path for urban renewal. Charlene Mires elucidates the potential that the project carried for real estate markets across the United States, documenting how municipalities and states competed to host the new organization. She demonstrates that architects, planners, and politicians all entered the planning for the UN Headquarters with different intentions and agendas, in the process shaping and refining ideas around the role that the physical headquarters would play for both the organization and the hosting cities.[21] But having an impact on an urban scale—which the UN undoubtedly ended up having—does not necessarily mean that this is what the organization's architects and diplomats had in mind. Quite to the contrary, I argue, the UN Headquarters was a building ultimately designed from the inside out.

To discuss the UN Headquarters, we also need to address the spatial histories and politics of diplomacy. Historians have explored in detail diplomatic architectures produced for the political economies of national contexts.[22] Jane Loeffler, for example, shows how the U.S. State Department developed a complicated building program of embassy architecture for cultural imperialism, embedding U.S. intelligence and administration across the world.[23] She explains that these architectures, reflecting shifts in foreign policy and diplomatic agendas, moved away from purportedly open configurations in space to embrace highly controlled and closed space typologies. But multilateral institutions require a move beyond questions of national representation, especially if one is to address the political and aesthetic challenge of internationalism within a broadening multimodal world, where nations constituted only the modular parts of a larger system of diplomacy.

Declarations of the complex as a monument or a symbol of peace, often delivered by diplomats and politicians to the press, speak to the incentives but fail to register the gap between ideals and realization. I maintain that these debates inadvertently produced a new kind of monumentality centered on infrastructures of work and circulation rather than symbolic forms. Underway was a hesitation toward monumental scale and a desire for a space to present diplomacy as grounded and democratic.

My story shares intellectual and structural affinities with architectural histories of bureaucracies and corporations, although it covers an entirely different organization, the United Nations.[24] More than spaces of governance, these public interiors reflected a profound belief in the capacity of management and organization theories to figure out systems of world order, ultimately harnessing new technologies of communication to implement them. Histories of development, environmentalism, immigration, and reconstruction demonstrate the entanglements of the organization with policy, planning, and the control and management of technical knowledge, arguing that the international institution's power and value lies as much in paper as in stone.[25] Yet, maybe with the exception of Lucia Allais's interrogation of UNESCO's architectural form and the corridor politics of cultural diplomacy, we have yet to understand and convey how the Headquarters' architecture and spatial politics participated in shaping the UN's organization mechanism at work. To do so, I interrogate the tactics of institutional internationalism vis-à-vis the cultures of assembly and governance that architectural and spatial decisions helped implement on the ground.

Diplomatic Interiors and the Public Sphere

This book delves into design histories of diplomatic interiors and the political power they frame. Interiors order power and relationships, governing through the organization of life and political representation. Design scholars and historians, who research partnerships between designers and governments, speak of the "political agency" of objects and their capacity to articulate meaning.[26] Others show how politicians and diplomats used design as a backdrop to ideological debates over social organization.[27] And others illustrate how interior design and furniture acted as agents of foreign policy to steer publics away from communism, practicing what Joseph Nye calls the "soft power" of culture.[28] More recently, Iris Moon has noted the political significance of interiors vis-à-vis "imperial ideology." Bringing attention to Napoleonic interiors, Moon argues that interior design historically allowed empires to claim sovereignty and power even with limited resources.[29] When employed in the service of colonial powers, she states, interiors install images of sovereignty and models of government, even if there is no building to enclose them, as was the case in the famous Napoleonic tent (an icon of nomadic life that Muammar Gaddafi mobilized from the grounds of Donald Trump's estate to antagonize the 2009 UN General Assembly and its diplomacy).[30] This book takes up this conception of the interior as an agent of political power to examine how it served (and articulated) liberal internationalism in global institutions.

The UN deployed global interiors to produce and reproduce its institutional approach to liberal internationalism. Although a public space in its constitution, the United Nations Headquarters purported to make a "home" for this new global polity. This mashing up of the private and public sphere might initially appear as an anomaly to the liberal order that institutes itself on the separation of the two.[31] But maybe it is not, particularly since the global interior, although presenting itself as a public sphere, lacks the political capacity to reinforce its own resolutions. In this sense it is a space that reproduces, for the most part, the orders and hegemonies that shape it, even when they shift.

Social histories and histories of science implicate interiors with architectures of power deployed in laboratories, courtrooms, and prisons.[32] These accounts remind us that interiors have not only been the domain of home economics, but also of state power. Behind that spatial research lies the specter of Michel Foucault, who in his own study of knowledge and power used those spaces and the way they organized bodies as hermeneutic tools to examine apparatuses of social control and their shifting paradigms. My book builds on this articulation of interiors as political sites of power sanctioning, at the same time that it departs from the Foucauldian model to argue for the representational value of global forums as media through which the UN constructs and circulates certain forms of social organization endemic to the institution's operational logic.

Peter Sloterdijk places interiors at the center of capitalist development, which he argues started with the colonization of the Americas. Sloterdijk claims that interiors are a symptom of and a tool for capitalism's expansion. It is through interiors that the "most effective totalization" took place; he points to the spheres of the self, the traveling pods (and cultures) of settler colonialism, and the stadiums and assembly halls of the new mass public.[33] Sloterdijk's interior is a means to resolve the paradox of a global assembly. He maintains that a democratic "world interior" is an oxymoron, since the world constitutes a "non-assemblable entity" that cannot gather in one place. Therefore, he says, democratic governance can only be organized in parts, as a system of subordinate structures. "One can observe that everything has a capacity for congress," he asserts, "except for the whole," which for him is the hallmark of the tragedy of the social in an era of globalized markets.[34] The UN interiors similarly promise expansion of the organization's publics while struggling with the desire to engage the world. This was a drive and conundrum that mobilized architectural decisions even when architects ended up delivering the world only as a denotative representation.

At the same time, I complicate previous readings of the post-1945 condition as the "closed world" or the "inner world" to explain that the exclusionary forces at play were predicated upon a promise and an invitation to engage, albeit remotely, with world affairs.[35] The Headquarters framed the political activity of the United Nations, but also endowed the organization with metaphors of transparency and equity on a global scale even while concealing liberal political and economic forces installing new asymmetries in the background.

Most importantly, diplomats and bureaucrats used UN interiors to bring a global polity within the mechanisms of liberal internationalism, an effort to create an international public around U.S. ideas about democratic structures. World War II and the masses-as-publics of the Third Reich forced thinkers, politicians, and sociologists of the time to rethink public life. Fred Turner notes that these conversations had started in the United States among a group of anthropologists, educators, designers, and artists who, taken aback by the success of Adolf Hitler's indoctrination, set out to research modes of cultivating the "democratic" persona and its attributes.[36] Explorations of how publics form and transform proliferated in postwar political theory. In *The Human Condition* Hannah Arendt theorized the public realm as the space of politics-making, constituted by its separation from the domestic sphere, although dependent upon it.[37] Just three years later, Jürgen Habermas described "the public sphere" as the spaces (theaters, coffee shops, and so on) and media (newspapers, books) where the emerging bourgeoisie addressed public concerns despite and at times antagonistically to the state.[38] According to this genealogy of political thinking, the formation of publics entails (and is entangled with) certain spatial configurations of the social.[39]

Rather than disregarding UN interiors as solely vestiges of institutional power—which they also are—I approach those spaces as platforms for speech acts and moments of articulation within the aggregation of systems and networks that constitute the UN. The ultimate goal is to demonstrate that, during the building of the UN (both the institution and the actual Headquarters) interiors constituted critical nodes that structured key functions of the new world order, while allowing counter-alliances to form and claim the stage, bringing about new systems for producing international publics.

Of Media Infrastructures and World Orders

Media and communications infrastructures feature centrally in architectural figurations of the global interior, tethering the interior to the exterior world. When deliberations over the UN's organizational structure pivoted toward a centralized institution with an expansive reach, diplomatic discourse introduced communications as both the metaphor and structuring principle to network institutions and people beyond national borders and regions. Channels of communication connected the main organs within the UN, as well as the organization with its specialized agencies, member states, local publics, and international institutions outside the UN frame.

This idea of communications-as-structure is not new. In his field-defining *Empire and Communications* (1950), political economist and media scholar Harold Innis held that empires and media coarticulate one another.[40] Communication systems built around cod, timber, and fur in Canada, he noted, defined the operational characteristics of empire and established hegemonies.[41] Media histories, emboldened by calls to unearth the longer historical and material processes that frame the emergence of media, have been pinpointing communications' continuous entanglement with colonial politics.[42] Winseck and Pike, in particular, demonstrate how communications infrastructures such as postal and telegraph services enabled colonial strategies that tied metropoles with peripheries in administrative and economic ways.[43] In her research on telecommunications networks, Starosielski locates the foundation of Internet infrastructures back in the imperial routes that forged the way for an initially telephonic and later fiberoptic flow of information.[44] Borrowing from the colonial playbook, I argue, the UN established itself through communications systems, with architecture feeding this sprawling system moments of ordering representation and coherence.

The United Nations communications infrastructures and its logic had also been epistemologically grounded in military techniques and practices. Media scholars have been describing the ways in which applications and theories developed during World War II formed the epistemological basis that transformed not only information theory and computer science, but also how scientists understood language and communications writ large. Lisa Parks implicates military technology in the development of a global communications systems and the production of the world citizen as "remotely present" and "globally mobile."[45] The UN's infrastructures of communication did not develop outside this military-industrial complex, but rather within, with UN bureaucrats actively seeking military advice on information systems, transfusing military knowhow into the UN's modalities of engaging and organizing publics for peace.

Military ideas also informed conversations on governance and social structures, most notably in the immediate aftermath of Norbert Wiener's publications and the Macy Conferences. Sociologist and cybernetician Karl Deutsch, who spent a good amount of his career studying political structures, urged political theorists and sociologists to approach the question of government not so much as "a problem of power," but rather as "a problem of steering" and a "matter of communication."[46] Governments, as historians of science show, deployed similar ideas about communication and control to organize administrative and executive branches of government, transforming technocratic states across Europe and North America.[47] This idea of governing as steering, I argue, was fundamental to the imaginary constitution of the UN, allowing bureaucrats to plan the new organization as simultaneously an organism and a communications technology.

Information—its production, management, and circulation—has been and remains at the core of the UN's mission. The UN's communications apparatus builds on earlier twentieth-century information science pioneers—Patrick Geddes, Otto Neurath, and Paul Otlet—and their globalist attempts to create a universal system for the storage and circulation of information.[48] The introduction of standards and regulation that this unification of the sciences resulted in has been dwelled upon in the history of science and technology.[49] These accounts demonstrate how an internationalist imperative, promulgated by expanding global markets, shaped the media and techniques whose universality we take for granted, installing rational structures that connect scientists and laboratories across institutional and national boundaries. Tools, media techniques, and standards, often embedded within local contexts, not only coordinated but also ordered a global knowledge production. Think here of the Dewey library classification system, or artificial languages and standardized measurement units.[50] Building on those interrogations of the media of internationalism, this book explores how the architecture of global interiors shaped the rules of engagement and exchange in multilateral institutions.

Until recently, international institutions and organizations stood outside the scope of media studies, with scholars tentatively addressing them as sites of implementation and carriers of media practices and techniques developed elsewhere. Jonas Brendebach, Martin Herzer, and Heidi Tworek broke this pattern to open up an important conversation on the intersection of media and international institutions.[51] They argue that debates over communications and their techniques shaped the diplomatic imaginary, especially as international institutions were adopting a functionalist approach that targeted shared interests and problems to connect states within structured systems.[52] They note that international institutions steered media to massage public opinion at a time when their existence and operational success depended on it. Just a few years earlier, during the 1939–40 New York World's Fair, panoramic interiors used media to create the "world of tomorrow" as a spectacle. By 1945, desires for rational and effective structures of communication emerged to organize the political spaces of appearance and their representations. This book expands this work to show that the design of the global interior at the UN sought to shape public opinion as much as the news circulating the organization's expansive—and unstable—media infrastructure, schematizing for the public the image of postwar institutional multilateralism.

Reckoning with media and publics in the age of globalization, sociologists have been pointing to the networked form that the globalized public sphere has been acquiring, directly connecting global polities with communications theories.[53] Manuel Castells, whose work on *The Network Society* brought him inside the UN, professed that the emergence of a global civil society and a network state require a "communication space" for global diplomacy, where "a new, common language could emerge as a precondition for diplomacy, so that when the time for diplomacy comes, it reflects not only interests and power making but also meaning and sharing."[54] Joining Castells, Danielle Allen deemed the older spatial metaphors of the "public sphere" inadequate frameworks for analyzing the dynamic systems of communication behind polities.[55] Yet, this book claims that, even in their aspiration to launch an ever-expanding and interconnected system of institutions, UN bureaucrats anchored those networks in the very physical space of global interiors. Those interiors defined the "communication space" the organization enabled at its core, ultimately spatializing before liquefying international publics.

Another way of addressing these UN platforms would be to examine them as "mediascapes," horizontal structures that organize and are organized by media. Mediascapes, Appadurai explains, enable "global cultural flows." They are situated and relational; they are messy outcomes of a complex set of institutional, corporate, and multinational actors. By bringing together infrastructures and representations, he notes, mediascapes create "the image of the world," with all their disjuncture, contradictions, and situatedness.[56] Thinking of the UN Headquarters as a "mediascape" brings attention to the media institution of global governance, but also to the nodal and organizational function that the architecture of those public interiors played. The architecture of those global interiors, I argue, not only organized media in space, but—with media in mind—delivered a critical representation of world organization and its publics of multilateralism as a coherent and graspable reality at work, rather than an abstract figment of imagination. This was a meaningful representation that also held the organization—an otherwise disparate and waggling body of agencies and organs—together. In that sense, the UN Headquarters and its global interiors participate as nodes within a much larger mediascape they aspire to create. These global interiors deliver a "structuring structure" for world order and for political representation.[57]

To produce the UN mediascape, diplomats and architects turned to broadcast and film studios. These studios offered palpable solutions to the programmatic and typological problem that the UN Headquarters presented. Lynn Spigel, Brian Jacobson, and other media scholars have discussed how studio architecture—either for television or film—created imaginaries by concealing the labor, service, and infrastructure supporting whatever is taking place on stage.[58] Broadcast studios taught the architects planning the Headquarters, I hold, how to introduce the hierarchies necessary in the production of images of world order without compromising calls to phenomenal transparency and political integrity. Studying the translation of those broadcast and recording architectures allows us to unpack the theatrical politics and logics of spectatorship embedded within the UN interiors, as well as the audience cultures they cultivated.

At the same time, media within those platforms, I claim, did not only structure the public sphere visually, but also acoustically. Kate Lacey demonstrates that listening is formative, if not constitutive of publics. Media technologies such as the radio and the phonograph historically transformed the terms of participation in public life, essentially producing "listening publics."[59] Extending Lacey's view on listening practices and public formation to the spaces of the United Nations points to the role that acoustics played in the institution of the international public sphere.

Not all acoustic spaces, however, are the same. Nor are they all driven by the same political imperatives. Exploring how the Third Reich deployed acoustic strategies for propaganda, Carolyn Birdsall poignantly identifies the totalitarian implications of the centralized and amplified soundscapes of Nazi Party rallies in Germany.[60] These soundscapes often form the historical past against which new soundscapes emerge. A case in point is Fred Turner's historical account of the "democratic surround," where he shows how, in response to the apprehended fear of totalitarianism, U.S. educational and cultural institutions did away with centralized configurations and master narratives, producing multimedia and multifocal environments for museums and galleries. Those attempts at a "democratic surround" fed individuated experiences and celebrated subjective interpretation and synthesis of information.[61] The UN was not an exception to the democratic imperative. In fact, UN engineers and architects similarly conceived the soundscape of global interiors as a response and an antithesis to the totalitarian soundscapes of the Third Reich, often being particularly wary of the political economies that high reverberation rates evoked.

These spaces differed from the concert halls and theaters that Emily Thompson and others examine in histories of modern architectural acoustics in North America and Europe. Rather than being built for music and its diffusion throughout space, the UN's global interiors aimed to transmit intelligibly and clearly the spoken word at the podium or the table.[62] Debate and assembly required a thorough yet different consideration of sound in terms of communication and transmission. These were (and still are), after all, sites where conversations, debates, and filibusters happened against the environmental noise of the infrastructure that supported them: air-conditioning systems, typewriters, and the noise of the city. Architects and designers spatialized these acoustic relationships, defining who enunciates and who listens, but they also used this language of amplification and transmission to imagine the UN as a broadcast architecture.[63]

International in their constitution, the UN's global interiors posed in addition the problem of language. Unlike national public spheres that often use a single official language, the UN's global interiors required a system to organize its multilingual diplomatic landscape in ways that ensured communication. The utopia that the UN aimed to be was telephonic. Simultaneous interpretation systems, often tying delegates to interpreters with a telephonic network, constitute an essential element of the global interior. I examine how these telephonic publics, stratified and complex as they were, transformed the UN fora. So apart from visual literacy, I argue, we need an acoustemological approach to understand the politics behind the design of the voice of the world.[64]

Situating Communications

I approach the UN spaces of diplomacy and international relations as indexical sites that embed and represent the organization's politics while also informing them. My goal is to interrogate the coproduction of the organization and its sites while studying how architecture imagined the space of global organization and assembly, ultimately shaping cultures of multilateralism in their temporary and permanent sites. I use "sites" as a hermeneutic tool that opens architectural inquiry to the social structures and cultural forms intertwined with the making of those spaces. Unlike buildings, sites can be closed or open, feature buildings or appear empty, be enveloped by architectural form or encounter it.[65] International affairs and global diplomacy happen in situ, even when this involves two strangers holding a telephone conversation from their offices within an embassy. Site analysis brings forth both the historical depth of the forms of political assembly mobilized and the breadth of epistemic cultures that were invited to order them. The diplomats and architects who worked at the site, as well as the engineers and bureaucrats, carried with them their own imaginary constructions of governmental structures, internationalist significations, and representations of universality that ultimately found their way into the form of the building. Hence, my job here is to examine how these conversations arrived and were woven into the site of global governance so as to understand the relationships that the United Nations hoped to implement and how these are different from or similar to the representations that were communicated to the public.

Pierre Bourdieu urges us to closely examine how social systems inhabit space. Through the study of the spatial configuration of power and hierarchy, he argues, we can gain insights into social stratifications at play, as well as the distribution of resources and power that enforce them.[66] In this sense space is a sort of sociological evidence. Yet built structures also determine in a way how power and publics form. Narratives that focus on professional actors say more about the social construction of value in modern architecture and its historiography, and less about how a massive international institution used its headquarters and media to come into being. To understand the headquarters as a site of liberal internationalism is to examine the practices that structured it, but also the ones it aspired to shape. Although the primary focus of this book remains the UN, the framework is expanded to include the conversations and debates that resulted in the mythmaking of liberal internationalism, which I argue starts with the theatrical construction of the spaces of political representation. In this sense, I treat the UN as an aggregation of sites of operations, exchanges, translations, and representations, an aggregation that I study through its global interiors, the spaces where the organization appeared to a global public.

Architectures of Global Governance: A History

The United Nations Headquarters was not the first time that architects got involved in the configuration of the spaces of international institutions. Attempts at global governance have been stirring up architectural debates on world capitals since the Peace Conferences of 1899 and 1907, when mostly European colonial powers pursued more permanent forms of international organization and world order to replace older imperial structures.[67] A 1904 architectural competition gave Louis-Marie Cordonnier the opportunity to design the Peace Palace, the seat for the Permanent Court of Arbitration in The Hague that the steel mogul and internationalist Andrew Carnegie funded believing, like other industrialists and businessmen of his time, that institutionalized international law and bilateral arbitration treaties would benefit the globalization of markets.[68] Architects and planners injected themselves into these conversations, proposing capitols and entire cities where an international body of bureaucrats would organize and administer policies, imagining sites of cultural, artistic, and scientific exchange. They repurposed old conversations on model cities and Beaux Arts projects for parliaments and people's palaces, evoking a mostly abstracted and transcendental cosmopolitanism, as Shiben Banerji notes.[69]

In these projects, the city was the medium of "peace" and "internationalism." Alfred Fenzl, who proposed a Peace Congress Palace on the Island of Lacroma

Figure I.3. Hendrik Christian Andersen and Ernest Hébrard, bird's-eye view of the proposal for a World Centre of Communication, 1912. Courtesy of the Library of Congress.

(1900), described his project as a communication apparatus in and of itself, "radiating electric light at night and signaling the message of salvation and peace to the wide world."[70] Similarly, Dutch theosophist and architect Karel Petrus Cornelis de Bazel imagined a world city-broadcast in The Hague, where "ideas that originate in the heart of the world radiate from it."[71] But it was Ernest Hébrard's and Hendrik Christian Andersen's World Centre of Communication (1913), a project generously supported by Andersen's sister-in-law and matron of the project Olivia Cushing Andersen, that tied communications with the project of internationalism.[72] Their idealistic world center proposed a city, where a global community of scholars, scientists, and artists would take on world peace. Hébrard repurposed the Rue des Nations of World Expositions for museums, universities, libraries and other cultural institutions.[73] Systems of transportation such as roads and railways wove the landscape together, connecting the site via cars, carriages, and boats.[74] There, Gabriel Leroux forestalled architecture as the "signals" and "signs" to carry the project of world conscience.[75] Part homage to the Tower of Babel, part celebration of towers and spires as communication technologies, and part evocation of wireless communications, a Tower of Progress at the city center ever more forcefully placed media and communications at the heart of the internationalist imperative in the beginning of the twentieth century (Figure I.3, I.4). Andersen's indefatigable attempts at creating traction around his ideas repeatedly failed, but the end of the World War I found architectural journals revisiting the project as a model for the future of global governance, calling it "prophetic" and a well-fitted model for the future of institutional internationalism.[76]

Figure I.4. Hendrik Christian Andersen, sketch of the Tower of Progress with outline of Eiffel Tower in the background, n.d. Courtesy of the Library of Congress.

The announcement of the League of Nations in the aftermath of World War I propelled architects to think about the spaces of global assembly and their interiors, responding to a series of studio briefs in architecture schools and later on to the competition for the Palais des Nations. The Académie des Beaux-Arts and its U.S. branch, the Society of Beaux-Arts Architects, both issued calls for capitols that yielded palatial neoclassical proposals for corridor diplomacy.[77] The 1926 competition brief for a Palais des Nations reinforced the idea of a centralized global governance, anticipating the concentration of all League of Nations organizations and institutions on one site. The brief described the Plenary Hall as a public global interior that would accommodate an audience of 2,600 participants, with press and general public outnumbering the convening delegates, challenging architects to consider the forums of the new international organization in terms of communications.[78]

However, the prioritization of press and radio that the League diplomats imagined had little impact on most entries. At the time, architects considered communications for the most part a technical rather than a design question. In an otherwise conservative pool of competition entries that for the most part firmly grounded the new world order in the old, the design of the Plenary Hall was the only place to steer a conversation on communications.[79] As Sabine von Fischer notes, the Assembly Hall presented an acoustic challenge that diplomats already thought of as cardinal to the operation of the organization.[80] The body politic could not assert its operations without establishing communication. In a detailed report for *The American Architect* acoustician F. M. Osswald, who condemned the majority of the entries as acoustically problematic, proposed the reduction of the overall size (which inevitably happened) and the use of a loudspeaker system for the controlled diffusion of speech (Figure I.5).[81]

But signs of an architecture of internationalism that conceives itself as a broadcast infrastructure appeared in Hannes Meyer's and Hans Wittwer's proposal (Figure I.6). With its glass dome and literal transparency, the proposal stood out for its appearance and externalized tectonics, in ways that underpinned the desire for a new relationship between publics and bodies of governance.[82] The entry featured a radio station on the roof and a news billboard on the exterior of the building, giving architectural form to the communication machine that international institutions aspired to be. Meyer believed the League to be one of the "expressive forms of modern social agglomerations," with press and radio serving its internationalist goals of cooperation.[83]

Architectural historians have extensively documented the story of the competition and the crisis of judgment that ensued.[84] What is of interest is that this crisis of judgment pushed a group of diplomats to engineer a "Board of Design" consisting of the architects behind the winning entries, a model of collaboration

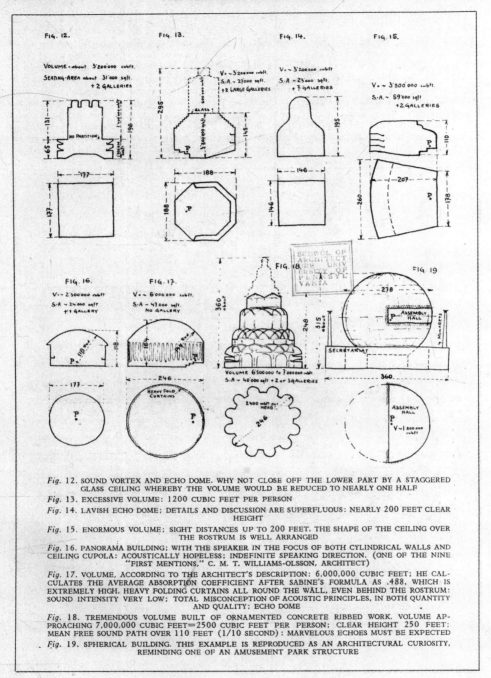

Fig. 12. SOUND VORTEX AND ECHO DOME. WHY NOT CLOSE OFF THE LOWER PART BY A STAGGERED GLASS CEILING WHEREBY THE VOLUME WOULD BE REDUCED TO NEARLY ONE HALF

Fig. 13. EXCESSIVE VOLUME: 1200 CUBIC FEET PER PERSON

Fig. 14. LAVISH ECHO DOME; DETAILS AND DISCUSSION ARE SUPERFLUOUS: NEARLY 200 FEET CLEAR HEIGHT

Fig. 15. ENORMOUS VOLUME; SIGHT DISTANCES UP TO 200 FEET. THE SHAPE OF THE CEILING OVER THE ROSTRUM IS WELL ARRANGED

Fig. 16. PANORAMA BUILDING; WITH THE SPEAKER IN THE FOCUS OF BOTH CYLINDRICAL WALLS AND CEILING CUPOLA: ACOUSTICALLY HOPELESS; INDEFINITE SPEAKING DIRECTION. (ONE OF THE NINE "FIRST MENTIONS," C. M. T. WILLIAMS-OLSSON, ARCHITECT)

Fig. 17. VOLUME, ACCORDING TO THE ARCHITECT'S DESCRIPTION: 6,000,000 CUBIC FEET; HE CALCULATES THE AVERAGE ABSORPTION COEFFICIENT AFTER SABINE'S FORMULA AS .488, WHICH IS EXTREMELY HIGH. HEAVY FOLDING CURTAINS ALL ROUND THE WALL, EVEN BEHIND THE ROSTRUM: SOUND INTENSITY VERY LOW; TOTAL MISCONCEPTION OF ACOUSTIC PRINCIPLES, IN BOTH QUANTITY AND QUALITY; ECHO DOME

Fig. 18. TREMENDOUS VOLUME BUILT OF ORNAMENTED CONCRETE RIBBED WORK. VOLUME APPROACHING 7,000,000 CUBIC FEET=2500 CUBIC FEET PER PERSON; CLEAR HEIGHT 250 FEET; MEAN FREE SOUND PATH OVER 110 FEET (1/10 SECOND): MARVELOUS ECHOES MUST BE EXPECTED

Fig. 19. SPHERICAL BUILDING. THIS EXAMPLE IS REPRODUCED AS AN ARCHITECTURAL CURIOSITY, REMINDING ONE OF AN AMUSEMENT PARK STRUCTURE

Figure I.5. Plate comparing the acoustics of different competition entry plans for the Assembly Hall of the Palais des Nations. F. M. Osswald, "The Acoustics of the Large Assembly Hall of the League of Nations, at Geneva, Switzerland," *The American Architect,* December 20, 1928. ETH Bildarchiv / Image Archive.

that UN bureaucrats expanded and put to work. Henri Paul Nénot and Julien Flegenheimer were invited to revise their entry with the help of Carlo Broggi, Camille Lefèbvre, and Joseph Vago. The final team also oversaw the construction and decorative program.[85]

Architects continued treating the forums of international organizations as secondary to the exterior design of the headquarters, focusing almost exclusively on setting capitol complexes on the urban scale. During the ten years that the design and construction of the Palais took, new proposals for adjacent international institutions articulated the communications imperative that the League's architects did not.[86] Building on Andersen's and Hébrard's World Centre of Communication, Belgian lawyers and pacifists Paul Otlet and Henri La Fontaine proposed the creation of a Cité mondiale, an informational infrastructure for knowledge storage and circulation in the form of a global city.[87] They invited Le Corbusier and Pierre Jeanneret, whose League of Nations proposal was dismissed on a technicality, to give form to their project so as to propose it as an annex to the Palais des Nations.[88] Sprawled on the hillside of Lake Geneva beside the Palais des Nations, the Mundaneum complex, as they named it, would feature a prominent urban core with a gigantic ziggurat to host the World Museum, a proposal that was never realized (Figure I.7).[89]

The Palais des Nations in Geneva opened its doors to diplomats and the public in 1937, just three years before World War II would force the League to close them again. It left the architectural press relatively unimpressed, with some journals calling the complete project a fittingly "unfortunate disfigurement of a noble idea."[90] Although we think otherwise, the criticism was not unilateral. Some architects found the complex well-designed and functional. Howard Robertson, who would later join the team overseeing the UN Headquarters design, called the League's headquarters a utilitarian complex and complimented the design board for the tempering of "architectural oratory."[91] There were even critics, such as Alberto Sartoris, who recognized in it an emergent modernism, albeit not fully developed.[92] Yet after World War II, architects and institutions such as the Museum of Modern Art would publicly claim the League of Nations and its palace as the absolute opposite of what the UN Headquarters should look like.

During World War II, architects in the United States and abroad redirected their focus on the war front and reconstruction projects, as Jean-Louis Cohen shows.[93] That, however, did not halt conversations on international organization and communications. By 1942, a new organization, the United Nations Information Organization (UNIO), appeared, pledging to coordinate the circulation of news with a network of broadcast companies and news agencies. An outgrowth of the Inter-Allied Information Committee and the British Ministry of Information, UNIO systematized the clearing and distribution of press releases,

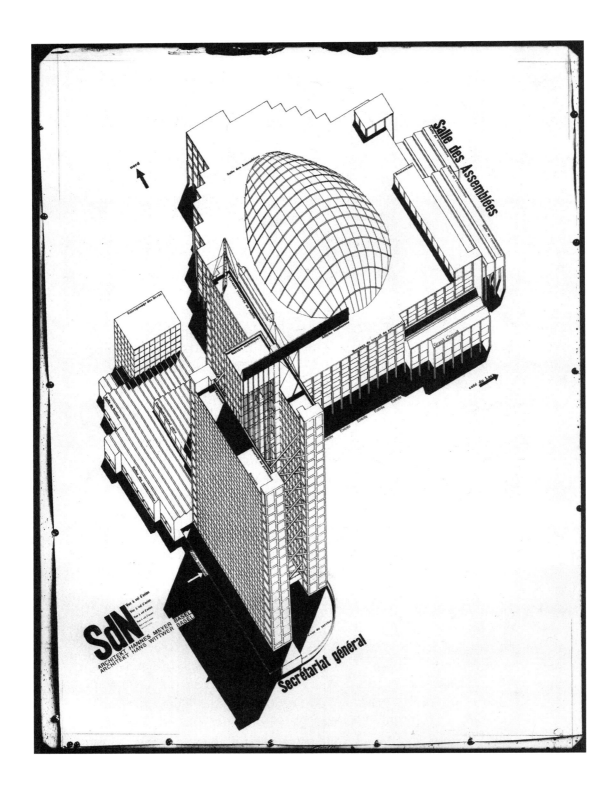

nord

Salle des Assemblées

Secrétariat général

SdN

ARCHITEKT HANNES MEYER BASEL
ARCHITEKT HANS WITTWER BASEL

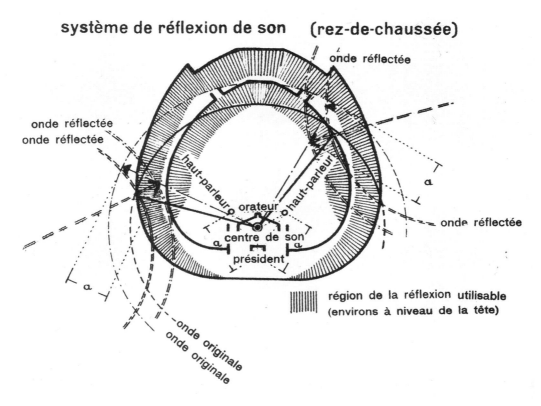

Figure I.6. Hannes Meyer and Hans Wittwer, axonometric of the proposal for the Palais des Nations and detail of plan of the General Assembly, 1927. gta Archives / ETH Zurich, Hans Wittwer.

broadcast programming, newsreels, and posters. The goal was to bolster support for the various war fronts but also further cultivate an internationalist sentiment around the world. The agency offered its library of photographs and images for the publication of pamphlets and posters, but also teamed up with cultural institutions such as MoMA to install exhibitions that propagated a cosmopolitan affect (Figure I.8). *The Road to Victory* (1942) and *The Airways to Peace* (1943), two traveling exhibitions designed by the Bauhaus émigré Herbert Bayer, expressed clearly this educational drive. If *The Road to Victory* aimed to strengthen patriotism and invite visitors on a one-way trip to world peace (mitigated, of course, by the U.S. military-industrial complex), then *The Airways to Peace,* with its open globetrotting panorama and Wendell Willkie quotes, effectually placed U.S. audiences at the center of a new connected world (Figure I.9). UNIO planted the seed for a reconceptualization of international institutions as mechanisms, and indeed communications apparatuses. This reconceptualization would also transform how

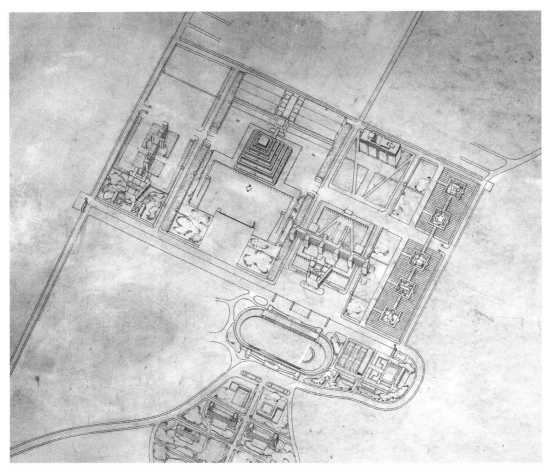

Figure I.7. Le Corbusier and Pierre Jeanneret with Paul Otlet, plan of Mundaneum, 1928. Copyright F.L.C. / ADAGP, Paris / Artists Rights Society (ARS), New York 2023.

the emergent organization would understand and articulate its relationship to the international community in space, in a new type of form, the global interior.

The Book in a Sketch

Chapter 1 examines how architects and designers, responding to the introduction of mass media and the call for transparency on an international scale, reconceived the UN spaces of international organization as stages with representational value. Unlike the early meetings in Dumbarton Oaks, where delegates met behind closed doors and design served as a visualization tool for administrators to debate, in San Francisco the UN sought to open its doors to the public eye and ear from its first moment. In doing so, the organization also invited a reconsideration of the

Figure I.8. View of *Know Your United Nations* exhibition at the Brooklyn Museum, 1947. Photograph by Kari Berggrav. Courtesy of the United Nations Photo Library.

symbols of internationalism and unity. In Nuremberg, the IBM telephonic system of interpretation organized the publics of international law, while constructing communications as central to the endeavor of liberal internationalism.

Chapter 2 explores how architects transferred the spatial systems and structures from the San Francisco Conference on International Organization and the Nuremberg Trials to the design of the UN Headquarters. The decision to favor a "headquarters" over a "world capital" for the seat of the new institution heralded a shift of focus from symbols to systems, and from centralized to networked models of organization. UN architects sought to install an infrastructural aesthetic that presented the UN as a communications organism and diplomatic labor as collaborative work in progress. I also discuss the emergence of new cultures of assembly and convening that the institution exported outside its Headquarters, showing how architecture and media framed political conversations and structured diplomatic labor.

Figure I.9. Installation view of the Outside-In Globe for the Airways to Peace Exhibition, 1943. Museum of Modern Art, New York. Digital image copyright The Museum of Modern Art. Licensed by SCALA / Art Resource, NY.

Chapter 3 notes that global interiors, insulated from their immediate context, re-established their connection to a global polity in terms of a regulated network of communication channels. Focusing on the design of the General Assembly, I demonstrate how, to ensure the intelligibility of the voice-as-signal, engineers and architects had to insulate the UN Headquarters from the outside, and its global platforms from external noise. I trace the acoustic design of the UN's headquarters back to military research on airplane communication systems and anechoic chambers. Media technologies such as the telephone, simultaneous interpretation systems, and the radio featured prominently in the public spaces of the UN, demonstrating the presence of a system that not only ordered the body politic, but also connected delegates with the rest of the bureaucratic machine and governments with publics outside those interiors. The goal was to establish the General Assembly as a site of both global and democratic listening and speaking.

Chapter 4 examines how the UN mobilized workshops, experts, and exhibitions to establish new communication channels and to plant the organization in the decolonizing world. Technical experts in seminars and conferences articulated the UN's ideas of political representation and procedure, which they carried from the Headquarters. In this sense I also consider how the distinction between the headquarters and the field instigated the communications systems of the UN.

The spatial apparatus of the global interior carried on to define multilateralism and governmental cultures in a variety of settings, from courtrooms to conference halls, delivering a new spatial vocabulary of communication and international organization. For global citizens around the world, those public interiors that assembled the United Nations coincided with the image of a modern cosmopolitanism, turning its furniture and interior design into hallmarks of internationalist projections and aspirations. Commercial films and television series recast those interiors as the sites of global governance for public consumption. But, also, these interiors transformed into a convening technique of internationalism that cross-contaminated organizations and ordered sites of multilateral exchange beyond its headquarters. My hope is that, in examining how diplomats and architects produced and used the UN global interiors, we will understand the role that architecture played in imagining and designing the assembly of national governments in a liberal world order. And maybe in doing so we will also learn something about what kind of space this mid-century utopia we call the UN forum is, and who it might serve.

1

Staging the World

During the final years of World War II, the planning for the post–League of Nations world order intensified with a series of closed but also well-publicized meetings: the Moscow Declaration (1943), the Tehran Declaration (1943), the Dumbarton Oaks Conversations (1944), and the Yalta Conference (1945). Newspapers printed lengthy reports, often accompanied by staged pictures of political leaders seated next to each other, either outside the venue, or more formally around tables set by the U.S. State Department. The multilateral character of the meetings denoted the international group of political leaders themselves, but also often underscored the tables they shared and a collection of flags in conspicuous places. Franklin D. Roosevelt's administration, nervous about the reception by the American public—especially in light of the Wilson administration's failure to endorse the League—used those events to launch a proactive campaign that prepared the grounds for the new organization in the United States and abroad. This effort to shape public opinion nationally and internationally structured the limited and planned admission of mass media to key sites and moments.

Unlike the early meetings in Dumbarton Oaks and elsewhere, which took place behind closed doors, the events to announce the United Nations to the world invited in the public eye and ear. First at the San Francisco Conference on International Organization, the inaugural event to finalize the charter and publicize the organization, and later at the Nuremberg Trials, where the allied forces gave judicial form to the new international order, planning committees offered unprecedented access to and support for mass media, with dedicated office space, studios, and even a U.S. Army Signal Corps–engineered communications infrastructure. Cameras, filming crews, journalists, and photographers inside and outside courtrooms and conference halls documented the two proceedings, interviewing delegates and soliciting insights. Yet both events had been planned in private, away from the public eye and with preplanned press conferences. The San Francisco Conference was outlined at Dumbarton Oaks, and the Nuremberg Trials were planned almost a year later in London. In fact, the Dumbarton Oaks

Conversations had already determined in broad strokes the shape of the new organization, and the outcome of the Nuremberg Trials was long foretold. What
then was the reason for a public presentation, if all was said and done behind
closed doors in London and Washington ahead of time? What did the Allied powers hope to achieve by inviting mass media inside these two events, and how did
this invitation transform the role that architecture and design would play for the
organization?

Architectural histories of the United Nations Headquarters often start with
the search for a site, leaving out the initial platforms where the organization's
global publics formed. This omission erases the informative experiments that
happened on the ground before architects started designing the headquarters itself. The truth is that opening those spaces to photographers, journalists, and
cameramen required a plan. Introducing the press at this moment of institutional
interpellation—the moment when the organization claimed a name and a body
in front of a public—posed critical questions of representation that architects and
designers were called in to solve. The task further complicated a desire to authorize and legitimize the United Nations in front of its publics and member states.

To answer those questions of legitimacy and authority, this chapter turns
to the new world order's inaugural platforms, examining them as architectural
events that outlined the UN's temporary figurations. In the mind of the diplomats
and politicians working out the postwar global order, an effective new world order
required an international law system as well. In fact, plans for the organization to
replace the League of Nations coincided with the formation of the United Nations
War Crimes Commission (UNWCC) that sought to examine the possibility of addressing war crimes, ultimately paving the way for the Nuremberg Trials and an
international criminal law system.[1] If the San Francisco Conference plenary hall
brought the new organization into being, then the Nuremberg Trials courtroom
presented it as a system with far-reaching tentacles. Inside the courtroom, architects calibrated the aural and visual conditions of globality, informing the future
configuration of the Assembly Hall. Seating, podiums, drapes, chairs, tables, and
benches ignited conversations on diplomatic form and political symbolism, but
also called for spatial solutions and design. These were the sites where industrial
designers, architects, and theater designers articulated a new vocabulary of internationalism, presenting communication as the operative rational structure to
triumph over the irrationality of World War II.

Designing World Organization

At the dawn of 1945, newly appointed U.S. Secretary of State Edward Stettinius Jr.
turned to General William J. Donovan with a quite simple request. At the time
Donovan was heading the Office of Strategic Services (OSS)—the military intelli-

gence division that Franklin D. Roosevelt had launched in 1942 for the production and circulation of information regarding various war fronts in Europe, Africa, and the Pacific. The State Department was engrossed in preparatory work for a new international organization, the United Nations, and Colonel Atherton Richards, formerly with the Office of the Coordinator of Information and president of the Hawaiian Pineapple Company, had tipped off Stettinius about the new presentation techniques developed within the OSS Presentation Branch. The Dumbarton Oaks Conversations had just concluded with the outline of a possible organizational structure for the UN, and a call for a larger conference at San Francisco to iron out and sign the charter. The State Department was also preparing the ground for the prosecution of Third Reich leaders, the trial that was anticipated to launch a more robust postwar international legal system with the preliminary blessings of Dumbarton Oaks. Stettinius asked Donovan to "loan" him illustrators, architects, and designers—at the time working for the War Department—for a number of projects the State Department was carrying out on "internal organization and management," "international conferences," "public relations," and "foreign policy."[2] He assured Donovan that the projects were of utmost importance to the United States, hence the urgency of the loan. The invitation did not give further specifications, but it sparked a frantic search for prospective personnel and a research trip to New York City to secure new hires for the Presentation Branch and the State Department.[3]

Design played an important role in the OSS, translating military intelligence produced by the Research and Analysis (R&A) Branch into valuable visual output for war operations.[4] The Presentation Branch, a hotbed of design and architecture within OSS, offered the R&A scientists "who had the facts and knew their meaning" a necessary "bridge" with the War Department generals "who needed the facts as a basis for decision and action."[5] In this sense, as Barry Katz expertly demonstrates, OSS architects, along with artists, illustrators, and designers, partook in intelligence production, supplying the military with tactical sabotage drawings, maps, flow charts, films, diagrams, and their architectures of presentation (situation and presentation rooms).[6] The State Department, anxious to see the UN successfully launched, entrusted OSS and the military with its presentation to the world.

OSS visualization techniques short-circuited disciplinary boundaries and translated field-specific expertise and language for a military audience in similar ways that corporations communicated with management, and advertisers with clients. The idea was not particularly new. As Gestalt theories infiltrated design education and practice, industrialists endowed their companies with dedicated design departments for the creation of recognizable corporate identities and advertisements.[7] The idea was that design can circumvent the limitations of language and successfully broaden one's audience and market. Think here, for example, how social scientists such as W. E. B. Du Bois and Otto Neurath used visualization methods and design to reach larger audiences: Du Bois to demonstrate the structural nature of racism and Neurath to overcome the obstacle of illiteracy in governmental educational campaigns.[8] These projects paved the way for the use of design as a universal language.

With the San Francisco Conference fast approaching, why couldn't these same techniques also get past the problem of language at a moment that the institution considered foundational? The Presentation Branch's visual communications work received glowing accolades from the military. Charts and maps had helped the War Department to comprehend and communicate a complex military operation with many shifting constituents, but also to convince Congress's politicians and solicit economic support for its projects. Couldn't designers and architects, State Department officials wondered, play a similar role in securing peace for a new world order? Although apprehensive, they saw in design the ability to condense and communicate core ideas, values, and structures across expertise and language barriers. Unlike, however, their work for the War Department, at San Francisco designers would have to design and communicate, to literally give form, to a plan in the making. The Presentation Branch's ability to present as real an organization still in "somebody's imagination" was not only alluring to governmental officials, but also constitutive of the new institution.[9]

The State Department put together a Conference Secretariat to organize and run the San Francisco Conference on International Organization. Alger Hiss, the State Department administrator and executive secretary of the Dumbarton Oaks Conversations, later accused of espionage, was appointed the Secretary-General of the conference. On the administrative side, the group of State Department officials supporting Hiss's planning included Charles E. Rothwell, Secretary-General of the U.S. delegation to the UN; Leo Pasvolsky, the Wilsonian chairman of the Coordination Committee at the San Francisco Conference; and Clyde Dunn. Meanwhile, Warren Kelchner from the State Department Division for International Conferences would collaborate with the OSS team on etiquette and procedure.[10]

On the design side, Oliver Lincoln Lundquist, an award-winning architect in his mid-twenties who had dropped out of Columbia University to join Raymond Loewy's industrial design office during the Great Depression, was appointed Presentation Officer.[11] Lundquist, who OSS filmmaker and writer Carl Marzani called the "idea man at large," had arrived at the War Department early in 1941, eventually enlisting in OSS's Presentation Branch.[12] His early work included illustrations and charts, as well as commissioned presentations for the War Department. Lundquist arranged with Hubert (Hu) Barton, Presentation Branch Chief at the time, to have OSS loan his buddy Donal (Mac) McLaughlin, divisional head of the Graphic Division, who had left Loewy's office to join OSS in 1942.[13] A third-generation architect from New York City, McLaughlin had attended the Beaux-Arts Institute of Design and Yale, apprenticing at the Atelier Lloyd Morgan and the Atelier Corbett-Smith.[14] After a short stint at the National Park Service drawing maps and park structures, followed by post office designs for the Treasury Department and plans for greenbelt towns for the Resettlement Administration, he had moved to Walter Dorwin Teague's and later Raymond Loewy's office, where he designed interiors, exhibits, and dioramas for department stores and the 1939 New York World's Fair.[15] Both Lundquist and McLaughlin had impressed the War Department generals and colonels with their animation techniques.[16]

For the San Francisco crew Hu Barton also enlisted an impressive roster of talented architects, artists, illustrators, and editors: former editor of Viking Press and Modern Age Books, David Zablodowsky headed the Editorial Division,[17] and film director Richard (Dick) Wilson served as the photographic officer.[18] The team supported OSS historian Marian Emrich, public opinion analyst-turned-communications professor Edward Norton Barnhart, and literary scholar James D. Hart, with the generous administrative support of Marie Barton and Ruth Mandelbaum. Pamphlets, plans, and charts were prepared by a stellar line-up of artists that included New Deal muralist Eric Mose, celebrated children's book illustrator Joe Krush, African American television graphic designer Georg Olden, modernist landscape architect Lou Bernard Voight, abstract painter Charlotte Park, caricaturist Sam Berman, and illustrator Alice Provensen, to name a few.[19] By general admission, the team worked well together as a "congenial gang of brains, good humor, and a progressive orientation."[20]

If design was the means through which the organization would acquire form and structure in front of its delegates, architecture would be the medium to give this new organization and its international public sphere a stage. The conference would be hosted at the San Francisco War Memorial Opera House and Veterans Building, a pair of neoclassical buildings in front of the City Hall that Arthur Brown Jr. had designed to replace the earlier hall destroyed in the 1906 earthquake. These twin buildings comprised a municipally owned complex that was at once war memorial, cultural institution, and epicenter of the local political and cultural elite (Figure 1.1).[21] The Opera House would accommodate the opening addresses and the plenary sessions, while the Veterans Building, serving as the headquarters of the Conference Secretariat, would conclude the conference with the ceremonial signing of the Charter.[22] The choice of venues revealed a yearning for theatricality and staging that the Presentation Branch minutes confirm. During those "production meetings"—a willful fusion of film industry and show-business parlance with diplomacy—the Presentation Branch designated "staging" as the main task, particularly in relation to the design of the plenary hall

Figure 1.1. Exterior view of the San Francisco War Memorial Opera House and Veterans Building where the San Francisco Conference on International Organization took place, 1945. Courtesy of the United Nations Photo Library.

and the setting for the signing of the Charter. OSS architects and designers would not only support the conference in material and technical ways: they would produce it.[23]

And in all truth, the San Francisco Conference was conceived as a media event for an international public, admitted in a structured way that designated levels of access. The Conference Secretariat limited public admission to representatives of international organizations, both UN–affiliated and nongovernmental, leaving very little opportunity for the general public to enter this new global space. Instead, the place of the general public would be taken by photographers, filming crews, and journalists, who were offered prominent but organized placement within the galleries, removed from the floor yet with abundant access to the proceedings (Figure 1.2). The Veterans Building would accommodate press and mass media, offering office space for journalists, studios for radio broadcasting networks, as well as full telephone, telegraph, and radio services for wireless and

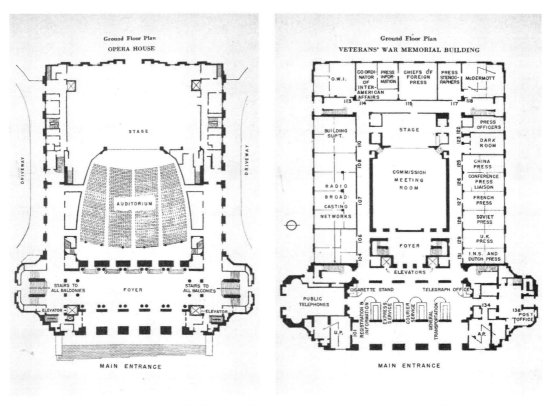

Figure 1.2. Plan of the refurbished Opera House on the left and plan of the Veterans Building on the right, circa 1945. *Guide: The United Nations Conference on International Organization, San Francisco, 1945* (Washington, D.C.: U.S. Government Printing Office, 1945). Archive of Oliver Lundquist, AIA, at Bard College.

cable messages. In addition, the Presentation Branch installed a pressroom on the second floor for interviews with statespersons, and cleared three boxes in the Opera House galleries opposite the center stage for the newsreel crews of Pathé, Paramount, and Universal, while bringing along Hollywood pioneer Peter Mole to supervise stage lighting for filming (Figure 1.3).[24] In this sense, the presence of mass media was ubiquitous and ultimately determinative of the organization's claims to globality and authority.

In designing the stages of the UN's constitutive moments, the Presentation Branch directed how and what media representatives (and by extension, the world) would see. During the preparatory meetings in Washington, the presence of mass media had challenged OSS architects and designers to bring front and center questions of visual identity. The organization needed to not only build those international platforms for multilateralism, but also to turn them into representations of the institution itself. State Department and UN bureaucrats

Figure 1.3. Dorothea Lange in the galleries of the Opera House covering the San Francisco Conference on International Organization for the Office of War Information, 1945. Courtesy of the United Nations Photo Library.

anticipated that design would authoritatively frame the organization for its publics.

At the San Francisco Conference, the Presentation Branch repurposed the streamlined aesthetic of industrial design for the pictorial needs of the postwar world order.[25] The full list of design tasks ahead—some identified by the designers themselves and others commissioned by the State Department—included passes, press badges, admission buttons, nameplates, handbooks and guidebooks. No matter how small the task, Lundquist assigned a team of editors and designers to address it, with State Department officials and R&A analysts intervening with feedback at critical production stages. The result was the creation of dedicated teams with affixed leaders, while artists, architects, and writers moved from one team to the next depending on need, availability, and priorities. Apart from staging the conference, designers transformed those objects of assembly into material signifiers of the larger world structure that representatives, journalists, and politicians entered when passing the conference gates. Together those objects would make up the visual language of internationalism, presenting as coherent an organization that was yet to have a body.

Among those tasks was the translation of the Dumbarton Oaks Proposals into communicable schematics to guide the conversations inside committee rooms and the plenary hall.[26] In an attempt to control the negotiations, the State Department had asked the pamphlet designers to schematize the Dumbarton Oaks Conversations in diagrams. The task was to outline the overall organizational structure without, however, presenting it as fixed or detailing hierarchies among organs. In addition, the State Department called for diagrams and charts to depict a democratic, decentralized, nonhierarchical structure, regardless of initial conversations indicating the prominent place of the Security Council within the institution. In fact, the goal was to visually downplay the centrality of the Security Council and instead emphasize the General Assembly. Published in a pamphlet, the diagrams set each organ on a radial flow chart to describe its role and place within the organization. These radial flow charts illustrated the diffusion of authority and power among the three main organs at the time—the General Assembly, the Security Council, and the International Court of Justice—while graphically communicating the new organization as a collaborative enterprise. The intention behind, and the result of, the ask was to separate the reality from the representation of the organization. Ironically, the illustrations revealed more than they hid: the charts implicitly evoked a layered organization, with its core parts visually fortifying an empty center and being surrounded first by a second band of organs (the Economic and Social Council, the Secretariat, and the Military Staff Committee) and a third outer band of even more remote yet affiliated specialized agencies. The language of periphery and center organized OSS's visualizations of the new institution. The charts contoured dependencies and relationships, eventually introducing a globe as an external yet malleable object that the organization swung one way or another, transforming the UN into a pendulum and the Security Council into its fixed point (Figure 1.4, Plate 1).

The Dumbarton Oaks publication received rave reviews from the State Department, which welcomed the pamphlet for its ability to sketch out the organization for a wider audience, setting a somewhat fixed foundation for all negotiations to follow without, however, claiming to do so. The Secretary of State found the diagrams clear in explaining the structure and setting the visual language of this new international bureaucracy, while the Conference Secretariat ordered enlarged charts for San Francisco. Excited State Department officials saw potential for the department's own publicity needs. An enthusiastic Dorothy Fosdick, a foreign policy expert and one of the few female employees at the State

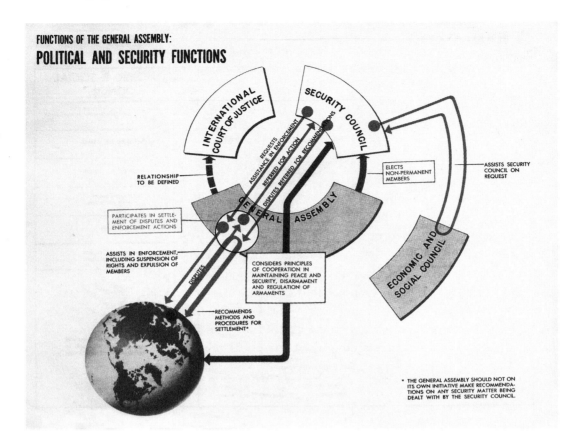

FUNCTIONS OF THE GENERAL ASSEMBLY:
POLITICAL AND SECURITY FUNCTIONS

Department, requested the production of similar charts for promotional purposes targeting the U.S. public.[27] The charts' mass circulation would help cultivate an internationalist sentiment among the U.S. audience, serving a purpose beyond the conference.

But charts also allowed the Presentation Branch to present the conference as a well-oiled, efficient, and frictionless operation, leaving no doubt about the legitimacy of the enterprise. In a twenty-minute motion picture, Lundquist combined those flow charts to imply the engineering nature of the new organization and to interpellate the globe as its zone of operation.[28] The press praised the Presentation Branch as a central agent to the flow of diplomatic work, attributing the smooth operations of committees to their designs and charts.[29]

Stettinius asked the Presentation Branch to produce visual aids for the various San Francisco committee meetings (Figures 1.5 and 1.6).[30] During the couple of months that the San Francisco Conference lasted, commissions of delegates would discuss the structure, procedure and policies of each United Nations organ. Commission I addressed general procedures; Commission II the General Assembly

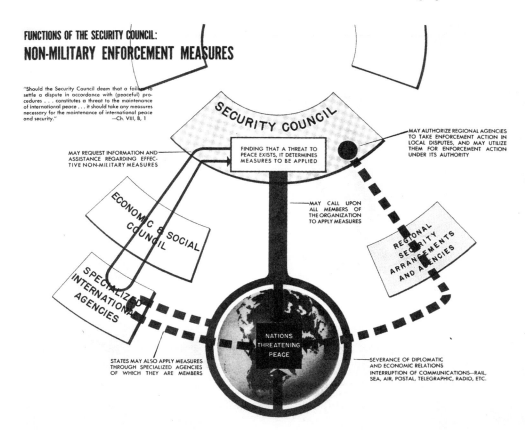

Figure 1.4. Department of State, *Proposals for a General International Organization as Developed at Dumbarton Oaks 1944* (Washington, D.C.: U.S. Government Printing Office, 1945).

structure; Commission III the Security Council; and Commission IV the judicial organization.[31] Stettinius hoped that the charts would direct diplomatic discussions and structure meetings the same way that they guided military strategy.[32] But diplomatic conversations did not need visuals to establish their conclusion. In fact, State Department officials advised against their use inside meetings, wary that their presentation as *faits accomplis* would result in their contestation. To the disappointment of the Presentation Branch personnel who longed to see their work put to the service of peace, State Department officials argued that illustrations did not leave enough "elbow room" for negotiations.[33] Unlike war operations, diplomatic labor thrived in abstraction, turning OSS visualization techniques into an obstacle rather than a tool.

OSS designers also determined the symbols of the new organization, particularly its emblem. For example, proposals for a United Nations flag began arriving in 1943, as early as plans for a new organization started circulating in the

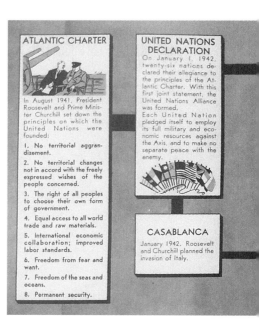

Figure 1.5. Flow chart prepared by the OSS Presentation Branch declaring the United Nations Conference on International Organization as the outcome of diplomatic negotiations starting with the Atlantic Charter, 1945. Courtesy of the United Nations Archives and Records Management.

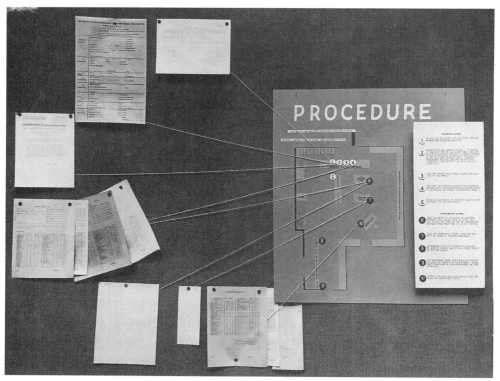

Figure 1.6. Exhibit wall showing the procedure for the preparation and distribution of documents for the United Nations Conference on International Organization, 1945. Courtesy of the United Nations Archives and Records Management.

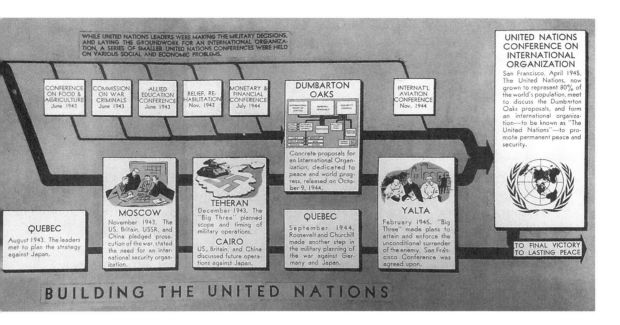

Figure 1.7. Sketches of lapel pin proposals by Donal McLaughlin. Donal McLaughlin, *Origin of the Emblem and Other Recollections of the 1945 UN Conference.* Edited by Jennifer Truran Rothwell, 1995. Courtesy of Brian McLaughlin and Donna Firer.

press. Boris Artzybasheff's rainbow flag, and even more so Brooks Harding's "Four Freedoms" flag proposal, stirred up conversations on symbols for the new organization.[34] As Biddiscombe shows, however, it was the lapel admission pin for delegates and visitors that would eventually win the UN seal of approval for the organization's emblem. Donal McLaughlin, who led the team of designers responsible for the pin, found the initial proposals ambiguous and at times inappropriate: a chain around a globe to link all nations connoted slavery and imprisonment; the corner of a brick-and-mortar wall with an olive branch behind pointed to the "building" of peace but also its containment; a bundle of rods with olive branches to symbolize unity was too close to fascist iconography; and the initials "UN" would be illegible (Figure 1.7). He approved instead of an azimuthal projection of the globe for its ability to present all landmasses at once, surrounded by a laurel wreath as a symbol of peace.[35] The Bastian Brothers manufactured the lapel pin with jewelers' enamel in light blue hues (Plate 2).[36] Larger versions of the insignia also appeared on the stage at the Veterans Building and later in the temporary venues that the UN inhabited before moving into the permanent Headquarters.

The San Francisco buildings served as the stages where the Presentation Branch would elaborate a new visual language for international bureaucracies, along with its symbols, textures, and color palettes. In hopes of further reinforcing a uniform appearance in front of delegates and mass media, Alger Hiss and Oliver Lundquist asked that all furniture be made out of high-end plywood and all floors be carpeted.[37] Dazian's Theatricals, a draping and costumes supplier for Broadway theaters, provided the drape for the stages in the blue-gray hue that came to be known as "Stettinius blue."[38] The stamp of the U.S. government was now everywhere, from the drapes to the pamphlets, and from the selection of the color tone to the linen-cotton blend for official documents.[39]

Regardless of all the rhetoric on uniformity, the San Francisco Conference stages revealed representational and design divergences. For the plenary hall, where the State Department anticipated sustained press interest during the opening, the closing remarks, and the main sessions, Hu Barton brought back theater designer Jo Mielziner,[40] who had recently concluded a stint with the camouflage corps and OSS.[41] His background in military projects, as well as his work on Broadway productions and stage design, qualified him for the job. Mielziner collaborated with Lou Voight and Lundquist, as well as theater lighting expert Ed Kook, to stage the plenary sessions for the press. The setting of the Veterans Building central hall, where the signing of the charter would take place, was taken over by Donal McLaughlin, with the help of State Department official Warren Kelchner, who had previously staged the Yalta conference on a circular table at the center of the room. The two approaches would ultimately result in two different directions for the architecture of international institutions.

On the one hand, Mielziner built on a long history of governmental architecture. To juxtapose the fragile and volatile moment that the end of World War II presented, Mielziner appropriated a more or less classical language to convey—and in this sense also to endow the new global institution with—power and authority.[42] Initial sketches showed four freestanding golden pylons rising to the sky uncapped, implying an untapped potential for growth, with flagpoles plumed on their sides and garlands connecting their tops (Figure 1.8). The structure intertwined Franklin Delano Roosevelt's "four freedoms" with the UN's framing device, metonymically conflating the United Nations with an American liberal understanding of freedom and democracy.[43] Mielziner covered everything in cotton velour: the podium, the rostrum, the pylons, the stage floor, the desks' aprons, and stair risers and treads, creating a shared color and texture palette for the UN commissions and meetings.[44] The setting foregrounded the pylons and presented the emerging international institution as the anchoring site for national identities, securing the distinct and equal place of each participating nation within the UN's structure.

Mielziner's initial plan to affix flagpoles to the freestanding pylons met resistance both on technical grounds (the hollowed pylons could easily tip over, endangering the very representation of stability and security the organization wished to broadcast) and on symbolic grounds (the structure implied a dependency on the United Nations that was neither desirable nor truthful). Instead, the team placed the national flags in front of the signature gray-blue drape behind the podium, producing internationalism as the horizon and the nation-state as its elemental unit (Figure 1.9).[45]

The rest of the plan defined diplomatic protocol and process. In this sense the space did not diverge from years of plenary hall design, not even in how elevated podiums and secretarial pits demarcated hierarchies of work. Conference protocol officer Gerald A. Drew asked for a speaker podium just below and in front of an elevated "long table" for the President, Secretary-General, and other Secretariat officials leading the plenary sessions. He also placed verbatim reporters and typists in a sunken pit before the stage, hiding the infrastructure that supported the proceedings for an unobstructed view of the podium.

The theatrical element in Mielziner's and Lundquist's design, however, was more covert. Theater, for Mielziner, was not a spatial affair, but rather a relational possibility. It materialized wherever somebody was watching something happening, wherever there was an audience and a performance at play.[46] His career had marked a departure from strict realism and an effort to "break the rigid, restricting straight line of the aprons of . . . twentieth-century theatres," extending theatrical events to the audience and establishing theater as an active act of secularization.[47] Although at a first glance the stage he created appears a far cry from his theories, heavy on symbolism and iconolatric representations of unity and peace, on a second read it reveals a complicated spectatorship architecture. For Mielziner and Lundquist, the convening delegates were not the audience but rather part of the spectacle that filming crews and photographers on the galleries would present to international publics around the world. The stage did not end with the secretarial pit and the presentation of the conference mechanism; instead, it extended to include the auditorium and its global polity that gathered to legitimize the UN's becoming.[48] Delegates and plenary hall speakers were equally participating in the performance for an audience residing outside the Opera House.

On the other hand, the modernist language of the central hall at the Veterans Building contradicted Mielziner's neoclassical setting, repurposing military

Figure 1.8. Jo Mielziner, sketches for the refurbishment of the stage at the Opera House, San Francisco, n.d. Jo Mielziner Papers, Billy Rose Theatre Division, The New York Public Library for the Performing Arts. Courtesy of the Mielziner Estate.

presentation technique—and its corporate ancestors—to imagine the representation of globality and the production of global space. McLaughlin, who was designing the stage for the Veterans Building, equally marshaled symbols, but in the place of neoclassicism, he offered abstraction and a new focus on function and procedure. He organized the plan as a "flow chart" similar to the ones OSS had been producing for the military.[49] The plan delineated the circulation of national delegations inside and outside the building, demonstrating how they would arrive at the Veterans Building; be chaperoned to the briefing room; and then be escorted outside. The plan-as-flow-chart successfully transformed the space of global presentation into a matter of organizational engineering, producing the signing of the charter as a frictionless move through space (Figure 1.10).[50] In this sense, McLaughlin designed the UN's global platform as a management and organizational structure that eliminated friction and static.

If at the Opera House Plenary Hall architects staged the global polity as audience, at the Veterans Building Central Hall they presented the new organization's public sphere through the synecdoche of the round table. In fact, for the signing of the UN Charter, the OSS placed the press near the entrance, with filming crews

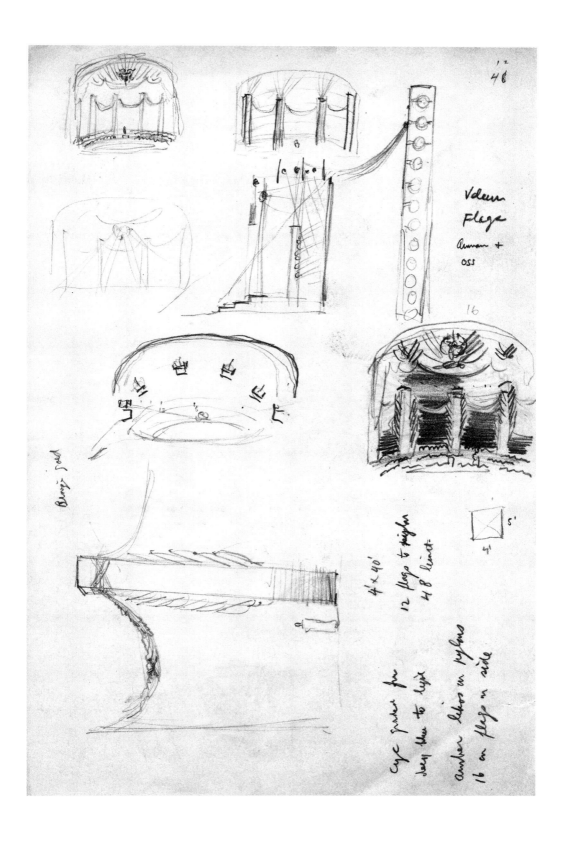

Figure 1.9. View of the plenary hall from the gallery, showing T. V. Soong, chairman of the Chinese Delegation, presiding, 1945. Courtesy of the United Nations Photo Library.

on the balcony above and journalists behind a rope on the floor. Building on the tables that the State Department had used to stage the preliminary international meetings, the Presentation Branch introduced a grand circular table on top of a thirty-six-foot diameter carpet that commanded the entire room and announced in front of press and cameramen, perhaps prematurely, the arrival of new, democratic cultures of assembly and diplomacy. The circular table framed a row of flags flanking the UN insignia mounted on another gray-blue drape behind the balustrade.[51] Designed by Donal McLaughlin, the table at the center featured a small recess to indicate the place of the signatory. Although alluding to a round table, the desk was not functional, but rather symbolic. To sign the UN charter, the fifty national representatives took their seats at the table only one at a time, claiming the place of each member state in the new world order and committing their countries to the organization.

Not all elements of the set, however, spoke to the OSS's modernist desires. Bearing semantic weight, the signer's chair had McLaughlin, Lundquist, and the

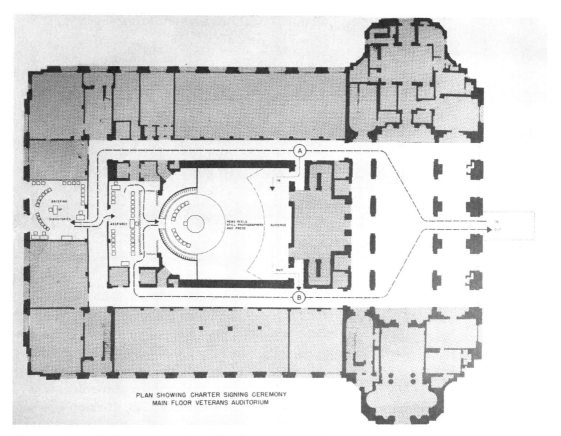

PLAN SHOWING CHARTER SIGNING CEREMONY
MAIN FLOOR VETERANS AUDITORIUM

Figure 1.10. OSS diagram produced for the signing of the UN Charter Ceremony, 1945. Courtesy of Brian McLaughlin and Donna Firer.

Presentation Branch scouring San Francisco for the appropriate piece. The curator of the de Young Museum proposed the big black-oak chair of federalist U.S. statesman Daniel Webster, a chair that the Presentation Branch loathed, calling it on record "a monument of ugliness." Despite some fleeting sentiment for a more modern design, the team settled for the Webster chair but asked it to be reupholstered to match the rest of the interior.[52] The OSS team also nixed an initial proposal to use an additional row of gilded upholstered chairs in the background; the chairs seemed incongruous with the rest of the design,[53] in addition to "clutter[ing] up the action" and clashing with McLaughlin's modernist aesthetic (Plate 3).[54] The symbolism of the round table was more important than the rather literal translation of diplomats taking a seat at the table.

On June 26, 1945, on the ground floor of the Veterans Building in San Francisco, representatives from fifty nations concluded their month of debates and conversation with a ceremonial signing of the UN charter. Signatories received an additional minute for newsreel addresses and photographs to mark the signing.

Writing from the Veterans Building, Donal McLaughlin talked about "an atmosphere of dazzling splendor."[55] Newspapers did not fail to notice the staging of the signing ceremony, remarking that the presence of cameramen, photographers, and journalists, as well as bright lights, induced a "Hollywood" atmosphere.[56] Reporting from San Francisco, Walter Winchell of the *New York Daily Mirror* described how the State Department transformed San Francisco into a stage, offering a full account of the Hollywood celebrities and studios involved in the affair. "This is not a Hollywood production, or San Francisco's either, but the world's and, especially, the State Department's," he said.[57] In this sense the San Francisco Conference also affixed certain symbols, typography, and visual syntax to the UN, turning the lapel pin into the official emblem and the round table into a metonymy for the organization's global public sphere. But in a more substantial way, the San Francisco Conference transformed those sites into stages, an important first step in the creation of the UN's "global interiors."

Landscapes of Justice

In early May 1945, and as Lundquist and his team were in the middle of the San Francisco Conference, President Truman summoned OSS to help with the preparation of another project to take place later that fall, the International Military Tribunal.[58] The USSR's initial desire for a swift extradition and the British government's insistence on "summary execution" of World War II criminals had given way, and the four governments of the Allied powers—the United States, United Kingdom, France, and the Soviet Union—were convinced that an international trial was the necessary prelude to the launch of the UN. At the London International Conference on Military Trials national representatives from the four powers negotiated a legal process, building on the framework that the United Nations War Crimes Commission had been developing during World War II.[59] The idea was to make the prosecution of "ruthlessness and unlawful force" in war public with an international tribunal. This way, the U.S. State Department argued, "world opinion" would regard the Allied powers as carriers of morality and the liberal cause of the emerging new organization as the only way forward.[60] By August 1945, the four governments had agreed on an international military tribunal to be held in Germany and signed off on the prosecution of major war criminals, modeling international justice and announcing the UN's commitment on human rights on an international stage.[61]

The desire for a public prosecution marked the preparations for the International Military Tribunal. OSS's Bill Donovan convinced the skeptical U.S. Chief Prosecutor Justice Robert H. Jackson to admit mass media inside the courtroom so as to afford the tribunal a global audience.[62] Admitting mass media meant, however, increased demands on office space and facilities, which complicated the search for a site. Justice Jackson relayed the apprehension of General Lucius D. Clay, who as a deputy military governor in Germany had been searching for possible locations:

> We shall have very great difficulties about physical arrangements for a trial of this kind. . . . The destruction is so complete that there is hardly a courtroom standing in Germany. We have got to have a place for prisoners. We have got to have a place for witnesses. There are many people who will want to attend—military men from all parts. We have communications to set up. The press are [sic] going to want to know about this. The public is interested. There will be at least 200 correspondents for newspapers according to our estimates who will insist on having some place to live and a place to work. That estimate includes a representation of the presses of the different countries. You will have representatives of other nations who will want to observe us.[63]

The built reality complicated matters. Dilapidated building stock, the ruinous state of German urban centers, and a desire for a swift trial left the Allies with very few options to house a function with ever-increasing spatial needs for offices, storage, and accommodation.

Among the cities proposed, Nuremberg, suggested by General Clay, seemed to fit the bill.[64] Although devastated by the British earlier that January, the city featured a relatively intact juridical complex on the outskirts of the city close to Fürth, the Justizpalast, with ample office space, courtrooms, and a four-wing panopticon prison adjacent to its rear for the defendants awaiting trial (Figure 1.11).[65] Bringing the tribunals to Nuremberg also served an illustrative function, marking the end of war with the application of reason at the "symbolic capital" of Hitler's Germany.[66] Hitler perceived Nuremberg as the built expression of German culture and national identity, relocating his Party Rallies there from Munich.[67] Between 1933 and 1938, the Nuremberg Reichsparteitagsgelände (the Reich Party Conference grounds) that Albert Speer planned for him became the epicenter of Hitler's nationalist delirium.[68]

National governments had already utilized courtrooms as sites of political restoration, publicly prosecuting Nazi collaborators both on the local and the global scale. Attending the trial of *Je suis partout* editor-in-chief and Vichy-regime supporter Robert Brasillach in Paris, Simone de Beauvoir argued that courtrooms entangled and triangulated the public in an architecture of repair. "It is in our name that they judge, that they punish," she claimed. "Ours is the public opinion that expresses itself through newspapers, posters, meetings, the public opinion that these specialized instruments are designed to satisfy." She contended that the restitution of victimized publics in response to "tyranny" necessitated the

Figure 1.11. Aerial view of the Justizpalast in Nuremberg, 1945. Stadtarchiv Nürnberg. Photograph by Ray D'Addario (November 20, 1945). City AN A 65/IV No. RA-141.

prosecution of crimes and the administration of justice to "reestablish the dignity of man."[69] Unlike other forms of retribution, courtrooms offered the public a sustained view of the *longue durée* of modern punishment, watching war criminals, once perceived as heinous tyrannical figures, slowly but steadily being reduced within a highly ritualized environment into "tired," "pitiful old" men.[70] De Beauvoir called this an architecture of revenge aimed at reinstating the victims of the Nazi atrocities as subjects with agency. Primo Levi, who declared himself disinterested in revenge, called these trials a settling of accounts, "the hour of colloquy," noting in retrospect that the military trials left him "intimately satisfied by the symbolic, incomplete, tendentious, sacred representation."[71] And this architecture of public retribution was necessary for the restitution of a liberal world order.

By hosting the trials in Nuremberg, the prosecution brought before the bench not only the criminal organization of the Third Reich, but also the cultures of spectacle and nationalist narratives of racial purity that nourished it, as well as the homogeneous vast publics it articulated through pictorial and film propaganda. This way the Allied powers would set the new public spaces of the UN world order against the vast centripetal spaces, spectacular celebrations, and military aesthetics of the Third Reich. This aesthetics would counter-propose, even if as a representation, a culture of democracy, transparency, and rationality to the totalitarian, conspiratorial, and spectacular logic that the Nazis had inhabited, while reifying international law as the agent and carrier of this new culture and practice of justice and diplomacy.

It is interesting then to note that the planning of the courtroom started in the absence of a building, as a floating interior. The memorandum that circulated among the U.S. Chief of Counsel's staff on May 17, 1945, invited interested governmental agencies and their teams to contemplate their possible contribution to the prosecution planning, particularly in relation to the production of evidence—pictorial, filmic, and textual—and the architecture of the courtroom.[72] This was also the first time that film was admitted as evidence in the courtroom.[73] Rather than focusing on the judges and the triangulation of power, the new courtroom would need to tend to the presentation of the evidence gathered.[74] This reconstitution of the courtroom around forensics, rather than the judges, speaks to what Jennifer Moonkin calls an emerging "culture of construction," which endowed media with evidentiary value.[75] The architecture of the courtroom was to participate in this production of evidence, but also in its global dissemination.

For the design of the Nuremberg courtroom, General Donovan asked the Presentation Branch to foreground visual evidence. Unlike military presentation rooms, where media produced a quantitative image of the world for a handful of strategists to analyze and interpret, the tribunal aimed to extract forensic value from visualization techniques for the entire world to watch, sealing World War II with a judicial victory over the Nazi party. In this sense the OSS presentation practices, but also architectures developed for presentation, aspired to be what Alejandra Azuero-Quijano defines as a "forensic practice" central in "demonstrating the rational, organized, and large-scale nature of Nazi war crimes as juridical evidence."[76] In other words, what for the military meant intelligence, information, and communication, in the hands of the tribunal would become evidence and facts for examination and cross-examination.

To spearhead the OSS team of designers for the military tribunal, Hu Barton appointed Dan Kiley, a young landscape architect with a small office in Washington, D.C.[77] Kiley had just joined OSS on the recommendation of Eero Saarinen, with whom he had been developing military housing in Washington, D.C., and Detroit, Michigan.[78] During his years at Harvard, Kiley had come to appreciate the Bauhaus tenets and functionalist principles behind Walter Gropius's teachings and writings.[79] Building on a multiscalar approach to design, Kiley proposed an integration of landscape and architecture. Along with fellow landscape designers Garrett Eckbo and James C. Rose, he declared that interior design and landscape should be in dialogue as "interchangeable and indistinguishable":[80]

> Landscape design is going through the same reconstruction in ideology and method that has changed every other form of planning since the industrial revolution. . . . The approach has shifted, as in building, from the grand manner of axes and facades to specific needs and specific forms to express those needs. . . . The technics are more complicated than in the Beaux Arts patterns, but we thereby achieve volumes of organized space in which people live and place, rather than stand and look.[81]

Kiley, who had visited the Pétain trials in Paris—a "really disorganized trial," in his view—realized the need for an ordered courtroom that organized the legal landscape around the scope of the beholder—in the case of the Nuremberg Trials, the press. Dan Kiley's team joined James (Jim) Johnson, a young architect who would draft plans and oversee the construction first in London and later in Germany, under the supervision of the Chief of Counsel.[82]

Building on the San Francisco experience, Kiley produced the courtroom as a "world stage" in his team's preliminary plans for the Chief of Counsel. "I thought it was going to be a world spectacle," Kiley recalled; "it wasn't just an ordinary trial."[83] Kiley considered how the cameras and publics of the courtroom would follow the tribunal, without, however, bringing the same kind of attention to the placement of the judicial landscape. While advocating for the Nuremberg Opera House as an alternative to the Palace of Justice site, Kiley carefully placed reproduction and photographic facilities, radio, and press, but without further defining the space of the courtroom (Figure 1.12). In another equally diagrammatic sketch, he imagined a "[b]ackdrop depicting strength of the United Nations interwoven with ultimate justice prevailing over 'might' n 'Force'," speaking to the desire to present, along with evidence, the victory of institutional organization and reasoning over aggression and war (Figure 1.13).[84] These initial plans rarely delineated the place of the judges' benches, or the witness stand, or the defendants' dock. There would be another architecture, another typology, to further determine the landscape of justice and its configuration of power presented to the world.

The architecture of courtrooms, in many ways, is an architecture of power and signification, where physical and visual forms structure jurisprudence as much as aesthetics.[85] Room acoustics, judicial dress, lighting, and the architectural construction of relations among defendants, plaintiff, and publics inside the courtroom matter.[86] Piyel Haldar calls the courtroom the *parergon* of law, the subsidiary (but no less necessary) apparatus that makes place for "legal judgment," defining the "topography" of law while constituting both its "internal, ritualized do-

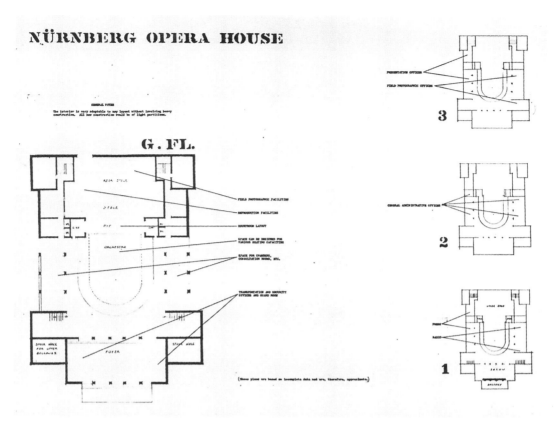

Figure 1.12. OSS provisional plan for the placement of the courtroom at the Nuremberg Opera House, 1945. Courtesy of the National Archives and Record Management.

main" and its "outside" jurisdiction.[87] And indeed, this topography of law, particularly within the context of European and North American courtrooms, as Linda Mulcahy and Katherine Fischer Taylor show, uses architecture to determine the relationships of power between the state and the public.[88] Changing legal systems often result in the reorganization of the courtroom, particularly when there is a need to demarcate a new authority in space.[89] Within these discussions the courtroom acts as a theater, either due to its performative character or due to its procedural nature and oral constitution.

In this sense, the Nuremberg trials courtroom also constituted a theatrical space designed for a dramatized experience of justice.[90] However, conceptions of what qualified as spectacle varied. The Nuremberg Trials prosecution teams resisted attempts at spectacular constructions of the space, while the press often found those attempts falling flat for not producing dramatic enough effects. Additionally, Nuremberg was not a court but rather a tribunal. Tribunals, as Cornelia Vismann demonstrates, mark a transitional period between different juridical

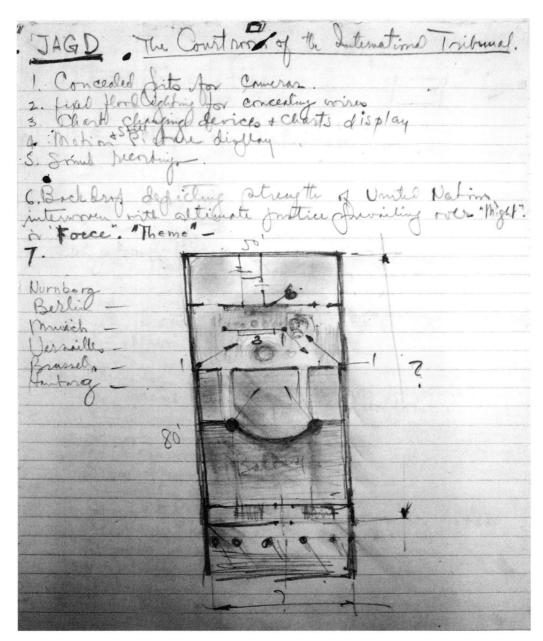

JAGD . The Courtroom of the International Tribunal.

1. Concealed slits for Cameras.
2. fixed flood lighting for concealing wires
3. Chart changing devices + Charts display
4. Motion & still picture display
5. Sound recording.

6. Backdrop depicting strength of United Nations,
interwoven with ultimate justice prevailing over "Might".
a "Force". "Theme" —
7.

Nurnberg
Berlin —
Munich —
Versailles —
Brussels —
Hamburg —

Figure 1.13. Preliminary sketch for the courtroom layout, 1945. Courtesy of the National Archives and Record Management.

domains. They are temporary spaces of adjudication that do not adhere to one es-tablished legal system. In architectural terms this means that tribunals, even when they invite the public eye, are not courts-as-theaters with well-established posi-tions for the stage and the auditorium, the actors and the spectators. In tribunals, the goal is to deliver a new power structure, displacing old authorities, in front of an audience that ultimately authorizes the court's predetermined adjudication.[91] As such, Courtroom 600 was primarily an ocular apparatus, a tool for seeing inter-national law—and by extension world order—at work. It instructed a global polity on matters of international law while constituting the tribunal's authority.

OSS architects had been working on such an ocular apparatus, while design-ing situation rooms for the military, long before Kiley inherited the design of the courtroom. Jean-Louis Cohen, building on Katz's foregrounding of presentation technique, notes that Kiley's designs acted as "a kind of retrospective situation room," delivering a juridical *"mise-en-scène."*[92] Situation and war rooms consti-tuted the main architectural contribution of the OSS Presentation Branch to the War Department.[93] In fact, the Presentation Branch formed out of efforts to furnish initially President Roosevelt and later the War Department with an "ar-chitectural flexible presentation building" that would endow think tanks with a "panorama of concentrated strategic information."[94] From 1941 to 1944, Henry Dreyfuss and Eero Saarinen had proposed and refurbished presentation rooms for the American Ammunition Plant, the Coordinator of Inter-American Affairs, OSS, G-2, the Deputy Chief of Staff, and the Bureau of Public Relations.[95] These interiors combined the modern American corporate conference room and the map room central to war operations to create an operative and quantitative image of the world for the military to act upon, setting the government and the various theaters of operation in feedback loops.[96] In the Joint Chiefs of Staff room—the most publicized situation room the OSS refurbished—maps and visu-alization boards took center stage, helping the strategists to see, assess, and plan war operations.[97] OSS designers, and in that sense the State Department as well, understood the value of those situation rooms for the production of intelligence and biopolitical operations beyond war—particularly as a quantitative, market-driven logic was taking over policy and administration—assigning Saarinen with the task to further develop a presentation room for the State Department (Fig-ure 1.14). This was the ocular architecture that the OSS architects aimed to deploy in Nuremberg.

The first proposal the Presentation Branch submitted to the Chief of Counsel in mid-July resembled those war rooms, introducing the logic of military situa-tion rooms into sites of justice. An "exhibition wall" foregrounded "evidence" for cameras on the opposite site, while retaining the centrality of the judges in the reconfiguration of power (Figure 1.15). In his letter to Justice Jackson, Gordon

PRESENTATION ROOM

Figure 1.14. Eero Saarinen, interior view of situation room for the State Department, circa 1944. Courtesy of the National Archives and Record Management.

Dean (soon to chair the United States Atomic Energy Commission) described that first proposal as "novel, if not intriguing," not only for its exhibit wall, but also for bringing film crews inside the courtroom.[98] The proposal responded to earlier directives asking for the containment of journalists and cameramen, while accommodating Bill Donovan's request for unprecedented press access.[99] Kiley would only have to install this situation room architecture on stage, centering the courtroom on charts and film, while reconfiguring the place of press, visualization easels, defendants, and judges.

The plan of the courtroom presented legal challenges, as well. There was the legislative problem: how to combine diverging national legal systems into a new foundation for international criminal law? There was, of course, the precedent of the Permanent Court of International Justice, but that organ had never aspired to attract the mass media in such a structural way. There was also the problem of representation: how to establish the international scope of the tribunal, not only in terms of its internal organization, but also in terms of its presumed jurisdiction, the world? The courtroom Dan Kiley had to design with the help of Jim Johnson did not have a single state as matron, but rather an international organization and the multilateral agreement that authorized the four judges on the

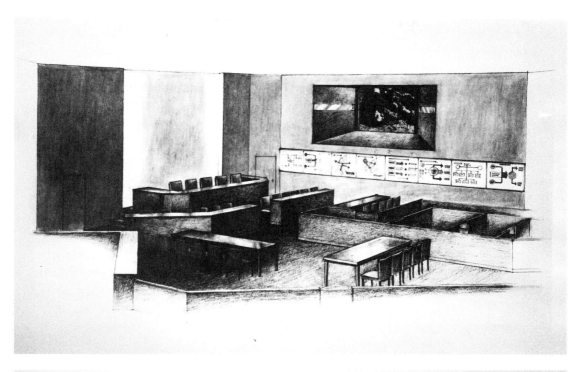

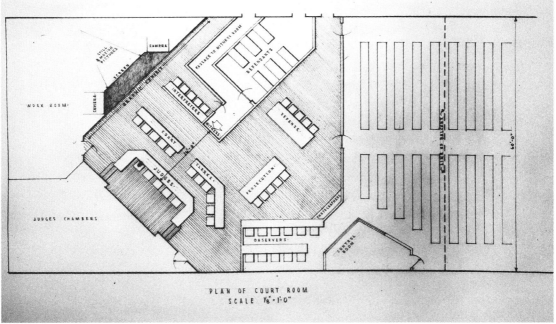

Figure 1.15. Perspectival drawing of interior view and plan of the first proposal for the tribunal courtroom, 1945. Courtesy of the National Archives and Record Management.

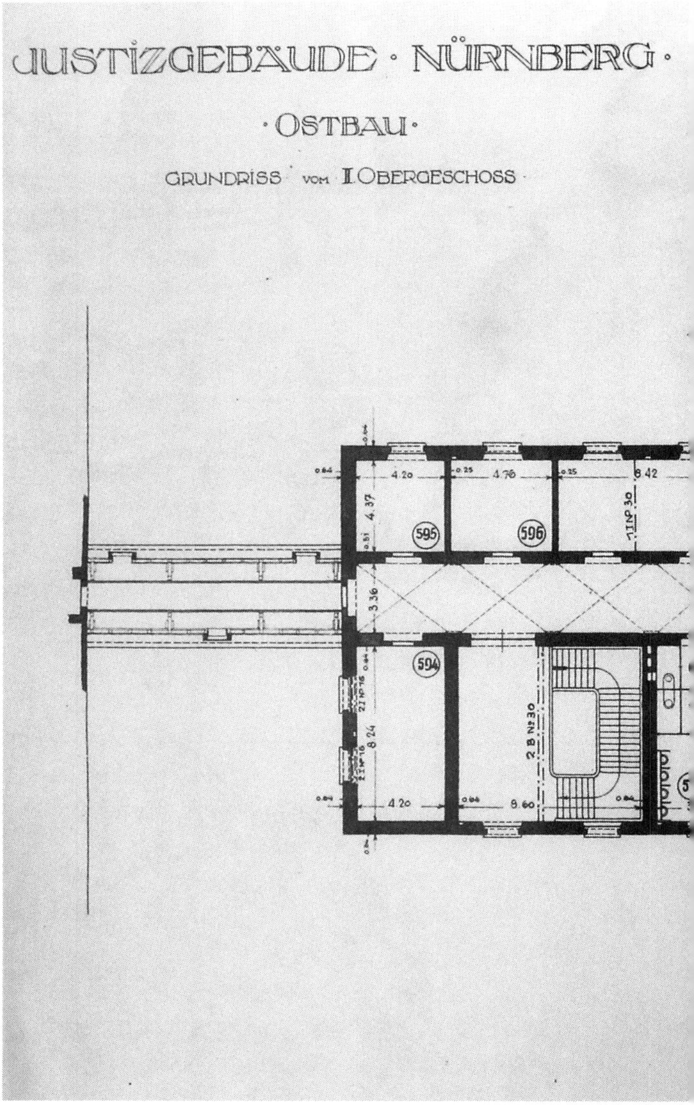

Figure 1.16. Original plan of Courtroom 600 on the second floor of the Nuremberg Justizpalast. Dan Kiley, 1912–2004. Papers of Dan Kiley. Nuremberg Courthouse. Folder: 0048. Courtesy of the Frances Loeb Library, Harvard University Graduate School of Design.

bench to issue adjudications in the name of the United Nations. Representation was at best provisional.

   Kiley declared the design of the courtroom a matter of economy and efficiency, not so much out of a desire to save time and money—although that was definitely a concern—but rather as a representation of new systems of reasoning.[100] Figuration, decoration, and monumentality would undermine architectural representations of reason, especially given the scarcity of material and human infrastructure. Instead, Kiley arranged all parts in terms of a landscape, while "struggling to meet everybody's requirements."[101] In early October, only a couple

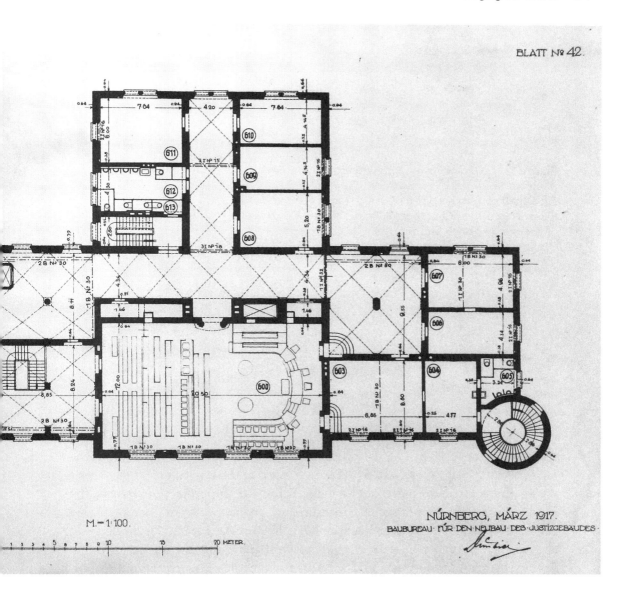

of months before the start of the trials, he submitted the final plan with provisions for furniture and media.[102] Courtroom 600 on the second floor of the annex to the Nuremberg Justizpalast, where the trials would take place, featured a central, elevated judicial bench facing defendants and prosecution with a "well"—an empty resonant space between the bench and the plaintiff for testimonies to be weighed and judged—separating the judges (representatives of the state) from the public (the ultimate witness to the application of law) (Figure 1.16).[103] Kiley kept the defendants' dock in the same place, by the doorway connecting to the prison, and moved the judges onto an elevated bench on the opposite side, facing

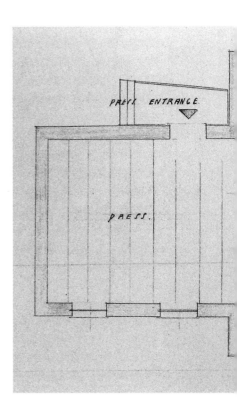

Figure 1.17. Plan of Courtroom 600 after Dan Kiley's modifications on the second floor of the Nuremberg Justizpalast. Dan Kiley, 1912–2004. Papers of Dan Kiley. Nuremberg Courthouse. Folder: 0048. Courtesy of the Frances Loeb Library, Harvard University Graduate School of Design.

the defendants. In displacing the judges from the courtroom's stage, a move that was strongly opposed by Colonel Robert J. Gill,[104] Kiley subsumed the figure of the judge within the larger system of justice arranged in the courtroom.[105]

In the traditional place of the judge Kiley put the projection screen, the board, the witness stand, and the interpreters, and across from them he placed the lectern, in front of the prosecution and the press (Figure 1.17). He centered the courtroom on the system of evidence and testimony on the background. Facing the projection screen, and with his back to the press, the chief prosecutor would address the data, assembling them into undeniable proofs of the war crimes committed. Behind the chief prosecutor, the prosecuting teams gathering and structuring information into narratives would present a well-organized machine at work, a system to bring justice.[106] This placement, as Mark Somos demonstrates, aligned the view of the press with the view of the prosecution, putting the public in the place of the prosecution interrogating evidence and defendants.[107] Justice would not be a matter of subjective interpretation, but rather based on facts.

In other ways, Courtroom 600 was no different from any other courtroom in Germany. Each party participating in the trials would enter the landscape of jus-

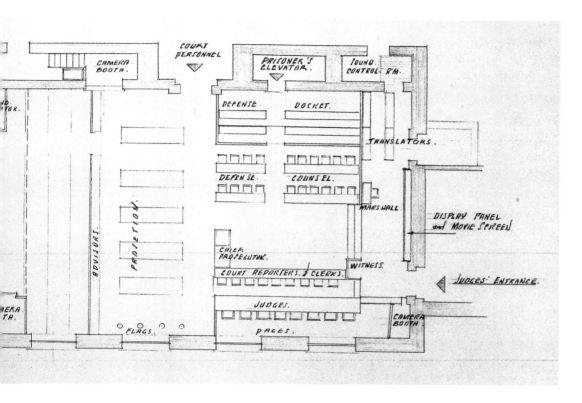

tice from a separate entrance: the press from a side entrance directly connecting to the seating area; the court clerks and prosecutors from the main entrance; the defendants from the elevator that connected through an underground passage with the prison; the interpreters from a door behind their booths; and the judges from the doorway leading to their offices. Four staircases served the courtroom, sequestering all parties moving through the judicial complex. The rationalization of the circulation system introduced press, lawyers, judges, defendants, and interpreters as distinct parts of the trial, arriving at the site of justice via dedicated pathways that did not cross-contaminate. These circulation paths also implied that the system as a whole amounted to something bigger than its constitutive parts, and that international law afforded multilateralism an infrastructure of justice.

It was in this fusion of judges, public, and media that the Nuremberg Trials' configuration of justice was produced. The international tribunal offered an opportunity to render "international law" visible to an exterior public, and at the same time to define how the public "would see it."[108] Courtroom 600 would instruct the values and structures of an international legal system in the making. "Unified, orderly, and dignified, that's what the courtroom should be," Kiley recalled later. There was the task of placing these different kinds of labor in space and delineating their relationships, generating a landscape of justice. There was the work of the defense counsels; the prosecution; the judges; the witnesses; the visual evidence; the interpreters; the clerks; the guards; and on a macroscale, the work of the press and that of internationalism, to be organized and presented in space. But there was also the additional semantic task of endowing the new international order with form and meaning, readily available to the journalists reporting back home and graspable in photographs, even if only to appeal to a collective subconscious. The U.S. State Department requested that the cases be "well reported to the world at large."[109] Apart from mediating this construction of a new justice system to the public outside, mass media would more importantly imply the presence of a mediated public in the courtroom.

To make space for the press, Dan Kiley demolished the rear wall of the courtroom, opening it up to the anteroom, and took down the wood paneling on the upper gallery to supply radio and camera booths with windows toward the courtroom (Figure 1.18).[110] The U.S. Army Signal Corps set up radio broadcasting in the attic, while cameramen filmed footage for newsreels around the courtroom.[111] The old media of the courtroom—its wooden paneling and figurative program—was covered with white walls to make space for the new media—radio and film (Figure 1.19).

More than a judicial landscape, the courtroom delivered what the Allies thought to be an important lesson in institutional multilateralism. Photographs providing glimpses into Courtroom 600 appeared in newspaper articles around the world. Often the photographs centered on the prisoners' dock, where the Nazi leaders sat under the vigilant gaze of the guards, and even more frequently the courtroom was erased altogether in favor of close-up portraits that attempted to attenuate the notoriety of those figures. But photobooks—books that used photographs to tell the story of the trials for a bigger audience—gave a slightly different account, presenting the courtroom as the instrument through which the Allied forces delivered retributive justice in the name of a global polity and liberal values.[112] During the trials the U.S. Army Signal Corps filmed the proceedings— although intermittently—for legal but also commercial reasons. Using some of that footage, Stuart Schulberg directed *Nuremberg: Its Lesson for Today* (1948), which reached movie theaters in Europe and the United States, and Elizaveta Svilova directed the USSR production Суд народов (released in English as *The Nuremberg Trials*, 1947), further reifying the image of international law and the global space of its annunciation.[113] But most importantly, Courtroom 600 fixed in place a mass media apparatus as constitutional to global interiors, challenging architects to further elaborate on the emerging new typology of public spaces while planning for the United Nations sites.

Figure 1.18. Photograph of the interior of Courtroom 600 before and after the refurbishment, 1945. Charles Alexander, Office of the United States Chief of Counsel. Harry S. Truman Library.

Figure 1.19. Photograph of Courtroom 600 after the renovations. Charles Alexander, Office of the United States Chief of Counsel. Harry S. Truman Library.

The Soundscape of Internationalism

But visual communication was not the only matter of concern. Although not immediately apparent, voice commanded the landscapes of media that OSS architects, broadcast networks, and engineers brought together in those preliminary spaces of global governance. The voice projecting from the podium constituted their political function, engulfing the polity it was addressing while feeding microphones and recording systems with signals to be transmitted, broadcast, stored, and archived as part of the organization's institutional memory. The voice was also the signal to circulate the world, turning those global interiors into its broadcasting instruments. All this attention and care around the spoken word also revealed its entanglement with the production of this new global public sphere. The acoustic formation of public spheres was apparent to the organizers of the San Francisco Conference, as it has been evident to anyone planning public speaking events. The desire to hear and be heard marks any attempt to articulate a public, even if as metaphor.

Acoustics were also important for the Nuremberg Trials. Voice and auditory technique hold a central place inside courtrooms—the spaces of elocution and testimony, as James E. Parker points out.[114] The acoustic nature of trials structures legal procedure and its temporality. Mladen Dolar argues that the "living voice" becomes the main medium through which the public gets to know and practice law, the main "instrument by which the legal system could be extracted from the hands of specialists" and brought into the public.[115] The voice of the judge implements the written law, with testimonies, examinations, cross-examinations, and closing remarks ordering the "judicial soundscape." Access to the courtroom depends on access to its soundscape, to be able to listen to the testimonies, but also to testify. To submit to the authority of the court a witness takes an oath, committing orally to speaking the truth. Visual evidence and testimonies, words and objects, intertwine in a complex audiovisual landscape, which judges (and sometimes juries as well) scan for their adjudication.[116] For a courtroom to work all parties need to be able to listen to but also to be heard by all.

What distinguished the soundscapes of San Francisco and Nuremberg from other courtrooms and parliaments was the problem of language. National juridical and political processes operate under the postulate of a shared and common language that orders the acoustic space. The San Francisco Conference and the Nuremberg Trials constituted, however, fundamentally multilingual spaces, where translation was necessary for equitable and broad access to the publics of the world. To solve this problem, the organizing committee in San Francisco turned to the diplomatic tradition of interpretation. Historically, interpreters had occupied public positions next to diplomats and politicians.[117] Diplomats' accounts presented interpreters as almost mythic machines, marveling in their capacity to memorize and translate on the spot. Stories recalled Paul Mantoux, Georges Clemenceau's interpreter at the Paris Peace Conference, and his "uncanny" ability to recite by heart very long addresses.[118] Interpreters themselves perpetuated this mythology. Arthur Birse, Churchill's interpreter, described his peers as "mouthpieces" with extraordinary capacities for focus and attention.[119] League of Nations and later United Nations interpreter Jean Herbert reveled in his own capacity to interpret even while falling asleep.[120] The metaphor of the machine served the interpreters well, particularly since it rendered them transparent mediums of transmission lacking subjective agency, as Laura Kunreuther argues.[121] But presenting themselves as machines also forged the path for their removal from the public eye and their integration into a mechanical sound system of speech transmission to structure any public space with internationalist aspirations.

Although French and English were the two official languages that diplomats adopted in San Francisco, the delegates were invited to use any language of their choice as long as they provided their own interpreters, who would take the podium and translate their speech immediately thereafter, a method known as consecutive interpretation.[122] A hallmark of bilateral diplomacy, consecutive interpretation had prevailed in international conferences and organizations in the early twentieth century. However, it was not without its own shortcomings. To begin with, consecutive interpretation substantially prolonged proceedings, doubling their duration. Time lags between a speech and its translated delivery—utterance and comprehension—disrupted the procedural flow. Delegates frequently used this additional time to prepare their own speeches or socialize backstage, disengaging and removing themselves from the process.

If for the relatively compact San Francisco Conference consecutive interpretation did not significantly affect attendance, for the Nuremberg Trials, which planned to bring on the witness stand twenty-two Nazi leaders and over a hundred witnesses for examination and cross-examination in four languages—let alone the trials of lower-ranking Nazi doctors and officers from 1946 to 1949—consecutive interpretation would double the duration of the trials, imperiling the swift delivery of adjudication. The success or failure of the process depended on an effective interpretation system. The other solution—to establish a lingua franca, so to speak—required diplomatic negotiations and threatened the fragile multilateral agreements that authorized the tribunal. A robust and effective interpretation system would short-circuit this crisis of diplomatic negotiation by eluding the establishment of a main language of communication, hence endowing the court with the appearance of equal power.

The only alternative to the consecutive interpretation method was an archaic model of simultaneous interpretation at the time installed by the International Business Machines company (IBM)—but not in use—at the League of Nations. The Filene-Finlay system of "telephonic interpretation," as the system was originally named, consisted of headphones, dials, interpreters, and a control room that monitored sound volume and channel distribution. Behind the speaker rostrum, interpreters translated each speech into one of the official languages; on the other end, each delegate, equipped with a headset and a dial, tuned in to the channel with the language of their choice. Interpretations did not interrupt the proceedings, but rather happened more or less simultaneously.

This system had been developed with the financial support of New England businessman Edward Filene, who noted at the 1919 Versailles Peace Conference and the International Chamber of Commerce founding meetings that consecutive interpretation was disruptive and dragged out the meetings. These disruptions were an unwelcome reminder that capitalism was not an organic frictionless force that moves steadily forward, regardless of the hopes of industrialists and businessmen. Looking at telephones, at the time seen as media of untapped broadcasting potential, Filene reached out to League of Nations Secretary-General

Figure 1.20. Gordon-Finlay tests "Hush-a-phone" attachment, 1927. ILO Archives, Geneva.

Eric Drummond in 1924 with an idea for a telephonic system. Given that most of the delegates prepared their speeches in writing, this telephonic method would allow the interpreters to deliver their translations almost instantly and relatively accurately. He hired British engineer Alan Gordon-Finlay, who was working for the International Labor Organization (ILO), and together they wired delegates to interpreters with "hush-a-phones," a cup-like attachment for telephones that insulated voices from background noise (Figure 1.20).[123] The goal was to produce communication as organic, instantaneous, and automated, eliminating any suspicion of friction, political or otherwise.

Since its installation at the Palais des Nations, however, the Filene-Finlay System had been in disuse, a disuse that reflected the suspicion with which international institutions had received it.[124] Perceiving it to be a threat to their profession, interpreters had abstained from working on it, actively sabotaging its use. League diplomats hesitated to adopt a system that had not been tested before. They also wondered how one could speak and listen to another speaker at the same time. The new system required that delegates stand still and speak

slowly in front of microphones, challenging early twentieth-century styles of ora-
tion and public speaking. But there was also an impending question of control.
The simultaneous interpretation system placed complete control with the interpreter, denying diplomats the opportunity to correct or revise the interpretation
of their speech. Half of the delegates proclaimed the solution ingenious and half
of them useless, leading to its abandonment. One small victory for IBM was that
the League of Nations founded a School of Interpretation at the University of
Geneva to train interpreters for its translation system, which later equipped the
Nuremberg Trials and the United Nations with interpreters.[125] Perhaps the largest problem was that—because consecutive interpretation continued while the
Filene-Finlay system was in use—League diplomats never realized the timesaving
benefits that the system was designed to deliver.[126] Instead, the predominant
consecutive model created the acoustic inferno that British journalist George
Slocombe described as a "babel of strange sounds."[127]

During the 1944 Dumbarton Oaks Conversations, OSS officials suggested the
"telephonic" method to avoid the "dull," "inefficient" consecutive interpretation
and the "cold voices of the interpreters, which painfully slowed up the proceedings" of the 1919 Paris Peace Conference,[128] but skepticism and inertia won the
argument.[129] Political leaders were reluctant to replace their own interpreters with
what looked like a mechanical system. One of the issues for Dumbarton Oaks
was trust. A set of interpreters translating out of view, with an additional engineer working the control room, undermined the sense of agency over one's own
words that the situation demanded. In addition, the number of delegates and politicians participating allowed for consecutive interpretation without testing the participants' endurance. The 1945 San Francisco Conference presented yet another
opportunity to implement the simultaneous interpretation system, but consecutive interpreters boycotted the attempt. There were not enough experienced simultaneous interpreters, and administrators preferred the safety of the known
over the unknown system, especially in such a public and outward-looking event.
Instead, the conference administrators designated two official languages, bringing past diplomatic traditions into the post–World War II world order.

The importance of a timely deliberation at the Nuremberg trials, however,
forced administrators to adopt the telephonic interpretation system over recur-
ring obstacles and people's suspicions. Ultimately, the signal architecture of the
telephonic system facilitated the broadcast of the proceedings to a wider audience,
rendering the tribunals a global event. For the Nuremberg trials, the prosecutors
hired IBM to design and build the simultaneous interpretation system they would
use. Telephonic wires and switch selectors tied together judges, witnesses, exam-
iners, and interpreters in communication channels that fed the entire courtroom
with instantaneous translations in four languages: French, Russian, German,
and English. Radio broadcasters would pick up interpreted recordings to use in

Figure 1.21. Sketch of the installation of the Filene-Finlay Translator for the ICC meeting. Both interpreters and control room are hidden behind the wall, with all chairs wired with switch selectors and headphones. Copyright and courtesy of the IBM Corporation.

their programs. The main channel was also projected in the room with loudspeakers that proved entirely ornamental, given that everyone dialed into the system rather than listened to the deliberations. Efficiency was not the only reason that prosecutors agreed on the telephonic system. By using simultaneous interpretation, the prosecution teams eliminated the additional time available for the preparation of the defense.

But the placement of the telephonic interpretation system presented an architectural challenge. The first two iterations of the system had kept interpreters in the public eye, close to the speaker's podium, but the final installation at the Palais des Nations had removed interpreters from the debate floor, arranging them behind walls to create the fantasy of organic and frictionless international communications.[130] Microphones picked up words; cables transmitted signals to a "concealed translating center"; headphones "relayed [each speech] to the auditorium," but interpreters—doing the actual labor of translation—were nowhere

Figure 1.22. Interpreters behind glass on the raised platform between the sound control room and the witness stand at Courtroom 600, 1945. Courtesy of the National Archives and Record Management.

to be seen. IBM had celebrated this architectural construction of invisible labor as a technological miracle. "The barrier of confused tongues . . . has been overcome," the press release claimed. "A speaker may now have the unique experience of having his thoughts immediately understood by an audience composed of people who do not understand the language in which he is addressing them" (Figure 1.21).[131] But interpreters, who perceived their removal from the public eye as an offense to their professional dignity, loathed it.

Kiley's architectural solution was telling of the special place interpretation held as an internationalist technology. Unlike IBM, Kiley moved the interpreters back to the spotlight, behind glass, on a raised platform next to the witness stand. Since interpreters had long been imagined as machines, with a "full command" of languages, "unusual memory," and an "exceptional faculty of concentration," Kiley decided to present them as pivotal parts of the technocracy that organized the tribunals (Figure 1.22). The placement was not functional, but rather representational. In making the presence of interpretation conspicuous and unambiguous for both journalists and the world community following the trials, Kiley constructed international law as the system ordering the "Babel of tongues," while

Figure 1.23. Interior view of the courtroom for the International Military Tribunal for the Far East. Courtesy of the National Archives and Record Management.

leaving little doubt as to how the system of international justice worked and who ordered it. He also reinforced the global and transparent character of the trials, articulating in space international law as efficient, fact-driven, and global. In doing so, Dan Kiley produced a judicial modern picturesque, in the sense that the image of international justice that the prosecution and the UN wanted to present to the world drove the design of the courtroom.

But in critically reducing the length of the trials, the IBM system also transformed the very structure of the juridical public. The interpretation apparatus required the use of headphones, but headphones acoustically isolated participants.[132] In this sense a global polity could exist only as an aggregation of individuals with atomized experiences of and relations to the legal system. Headphones, as Jonathan Sterne notes, produce an experience of listening alone-together, especially in public spaces.[133] Unlike previous courtrooms and their shared acoustic space, what participants experienced in Nuremberg was their acoustically "collectivized isolation."[134] The IBM system transformed the courtroom into a space of individuation, where all participants inhabit "their own private acoustic worlds," and share the experience of their individuation.[135] Everybody inside the courtroom could participate, but only as individuals. No global public space—not for international trials, or international conferences, or assemblies—could exist

Figure 1.24. Interpreters behind glass panels test the IBM system in its installation for the United Nations at Lake Success. Courtesy of the United Nations Photo Library.

outside the space where interpreters and headphones existed. Communication stopped the moment delegates stepped outside the room. Only within the room that interpretation systems organized did internationalism exist—not outside.

On November 21, 1945, Justice Robert H. Jackson took the podium. Across an empty witness stand and a presentation screen he inaugurated the Nuremberg International Military Tribunal, "one of the most significant tributes that Power has ever paid to Reason." Journalists and photographers anticipated a highly dramatized effect. Stuart Schulberg describes how OSS's Documentary Evidence Section proposed to line the docket with neon lights to illuminate the expressions of Nazi defendants as evidentiary film was screened. This lighting led journalists and reporters to perceive the trials as an encounter between the Nazi apparatus and its crimes. Joseph Kessel, describing it as a "unique moment in a lifetime," commented on the restorative power of the "confrontation" between the film and the Nazis, between the illustration of the horrific acts and the agents of horror.[136]

Yet the staging of the trials did not have the dramatizing effect that graphic photographs and sensational headlines in the world press promised. Routine and

Figure 1.25. Covered interpretation booths at the multilingual room at Lake Success. Ralph T. Walker Papers, Special Collections Research Center, Syracuse University Libraries.

boredom reigned in the courtroom, with testimonies dragging, legal terminology alienating journalists, and judicial etiquette tiring the public. The *New Yorker*'s Rebecca West described the courtroom as the "citadel of boredom," poignantly remarking:

> The nerves of all others present in the Palace of Justice are sending out a counter-prayer: the eight judges on the bench, who are plainly dragging the proceedings over the threshold of their consciousness by sheer force of will; the lawyers and the secretaries, who sit, sagging in their seats because they have been there so long, at the tables in the well of the court; the interpreters, twittering like sleepy birds in their glass boxes; the guards, who stand with their arms gripping their white truncheons behind their backs, as still as hard as metal, except for their childish faces, which are puffy with boredom. All want to leave Nuremberg as urgently as a dental patient enduring the drill wants to get up and leave the chair.[137]

The IBM system that was designed to shorten the duration of the trials had also slowed down the juridical process, forcing witnesses, defense, and prosecution to

Figure 1.26. Interpreters inside booths below the galleries in the Plenary Hall for the second part of the First General Assembly in Flushing Meadows, 1946. Courtesy of the United Nations Photo Library.

follow the pace of the interpreters. Yes, the interpreters could translate almost instantaneously, but to do so everyone else needed to adjust to a slower pace. Interpreters ordered the temporal reality and social life of the courtroom with "stop signs" and light bulbs on the podium, red signaling to stop and orange to slow down (Plate 4). In addition, the interpretation system forced all constituent parties to stay put in their posts behind microphones. Moving away from one's microphone equaled losing access to the legal system and the right to participate. Lawyers could not improvise and interrupt the process, creating dramatic performances to lure the judges. Judges could not lean in and whisper to secretaries or their colleagues without being recorded or interpreted. They had to announce they wanted to be "off the record."[138] Hence, the IBM system disciplined all participating bodies, transforming the courtroom into a technocracy.

Following the Nuremberg Trials, the IBM system of simultaneous interpretation became an integral component for any event or space claiming an international character. Even Justice Jackson, who had doubted the success of the

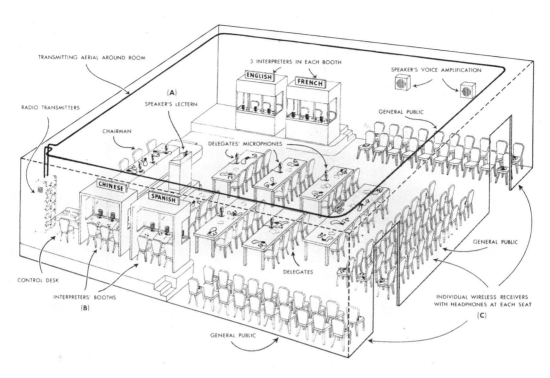

Figure 1.27. Diagram of the wireless IBM system deployed inside room, n.d. Copyright and courtesy of the IBM Corporation.

system, anticipating that the trials would be "a confusion of tongues" and "ridiculous,"[139] enthusiastically endorsed simultaneous interpretation by the end of the tribunals.[140] At the same time, General MacArthur was transplanting the spatial configuration of the Nuremberg trials to Japan for the International Military Tribunal for the Far East. When the trials launched in Tokyo later that spring of 1946, the prosecutors used Dan Kiley's diagram to organize the courtroom. The agonistic framing of the defendants against their judgment remained the same, but instead of a screen and interpreters the stage was taken over by dignitaries. Interpreters initially appeared in ad hoc places on the sides, but soon moved to a more formalized glass booth facing the press and the general public (Figure 1.23).[141] Ralph Walker, who was at the time retrofitting the Sperry Gyroscope Plant at Lake Success, adopted Kiley's glass interpretation stations but arranged them on the sides rather than the back of the hall (Figure 1.24). This initial configuration offered a productive opportunity to negotiate transparency and function, but noise complaints from interpreters forced Walker to enclose the interpretation stations later in 1946, effectively turning them into boxes (Figure 1.25). By the time that the UN Security Council moved to its temporary headquarters in Lake Success after a short stint at Hunter College, the place of the interpreters was affixed inside booths. The presentation of transparency was no longer constitutional to questions of security in the same way that it had been in the application of law. Later in 1947, when Flushing Meadows hosted the United Nations Assembly for the first time for a special session on the Palestinian occupation, UN bureaucrats fastened the place of interpreters inside booths, below the radio and film galleries flanking the plenary hall, making sure that the interpreters had visual access while remaining relatively invisible, hence enabling the fantasy of organic communication at a moment of diplomatic crisis (Figure 1.26).

From 1947 to 1953 requests for the IBM system rose from around nine to sixty per year.[142] In 1954 the company boasted that the system had made possible almost "258 international meetings" in "120 cities" in "34 countries," serviced by the "entire IBM family around the world."[143] The system would no longer be tied to buildings, chairs, and tables, but rather to the people using it, divorcing the acoustic space of international communication from the space it organized. Technicians would carry interpreters' booths, switching selectors, headphones, and microphones from conferences to meetings, and from assembly halls to courtrooms. This divorce was instrumental in widening the horizons of where and how simultaneous interpretation could be used, making possible the imagination of its future installation in conference venues, museums, and tours (Figure 1.27). Kiley's plan for Courtroom 600 transformed transparency into an integral value of the global interior, denoting the desire to reach and involve an international public residing outside the courtroom.[144] In this sense, the simultaneous interpretation system changed the presentation of international institutions, placing an emphasis on physical interiors and turning them into the de facto site of institutional internationalism.

In the San Francisco Conference and the Nuremberg Trials, the United Nations called the new global structure into existence, but also determined that the engagement with the larger public would be structured via communications and mass media. The path for the UN's representation of liberal internationalism was forged by the San Francisco Conference, where the Conference Committee, in order to qualify its platforms as international and global, had opened its doors, inviting the public (if only as eyes and ears) inside its plenary halls, the spaces that articulated the new global polity, its structures and its organs. After the conclusion of the conference, Stettinius asked Donovan to lend him Oliver Lundquist to create a UN division along the lines of the OSS Presentation Branch—the Department of Public Information, where Lundquist would serve as a "Special Services Officer" overseeing the production of films and establishing visual continuity between the Dumbarton Oaks Conversations and the United Nations.[145] Following the warm reception of the delegates' badge, David Zablodowsky, who also moved on to serve in the Department of Public Information, adapted and revised the lapel pin design to become the United Nations emblem that we know today.[146]

The American prosecution team used Courtroom 600 for twelve further military tribunals with a gloss of global authority and international affect. The French, Russian, and English prosecution teams withdrew from this second round of trials due to growing differences over jurisprudence and legal procedures. However, the power of Kiley's courtroom to signify and represent international order had superseded the need for a multilateral agreement to authorize these tribunals. The authority of the tribunals, in turn, established the plan of the courtroom. The Nuremberg courtroom laid the grounds not only for the immediate future (the International Military Tribunal for the Far East) but also for the post–1989 human rights project and the International Criminal Court, reified in its permanent seat in The Hague. There, architectural firm Schmidt Hammer Lassen implemented a historically global space, while actively internationalizing the spaces of law. "The most significant thing about Nuremberg is that it happened," claimed Whitney Robson Harris, the U.S. attorney and prosecutor.[147] He was not the only one. In fact, as legal historians and scholars have repeatedly argued, the prosecution of the Nazis was gratuitous in the first place. The significance of the event lay in its presentation of an operative system for international law, a new territory to be explored and navigated by international organizations, bureaucrats, and diplomats.

Inside those initial platforms, architecture produced two spaces: the lived space where new public spheres were formulated in the name of a global polity, and their representation through media. Between the two, the space as image and the space as practice, the separation was resolute and complete, allowing for institutional internationalism at large to acquire the image of a systemic, transparent, and just bureaucracy without lived experience undermining its efficiency and authoritative power. Above all, these initial configurations of public platforms placed an imaginary global polity inside the new institutions, while keeping publics-as-bodies outside. Those physical interiors, although global in their reach, were still impermeable as spaces, leaving mass media with the constitutive function of establishing connections with the larger world community.

2
Cultures of Assembly

Following the signing of the United Nations Charter at the end of the San Francisco Conference on International Organization (1945), a Preparatory Commission started planning the launch of the organization. The experience at San Francisco had made abundantly clear the centrality of platforms for diplomatic work in the emerging international order. Those platforms would sustain the UN's institutional multilateralism, determining the shape of the new global polity, and in doing so, also delineating its structure and function. Conversations on assembly cultures and their spaces were familiar to diplomats and high-ranking UN officials. Already involved in setting the stage to legitimize the organization, architects would design both temporary and permanent platforms based on institutional approaches to democratic form. As such, the design of these new platforms entangled discussions of aesthetics with politics, giving form to—and ultimately presenting as complete—the still unfinished project of the United Nations and liberal internationalism.

The inaugural events in San Francisco and Nuremberg revealed the UN's reliance on media conglomerates and communication technologies both for structuring its public sphere and reaching out to a broader global polity. Debates on the location of the headquarters and its structure affirmed the importance that communications infrastructures would play, as well as the volatility of the organization in the absence of permanent headquarters. Diplomats used communications as the framework through which they addressed issues central to the organization and its structure—development, decolonization, reconstruction. They challenged architects to do the same, to think of the space of global governance in terms of communications. Characteristically, Secretary-General Trygve Lie referred to the future headquarters, before a plan was in place, as the "nerve center," implying the existence of a much larger communications organism with far-reaching institutional tentacles including field stations, regional offices, and specialized agencies deployed around the world.[1] But how was communication as a function and institutional requirement to become architecture, and how was the building itself, the Headquarters, to produce that new organization?

Configuring both temporary and permanent headquarters would offer some answers, but also endow the organization with the aura of the stability necessary for its expansion. At the heart of those conversations was the form of the global polity that architects and diplomats would articulate in the Headquarters, sometimes in real time. Often tested in the organization's temporary locations, those figurations of the UN's public sphere determined the physicality of the Headquarters and ordered its constituents across the world in a causal relationship where the imagination for the latter would already be anticipated in the former. Through those cultures of assembly, the UN defined and determined how different publics interacted with the organization, modeling platforms for institutions of multilateralism in the post-1945 world order.

The World's Navel

In the years leading up to the first UN General Assembly at Church House and Central Hall in London, national delegates and their advisers occasionally touched on the topic of the headquarters, considering probable locations and spatial arrangements. Mentions of possible sites offered glimpses into the latent cosmopolitan and colonial desires driving the engines of international organization. For example, there was a persistent belief that leisurely landscapes often eased diplomatic negotiations, a belief that concealed the classed realities of the world of diplomacy. But at other times, those same conversations shed light onto new modes of diplomatic being and world organization that aligned the new institution with corporate America and its bureaucracies.

These first conversations entangled the structure of the new institution with geopolitical concerns. Since the Dumbarton Oaks Conversations, Franklin D. Roosevelt and his team had intertwined the question of location with different models of world order. His initial proposal for a federalist approach divided the world into zones of regional control with four designated "policemen" states heading them: the United States, the Soviet Union, China, and the United Kingdom. Apart from maintaining an overview of regions, the federalist model's decentralized bureaucracy required multiple regional capitols with equivalent administrative and executive power to install its network of world governance.

When Roosevelt purged the "four policemen" plan in favor of a globalist model centered on one international institution managing all political and territorial conflict, the project of institutional quadrupling started making less sense.[2] But Roosevelt insisted on avoiding a fixed center, proposing a peripatetic assembly and the dispatch of less critical components of the organization to regional centers to counteract the centralization of power.[3] During the Dumbarton

Oaks Conversations, he repeated his proposition for a dispersed institution with a permanent Secretariat, a traveling assembly, and a council of the major powers alternating among two or three sites. Roosevelt also assigned locations, putting the Secretariat somewhere in the United States and the Council on an island, with a roaming General Assembly moving from the Northern to the Southern Hemisphere. He pointed to the Empire State Building or the Pentagon as possibilities for the Secretariat, indicating his desire for a powerful bureaucracy, and proposed the Azores or Hawai'i for the new Council.[4]

Roosevelt's plan resonated with the utopian aspirations of proposals arriving at the Preparatory Commission's office. Some of them even suggested, in truly peripatetic fashion, that the new headquarters should take the form of a ship traversing the oceans.[5] However, unlike the utopian drive behind the many proposals that U.S. citizens put forward at the time, Roosevelt's project constituted a calculated political step toward American imperialism, with the administration anchored in the United States (the new aspirational center of the world); an isolated central council protecting the postwar world order away from press and public, yet close enough to the U.S.; and a detached open and international assembly in the role of the public front.

The UN Preparatory Commission, which was to translate charter principles into an operative organizational structure, arranged the first sessions of the UN organs and organized the Secretariat administrative structures. The commission had launched its operations in London, taking over Church House, Westminster, originally designed for the Church of England and its headquarters. Used occasionally by the House of Lords, Church House had already hosted the War Crimes Commission and part of the drafting of the UN Charter. There, the Preparatory Commission planned the new organization and held the first meeting of the Security Council. The commission populated a global diplomatic elite of statespersons, including eminent figures such as Peace Conference participant Wellington Koo (China), League of Nations veteran Nasrollah Entezam (Iran), and disarmament advocate Philip John Noel-Baker (United Kingdom). All committees were international in their composition; they received their charge from previous committees; and they produced reports, which they submitted for approval to the General Assembly. The location as well as the requirements for the UN Headquarters fell under the purview of Committee 8, the Preparatory Commission's technical committee for general questions, and later Committee 10, a subdivision within Committee 8 dedicated to the question of the headquarters.

The Preparatory Commission transfigured the debate between the regionalist/federalist and globalist model for world organization into a debate between centralized and decentralized institutional structures, where centralization stood for efficiency and decentralization for democracy.[6] Delegates inside the Preparatory Commission judged both models on their capacity to carry out a purported democratic and open world organization with an operational center capable of addressing the entire world as its public, a seemingly impossible task. While considering the "principle of centralization," they recognized the consolidation of political power this model would require.[7] They also quickly realized that the choice of location was both a political and a geographical matter. In choosing the location, delegates would ultimately determine a new political and diplomatic center, as the location would undeniably affect configurations of power networks within the new world order. These conversations shaped priorities not only on the level of legislation and organization, but also on the level of planning and design.

The problems that accompanied centralized institutions were clear to international policy think tanks, which had been trying to imagine ways of maintaining configurations of political power already determined before World War II. Among the handful of institutions to prepare guidelines for the new organization was the Royal Institute of International Affairs—later known as Chatham House, an institution that continuously inserted itself in the design of institutional policies and strategies for international organization. The Royal Institute, where historian Arnold Toynbee was serving as director of studies, produced and circulated several reports building on the experience of the League of Nations and the International Labor Organization. In its pamphlets, the Institute advocated for a globalist approach to foreign policy with a world state in mind.[8] Partly to establish continuities with the old colonial order, and partly due to the infrastructure already in place, the Institute championed the choice of Geneva, the location of the headquarters of the League of Nations.[9] Legal scholars and policy experts knew that centralized institutions necessitated expansive and effective communications systems for their global reach. Apart from infrastructural support (transmission centers, broadcast stations, switchboard centers, press accommodations), this meant in addition a need for the right legal and cultural conditions, "diplomatic immunity," and a robust Information Section akin to the United Nations Information Organization (UNIO).[10]

C. Wilfred Jenks's proposals piqued the interest of the Preparatory Commission delegates, who were curious to see how the Royal Institute translated the League's institutional structure into a new organization.[11] In *The Headquarters of International Institutions* Jenks, former legal adviser to the International Labor Organization, construed the new headquarters to be the center of a large communications network, and in doing so, he also demonstrated how vested the new organization needed to be in communications.[12] He condemned earlier proposals for decentralized and peripatetic institutions as wasteful, favoring the centralization of all resources and services instead. His proposal advanced an imagination of the new headquarters as a global communications hub, with a "world parliament," "libraries and records," "exceptional printing, telecommunication, coding and decoding, and other material facilities."[13] Jenks repurposed in his rhetoric ideas of world cities put forward by Andersen, Otlet, and others in the beginning of the twentieth century, emphasizing the communicative role that the seat of the new organization would play in the new world order.

Jenks's treatise steered the Preparatory Commission conversation toward communications infrastructure. The young international lawyer warned against all forms of isolation: "small island communities," "academic seclusion," and locations of racial or religious hostility. The new headquarters should be open and in touch with the global polity the organization hoped to address.

> It is these factors, and particularly the facilities for maintaining contact with the work of international institutions available to the press, the radio, the newsreels, publicists, educators, students, and representatives of organized opinion groups . . . which will determine the extent to which future international action will receive a solid backing from public opinion.[14]

Jenks even proposed the installation of television facilities to disseminate the message of the new organization.[15] His essay established communications as the problem and the answer for any attempt to launch a globalist world order. He did not prescribe form but left the planning for the physical headquarters to the "experts," without, however, avoiding speculative projections that oscillated between a robust headquarters complex and a fully developed "international city."

In the place of physical decentralization, the new global institution would rely on the circulation of information. The delegates of the Preparatory Commission discussed this new role of communication technologies and infrastructures early on in their meetings. Terms such as "diffusion" and "communications" appeared frequently in the verbatim reports. British diplomat Philip Noel-Baker noted that "international life in a material world must diffuse itself from an international centre where, without disturbance from national elements, it is permitted to breathe the international atmosphere."[16] He reasoned that centralized institutions managed resources more efficiently and that communications, both in terms of technical infrastructure and outreach programming, could weave a global community around the UN as well as—if not better than—a diffused constellation of regional institutions. Building on Noel-Baker's convictions, the commission approved the plan for a common and shared headquarters, believing that communications systems would sufficiently substitute for earlier regional plans and decentralized models.[17]

The conversation on communications infrastructure brought forward the operative tensions between the ideal of global connectivity and its local implementation, particularly concerning institutional independence and sovereignty. Communications infrastructures were complicated legal and political systems whose operation depended on multilateral agreements and negotiations among private and state actors. Even when institutions acquired their own radio stations, as was the case with the League of Nations, they depended on the local infrastructure to transmit their broadcasts and press releases, or even to make an international phone call. Delegates who placed the United Nations Headquarters within larger circulation systems realized that tapping into national communications systems would potentially compromise the institutional autonomy of the UN. Contemplating the question of sovereignty, members of Committee 10 pointed to Washington, D.C., and Vatican City as models for legal extraterritoriality and administrative independence from local legislation.[18] Extraterritoriality served autonomy, an autonomy that tapered the organization's infrastructural needs, since the headquarters would still have to establish a relationship with national communications infrastructures and energy grids, to mention only some of the technical landscapes involved.[19] Especially for communications, UN bureaucrats would have to create alliances and support fragile dependencies on national and private media conglomerates. Commission delegates maintained that proximity to established metropolitan centers that offered robust transportation and telecommunications infrastructures would address some of these needs.

The Preparatory Commission also understood the geopolitical significance of a centralized institution for international relations. An initial recommendation in favor of the United States stirred debate: European representatives, who perceived the proposal to be threatening to the relevancy of the old colonial order, used regionalist arguments to affirm Europe's continued centrality to the new world order. "It would not be desirable to centralise all international life in one country," noted Paul-Henri Spaak, the Belgian statesman who campaigned for the European Union and later served as Secretary-General of NATO. European representatives went as far as to cartographically misconstrue Europe as the "natural and inevitable communications centre of the world"[20] or to present it as "the cradle of modern civilization," building on colonial takes on history.[21] Middle Eastern, Asian, and Latin American representatives, who saw in the new headquarters the opportunity to shift the center of administrative and executive power,[22] persistently dismantled "European arguments" that sought to reinforce old hierarchies rooted at the League and to stratify certain state members as "second class" citizens.[23] Luis Padilla Nervo, the Mexican ambassador, acutely voiced his frustration:

> Let us not talk the language of 1920 or 1938. Let us not talk about the 'Mother of Civilisation' in relation with the issue before us, or we will have to engage in a historical debate about the 'Grandmother' and the 'Great Grandmother' of it. . . . Let us not talk of Europe as the centre of the world from which everything radiates and to which everything converges. The world to-day, Gentlemen, has not one centre any more, except that moral

centre to be built up by the common purpose and combined efforts of the United Nations.[24]

By the end of the discussions one thing was clear: the fight over institutional centralization constituted, in reality, a fight over European hegemony and its contestation.[25]

The site of the headquarters mattered for its semiotic capacity to denote the gravitational center of the new world order and the geopolitical affinities that order created. Driven by an anti-colonial sentiment to shift that center away from the European continent, the final vote affirmed a new world order on the rise with the United States at its center.[26] The old colonial order, initially supported through proposals for regional control, gave way to a new approach, both more expansive and more centralized. The promise that communications channels would hold the new institution accountable to its wider public resolved what started as a diplomatic and political debate by means of engineering and infrastructure.

The Preparatory Commission reframed the headquarters in terms of a brain managing and controlling the operations of this larger communications organism. Communications and transportation systems entangled the institution with the global polity it hoped to order and govern by proxy. A Technical Advisory Committee on Information proposed the establishment of a Department of Public Information to handle UN policy on news circulation.[27] At the same time, communications emerged as a central concept for organizing the building itself. The report asked for "corridors" as a spatial means of connecting departments with administrative infrastructure; for "service arrangements concerning messengers, and attendants"; "writing room"; and space to help with the "distribution of documents and notices." It also requested room for "radio, cable, telegraph and telephone facilities" and technical support in the form of "certain devices for speech transmission and recordings, and for simultaneous translations of speeches into the five official languages," listing all the ways in which communication would be instituted within the body of the UN. The headquarters would not only be the center of a larger communications system, but be itself a communications organism.

Starting with the Preparatory Commission, a battalion of committees and subcommittees took over the planning of the headquarters, turning its design into a bureaucratic process. Committee 10 put together a first set of guidelines for requirements; Committee 8 recommended specific site locations and refined the program; the Interim Committee and its Inspection Group further narrowed down the potential sites from six to two, and arranged for the temporary headquarters; the Headquarters Commission located particular plots of land within the two recommended areas; the Planning Commission outlined the project and coordinated the construction from the drawing board to the opening of the headquarters to the public; and the Board of Design developed the plans, sections, and elevations of the project. Drawings made the proposal a concrete possibility, but in that initial stage, text allowed UN diplomats to have a say in the organization's architecture, even if in terms of metaphors and requirements, feeding the emerging bureaucratic superstructure with their ideas. Within this context, the introduction of communication as a principle and requirement for world order constituted a recalibration strategy that allowed the centralization of international institutions to prevail in a postwar world critical of overgrown centers.

World Capital or Headquarters?

News of UN committees discussing the Headquarters location triggered a torrent of proposals. Perceiving the creation of the UN to be a U.S. affair, U.S. citizens flooded the office of Edward Stettinius—the Secretary of State turned U.S. ambassador to the UN—with suggestions. Architects, lawyers, contractors, and members of the public asked U.S. officials and UN committees to make space for them within the new headquarters. Charlene Mires discusses at length how private citizens, public administrators, communities, and city officials campaigned for their own cities.[28] She shows how local actors employed world-capital plans to convince the different UN committees of the viability of their sites, often building on earlier versions of world cities. Some communities, emboldened by the charter, used the opportunity to campaign for their rights. Ben P. Choate, a Choctaw Nation lawyer, offered the Choctaw Capitol plot in Tuskahoma in southeastern Oklahoma, a nomination that would be "no finer or nobler tribute" to "minority groups" in the area.[29] Proposals earlier dismissed resurfaced as possible solutions, as was the case with Paul Otlet's international city for scientists, artists, and scholars.[30] These projects ranged in scale and detail from vague suggestions to worked-out plans.[31] Petitioners often provided drawings and maps illustrating the fitness of the proposed sites, as was the case with the borough president of the Bronx, who put forward Riverdale, New York, an "isolated" yet "accessible to the heart of the City" site (Figure 2.1)[32] or another letter writer who appended a variation on the theme of the World Centre of Communication for the "United Nations Center," complete with plan and tower of progress in the middle (Figure 2.2).[33] The letter writers felt themselves part of the UN's public that they aspired to shape, willing the organization to enlarge its scope into world governance.

U.S. professional organizations and journals sparked a field-wide conversation not only on the location of the UN, but also on the possible role that architecture could play within international institutions. The UN appointed Howard K. Menhinick of the Tennessee Valley Authority to direct the Headquarters Planning Committee. U.S.-based architects and planners approached the Planning Committee with theories and suggestions. Professional societies such as the American Institute of Architects, the American Institute of Planners, the American Society

Figure 2.1. James J. Lyons, Bronx Proposal for the UN Headquarters, 1945. Courtesy of the NYC Municipal Archives.

of Landscape Architecture, and the American Society of Civil Engineers all lobbied for their representation in the process of the site selection.[34] Representatives of the Congrès Internationaux d'Architecture Moderne (CIAM) also hoped for an active role within the design process. Speculative articles appeared in all the major architectural publications at the time: *Progressive Architecture, Architectural Forum,* and *Domus,* to name a few.[35]

Regardless of references to "headquarters," the conceptual stupefaction over the scale and character of the building infrastructure persisted. UN diplomats inside the Preparatory Commission indulged visions of world capitals and international cities in an effort to speak to and formalize a global polity. UN press releases muddled state capitols and capital cities with the UN headquarters, confusing buildings for legislative organs and cities with sites of organizational management. The evocation of a "world capital" spoke to the diplomatic imaginary at work. A world capital created the illusion of world governance without necessarily legitimizing it. Like capital cities, a world capital offered to its citizens an open and living symbol of governance and sovereignty to visit and project themselves onto its built environment. Different delegations inside the Preparatory Commission were also sympathetic to the idea of a "world capital," believing that a city, rather

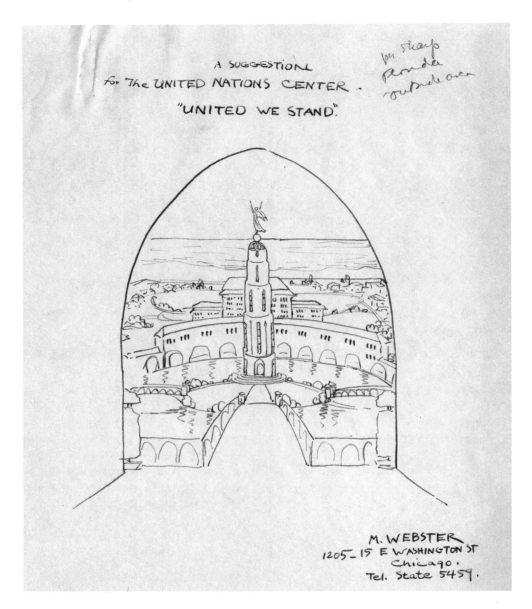

than a headquarters, would better denote the gravitational power that the seat of
the new global organization would carry. In memoranda, national representatives
drew comparisons with Geneva and entertained the idea of suburban locations.[36]
The UN Interim Committee on Headquarters and the Permanent Headquarters
Committee both anticipated a city forming around the seat of the new organization.[37] A world capital, unlike a headquarters, allowed fictions of a global federation of states to linger a bit longer, as well as offered national representatives to

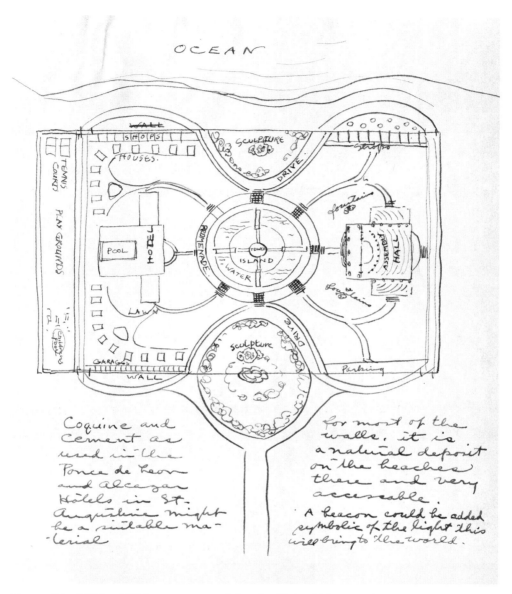

Figure 2.2. Mildred Webster, proposal for the United Nations Organization, 1945. Courtesy of the United Nations Archives and Records Management.

the UN an opportunity to reimagine their habitus and diplomatic work as tools of governance. An international polity could roam the streets of a world capital, feeding visions of a space that included rather than excluded publics. Contemplating urban forms and questions of an international city, a *polis,* meant examining also future forms of world citizenship, since, at least in the mind of the delegates, cities ordered societies and publics.

No project articulated this vision of a "world capitol" more forcefully than the proposal that Mayor O'Dwyer and Robert Moses put together for the nomination of the former grounds of the 1939–1940 New York World's Fair at Flushing Meadows (Figure 2.3). Gilmore D. Clarke, in collaboration with Aymar Embury II, Wallace K. Harrison, and Louis Skidmore, enveloped the General Assembly with an enormous cupola at the end of a monumental entryway and the rest of the capitol bowing in an otherwise classical arrangement of colonnades and art deco sentimentality. Hugh Ferriss's dramatic renderings illustrated the domineering cupola, marking in space the presence of the UN General Assembly, as both global and central to the new world order, denoting the intention to include the world by using the dome as an architectural symbol of universality. Within the General Assembly Hall, clearly marked with the laureled map of the world beaming light, the ocean of people gleaming under the dome left no doubt that the intention was to host the entire world (Figure 2.4).[38]

But how was a capital city to be global legally, functionally, and symbolically? Lewis Mumford, who had been thinking and writing about cities, had some suggestions. In his memorandum to the Inspection Group of the Interim Committee that was assessing sites, he talked about the "interior reconstruction" that a new world city would induce.[39] He believed that the mere existence of an internationalist space could instill humanist values in its surroundings, further pushing out the corporate and managerial drives behind urban development projects. The new city, "for it will be a city," he noted, "must be a City of Man; not a City of Western Man, not a City of North American Man, best of all, not an American City. It will be in America, but not of America, except in the sense that it is also of Asia, of Africa, of Europe."[40]

Mumford also gave voice to concerns and solutions aired within the architectural community, mapping out—and later rejecting—three major approaches. He opposed Philip Johnson's and Henry-Russell Hitchcock's strand of modernism as the sole appropriate expression of internationalism on the grounds of its reduction to a style with fixed elements. He sympathized with Andersen's idea for a World Centre of Communication, but regretted its purported "aesthetic expression of unity" for subordinating all parts to a "centralized authority." Capital cities such as Washington, St. Petersburg, and even the palatial complex in Versailles epitomized this kind of fictitious aesthetic unity to be avoided, as did Vatican City, a popular legal example of extraterritoriality. At the same time, he vehemently disapproved of the eclecticism of World Expositions and International Fairs, explicitly attacking the Rue des Nations planning feature for celebrating nationalism and reducing internationalism to a serial display of "variety" and "national idiosyncrasy."

For Mumford internationalism was a process and an organizational principle, not a form. Unity, he noted, could only emerge from a collective process, where "strife and turmoil and discussion" would eventually lead to a "new center of a

Figure 2.3. Hugh Ferriss, perspective drawing of a view of the UN project at Flushing Meadows at night. Flushing Meadows Proposal for the UN Headquarters, New York City Mayor's Committee on Plan and Scope, September 1946, Wallace K. Harrison architectural drawings and papers, 1913–1986. Courtesy Avery Drawings and Archives.

world organization" that synthesized the many historical, regional, or cultural references into one coherent physical arrangement for all.[41]

> For the unity to be sought is not an arbitrary, abstract, paper unity, to be imposed at the beginning and never departed from, but an organic unity, imperfect as all living things are imperfect, but serving as a principle of order, to be struggled toward, to be worked out, but never to be stultified by a surface perfection that allows no place for the further workings of time and mind.[42]

Mumford invited the Inspection Group and the Preparatory Commission to engage with "the collective mind," rather than assign the task to specialists. He advised against architectural competitions, a solution championed by MoMA

Figure 2.4. Hugh Ferriss, Auditorium of the General Assembly, perspectival drawing in New York City Mayor's Committee on Plan and Scope, Plan for Permanent World Capitol at Flushing Meadows Park, September 1946. Ralph T. Walker Papers, Special Collections Research Center, Syracuse University Libraries.

dignitaries and CIAM representatives. He proposed instead a planning process that involved the publics the UN wished to form, turning the temporary locations into the testing ground of spatial configurations for the different organs. And although in practice this process was never formalized to the extent that Mumford wished, parts of the proposal were. The various committees—including the architects participating later on—surveyed civil servants with experience in international administration and examined the temporary placement of fur-

niture and bodies in London, as well as Hunter College and Lake Success, New York. "World co-operation," Mumford wrote, should infiltrate the processes and drive the final result, from the conception of the headquarters to the final built form.[43] The organization filed away most of the externally produced reports that arrived from outside the UN's official channels, turning them into the archive of the institution's inability to address its publics outside their national containers. Mumford's proposal was no exception to that rule, being largely ignored despite assurances of its wide circulation, possibly fueling his later critical takedown of the Headquarters in his "Skyline" column.[44]

But committees, although often presenting otherwise, are not uniform. Not all delegates planning the UN envisioned world capitals with global polities roaming their streets. Inside the Headquarters Commission, members voiced concerns about this approach. The discord kindled Le Corbusier, the architect who had joined the commission as the French representative, and who hoped to create receptive conditions for his work and to forge a place for CIAM. Le Corbusier had inserted himself at an early stage, before any structures and design committees were set in place; he also understood that efforts to include the world, even as a representation, led to palaces and world capitals, programs antithetical to the architectural modernism he hoped to champion for the UN.

The machine metaphor was prevalent in descriptions of the UN organization and its seat. Official documents, minutes, and decrees had referred to the site as "headquarters" at least since the San Francisco Conference on International Organization—if not earlier, during the Dumbarton Oaks negotiations. Politicians and high-ranking officials often described the new organization as "an instrument" and not an "enchanted palace"; an "effective machine" second to none;[45] and later, on the eve of the Cold War, a "delicate machine."[46] Abe H. Feller, who was the legal adviser to the UN and participated in the planning of the headquarters, proclaimed the UN organs the "machinery of the Organization," with their "cogs and gears" waiting to be polished.[47] Building on the machine metaphors that UN diplomats and delegates put forward, modernist architects advocated for a functionalist approach to the headquarters design.

The term "headquarters" used in official documents and press releases spoke to the desire for a centralized control center to manage the passage from the old colonial to the new world order. The term "headquarters," reminiscent of military operations, suggests that the seat was also seen as the command post of a considerably larger unfolding enterprise. During the nineteenth century, inside "headquarters" commanders managed war theaters, missionaries organized expeditions, and colonial administrations planned strategies to further embed themselves within local social fabrics and markets while extracting resources and labor. By the end of World War II, the term came to signify corporate capitalism and the centralization of its expanding operations to global markets.[48] Corporate headquarters worked as the center that held together and commanded the company's dispersed body. Architects found in corporate America a welcoming ground for modernist experimentation with the physiognomy of office buildings.[49] But headquarters also denoted a relationship structured along the lines of a communications apparatus that further removed publics and placed them outside in abstracted zones of operations—the field. The existence of a headquarters suggested, not only a managerial approach to administration, but also an institution that organized its expansion and growth through communications centers.[50]

The term sat well with UN aspirations to install a worldwide system of management. Le Corbusier, who had joined the Headquarters Commission inspecting sites, affirmed that the UN assignment was for a "headquarters," establishing the design problem as univocally modern. In his personal report to the sixteenth meeting of the Headquarters Commission, proclaimed as the official opinion of France, he issued an ultimatum to Secretary-General Trygve Lie: "World Capital or Headquarters?" (Plate 5).[51]

> Words are bearers of their own destiny. The assignment is given to establish the Headquarters of the United Nations in the United States. Headquarters means an assemblage of persons and instruments at a given spot connected with the zone of operation by the most efficacious means of communication. The zone of operation is, in this case, the entire world, all points of which are known and accessible today.[52]

Le Corbusier proposed that the design of the headquarters, conceived as an instrument in the service of the UN, should "draw upon the prodigious resources of technics" and engage with the "mechanizing world."[53]

In advocating for "headquarters," Le Corbusier confirmed the latent presence of an almost military understanding of operations in the design of those spaces, especially evident in the temporary headquarters that the U.S. Signal Corps had been building for the organization in the Sperry Gyroscope Plant, Flushing Meadows, and Hunter College. He subsequently equated the UN's expansion with deployment strategies, and he theorized this new global space in terms of an "assemblage," a system of "persons and instruments" very similar to the systems that tied ships, aircrafts, and combat vehicles in communication loops with command centers. Architects were not to design palaces, but rather infrastructures for a new communications organism built to grow and manage theaters of operations globally. "One manages well only what one controls," affirmed Le Corbusier, anticipating that the organization would expand and install similar "control points" in geopolitically cardinal locations.[54] This theorization of the UN headquarters pointed to the emergent comprehension of the organization's seat as the brain of a communications organism that construed the world community, the publics the UN wished to address, as a "zone of operation."

Le Corbusier gave architectural form to his infrastructural vision. The drawing to illustrate his proposal for the General Assembly, the Council Chambers, and the Commission Halls brought together under one roof all the spaces for communal deliberations, hanging from a block of trusses in the ceiling (Figure 2.5).

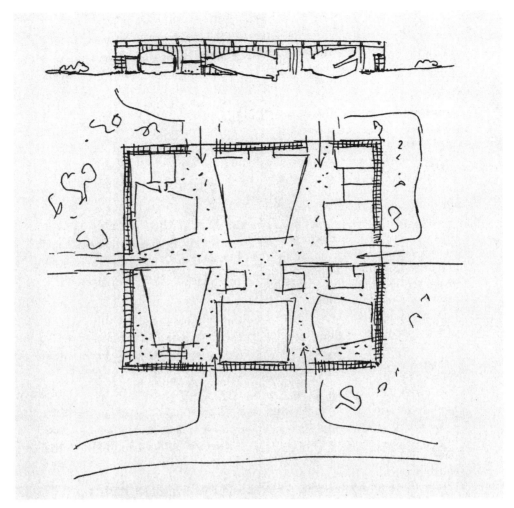

Figure 2.5. Le Corbusier, plan of proposed infrastructural block for the UN Headquarters, from his report published as Annex I in *Report of the Headquarters Commission to the Second Part of the First Session of the General Assembly of the United Nations* (Lake Success, N.Y.: United Nations, 1947). Copyright F.L.C. / ADAGP, Paris / Artists Rights Society (ARS), New York 2023.

First you see a group of bridge girders, destined to control the character of all possible ceilings and more precisely those of the halls, assembly, councils and commissions: Henceforth each ceiling is <u>independent of the ground</u>, suspended; the halls can therefore obtain any desirable size being neither bound down nor disturbed by the cumbersome presence of the supports. 'Façades' and 'silhouettes' need no longer be our concern. This important building, housing the Assembly, Councils and Commissions, will be a vast and regular quadrilateral mass.[55]

In reducing the outside to a box, Le Corbusier reframed architecture as systems management and articulated an entirely new—and unlike him—infrastructural approach to design. He drew attention to the spaces of assembly and collaborative work, the social spaces of the new global institution that the rest of the building would support with communications and technical systems. He also proclaimed those spaces the subject matter of technical knowledge (acoustics, lighting design, and air conditioning), positing that the headquarters would emerge in the conjunction of support systems with public forums. He continued advocating for a unified infrastructural block, or the "Forum" as he called it, all the way until April 1947, when the design of the UN Headquarters had moved to the hands of the Board of Design.

The chair of the Headquarters Commission, Sir Angus Fletcher, endorsed parts of Le Corbusier's report, agreeing with the criticism of the term "world capital," as did a confidential "critique" that circulated within the commission.[56] Additionally, the report received some unlikely supporters in Washington: congressmen, who, concerned with relinquishing U.S. territory to the UN, warned against "world capital" initiatives and the extensive internationalization of land they required. Instead, they lobbied for a limited "Headquarters District" that accommodated only the main organs and functions of the UN, with a more flexible—in terms of sovereignty—"zone" surrounding the international ground.[57] Within a matter of six months, the imagination around the UN Headquarters had moved away from palatial aspirations to infrastructural realities, placing communications and technological systems at the heart of the literal and metaphorical architecture of the UN.

A Workshop for Architecture

In January 1947, Wallace K. Harrison was given the most coveted job in the world—or the "world's number one job" as the *United Nations World* described it: to be the Director of Planning leading a team of designers, engineers, and contractors to design and build the United Nations Headquarters. The UN needed a manager-architect with experience coordinating large construction projects, and Harrison fit the bill. As a member of the New York Commission for the United Nations and the American Institute of Architects, Harrison had been entrenching himself deeply in the networks of real estate, diplomacy, and governmental bureaucracies growing around the UN. He had received his initial education at the Boston Architectural Club (one of the Society of Beaux-Arts Architects ateliers maintained in collaboration with the Worcester Polytechnic), and he had apprenticed in the ateliers of such prominent American architects as McKim, Mead & White and Harvey Wiley Corbett.[58] Having worked for some of the largest architectural offices at the time, Harrison recognized the managerial aspects of architectural work. His quick ascendance up the ladder of New York architectural offices brought more projects and new partnerships with Raymond Hood and later J. André Fouilhoux; a widening of his social circles; and a lucrative lifelong friendship with Nelson Rockefeller after Harrison's marriage to Ellen Milton, Abigail Rockefeller's sister-in-law. By the early 1940s, his designs for Rockefeller Center and the 1939–40 New York World's Fair, as well as his projects for real estate tycoons William Zeckendorf and the Rockefellers, had put him at the center of architectural production in New York.[59]

But what truly brought his candidacy to the table was the deal he helped secure between Nelson Rockefeller and William Zeckendorf for the UN Headquarters amidst a complicated and contested field of site nominations. By late 1946, just before his appointment, state and municipality representatives had offered plots of land from New Jersey to South Dakota, and from New Orleans to Hyde Park.[60] Reports on zoning, boundaries, transportation infrastructure, facilities, and topography deluged a group of delegates, who, surrounded by maps and drawings, found it exponentially harder to decide (Figure 2.6). If, in the Nuremberg Trials, graphic representation and visualization techniques helped prosecutors make the case (chapter 1), at the Headquarters Commission, they aggravated confusion, demonstrating that visual representation can only be effective when configured to present an argument. "Facts" rarely speak for themselves, and a productive comparison became increasingly impossible as technical descriptions and maps flattened all sites to equally problematic solutions.[61] Locations were vetoed on the grounds of racial discrimination (California nominations suffered due to the only recently repealed Chinese Exclusion Act of 1882, as did any area south of the Mason-Dixon line) or religious prejudice (a public speech against atheism and the USSR jeopardized Boston's case), with signs of local protest against the headquarters disqualifying nominations.[62]

The story of the final site selection is well known and has been widely documented. When the Headquarters Commission resolved to propose a site in Westchester, New York in early December 1946, delegates, who had been growing enamored with New York urban life and frustrated with their commute, frowned upon the idea of a suburban location.[63] But officials felt that the lack of a permanent home put at risk the organization and its stability. Mayor O'Dwyer, wanting to keep the headquarters closer to Manhattan, put together the United Nations Committee of the City of New York for his campaign. Faced with the possibility of losing the commission to another municipality, members of the committee, who coveted the investment and real estate opportunities that the UN Headquarters would bring to New York, rallied to keep it within the five boroughs.[64] On December 15, 1946, the UN General Assembly accepted Nelson Rockefeller's offer to buy the Turtle Bay plot from William Zeckendorf and donate it for the establishment

Figure 2.6. Permanent Headquarters Committee at Flushing Meadows, 1946. Courtesy of the United Nations Photo Library.

of the headquarters. Secretary-General Trygve Lie praised Harrison for his "forth-rightness, common-sense approach, and diplomacy" during negotiations.[65]

Meanwhile, after considering a number of venues from the Country Center in Westchester to Atlantic City's Convention Center or Boston's Symphony Hall (all of them dismissed for either involving long commutes, or lacking housing vacancies and office space),[66] the UN Inspection Group wound up recommending the Sperry Gyroscope Plant at Lake Success for temporarily hosting the Secretariat,[67] expecting alternative accommodations for the General Assembly closer to the city.[68] The directive motivated Mayor O'Dwyer to expedite negotiations and secure locations for the temporary headquarters in and around the five boroughs, first at the Bronx branch of Hunter College (present-day Lehman College) and later, when Hunter asked for the return of its campus facilities,[69] the Building of the City of New York at Flushing Meadows. These were the sites where the UN General Assembly, the Secretariat, and the three councils would test and configure their habitus, organize their public spheres, and define their relationships with the general public and the press.

By the time that Harrison took over the lead for the Headquarters design in early January 1947, the idea for an architectural competition had been aired and tabled for countering ideals of collaboration and unity. The truth of the matter was that UN high-ranking officials were trying to avoid the possible—and in their minds almost unavoidable—backlash from an international competition going awry, let alone the delay in construction that said competition would result in. And although UN bureaucrats at the Secretary-General's office kept their distance from the troubling (and misconstrued) legacy of the Palais des Nations competition, they did not hesitate to adopt the collaborative model used there to synthesize the finalists' entries, with Lewis Mumford's blessings.[70]

Harrison supported the idea of an international team of architects working together, especially since such collaborative efforts replicated the structure of commissions and specialized committees before them. The design of the headquarters was no different a problem than the planning for the organization of the Security Council or the General Assembly. National representatives, nominated by their governments and selected by the new Director of Planning, would present and debate their projects in front of the group, echoing the review and jury culture in architectural schools, but with the ultimate goal of synthesizing all solutions into the final project.

The UN could project the Board of Design as an open, democratic, and international structure precisely because the selection process had already either excluded or marginalized contingent voices that might have contested the process. Harrison immediately surrounded himself with confidants. He appointed Max Abramovitz as Deputy Director; George Dudley as liaison with Executive Secretary Glenn Bennett; Oscar Nitzchke as chief designer; and Hugh Ferriss, the illustrator responsible for the Rockefeller Center and X-City renderings, as the head of the drafting team to support the Board of Design with renderings. Invitations went out to all member states, requesting the nomination of architects for the board. Harrison launched a Research Section within the Headquarters Planning Office, headed by writer and dancer Faith Reyher Cook, who compiled meticulous candidate profiles, accompanied with biographies and portfolios.[71] In addition Cook solicited articles, books, and photographs of projects, helping Harrison to select the architects of the board based on their formal language and architectural approach.

This celebration of communication and inclusion was only to designate procedures rather than results. Although delegates welcomed the idea of promoting a collaborative ethos, dialogic procedures, and international participation, the board was marked by certain absences and Harrison's invisible work backstage. Not all member states were in a position to send a representative; El Salvador, India, Siam, and Syria all refrained from nominating due to lack of resources.

Chile, Czechoslovakia, the Union of South Africa, Ecuador, Iraq, Mexico, and Panama, to name a few, sent nominations that did not move forward or were replaced by a candidate favored by Harrison (and Le Corbusier).[72] The final composition of the board and the technical advisers tilted considerably toward the European and North American world, with the exception of Oscar Niemeyer from Brazil, Julio Vilamajó Echaniz from Uruguay, and Liang Sicheng from China.[73] Additionally, in requesting blueprints and photographs, Harrison ensured that the participating architects shared some foundational modernist language, eliminating candidacies with historicist and academic tendencies in their architecture. His process did away with the problem of judgment, since he had made sure that board members shared to a certain extent a modernist aesthetics and agenda. Finally, the discursive process of collective assessment he proposed complicated authorship claims and buttressed the authority of the Director of Planning over any one architect in the group.

The Board of Design, along with its entire infrastructure of draftspersons and model makers, took possession of the twenty-seventh floor of the Radio-Keith-Orpheum (RKO) building.[74] Harrison and Abramovitz cleared one side for mounting and debating working drawings, while moving the drafting room and office space on the other side, setting design production and critique in a continuous feedback loop (Figure 2.7). The two architects understood very well that, although the debate theatrics implied otherwise, power lay in the drafting room backstage, where conversations and abstract ideas were translated into architectural form. To manage the operation, Harrison and Abramovitz placed their offices next to the drafting room, overlooking the developing projects on the ground, yet removed from the conversation. "If you dropped into the Conference Room, any lunch-hour, you would see plans, sections, elevations being brought in from the drafting room," Ferriss remembered.[75]

Harrison spent most of February confirming the rest of the board members. In the absence of a quorum—the last architect to arrive showed up in early April—the Director of Planning prioritized the translation of requirements to spatial relations. Harrison's decision to limit conversations on the headquarters plan and to postpone decisions on architectural form constituted a strategic move that allowed him to suspend individual board members' ambitions to determine the external form of the building—often the site of contestation—and in doing so, to also manage conflict and debate. Buildings, the form they deliver, mattered. Elevations and facades fossilized the architectural gesture, inscribing metonymically the presence of the architect within the space of the city. Interiors, perceived as malleable and transient, did not carry the same weight for Harrison's board architects. George Dudley, who left the most complete record of those meetings, was surprised with the leniency architects demonstrated in discussing and revising their plans on the Headquarters interiors.[76] A couple of months later the external orientation and form of the Headquarters would spark debates over

Figure 2.7. Staff designers and architects in the drafting room preparing preliminary plans for the Board of Design proposals, RKO Building, New York, March 1947. Courtesy of the United Nations Photo Library.

monumentality and authorship, but for the time being, it would be designed from the inside out.

In the beginning, the board spent most of its time shifting around model rooms for the councils and the meeting agencies, even debating at times the importance that certain UN organs might take and their impact on form. The preliminary outline that Harrison shared with the Board of Design was surprisingly architectural in form, mainly reflecting the diplomats' eagerness to see the organization acquiring a body. The report on "basic requirements" detailed the number of floors, terraces and loading platforms, courtyards, and ponds, calculations for a General Assembly with "continental" type seating, and ample lobbies. The preparers had translated quantitative needs into buildings, giving the Secretariat the form of a slab and the UN council chambers a "Forum" bloc shape determined down to its conferencing tables (Figure 2.8).[77] The Committee on Requirements admitted their plan was too "specific," but reassured the architects of its "imaginary" nature.[78]

In contrast to the detailed plans for individual chamber and meeting room types, the report that the Headquarters Commission had submitted to the UN

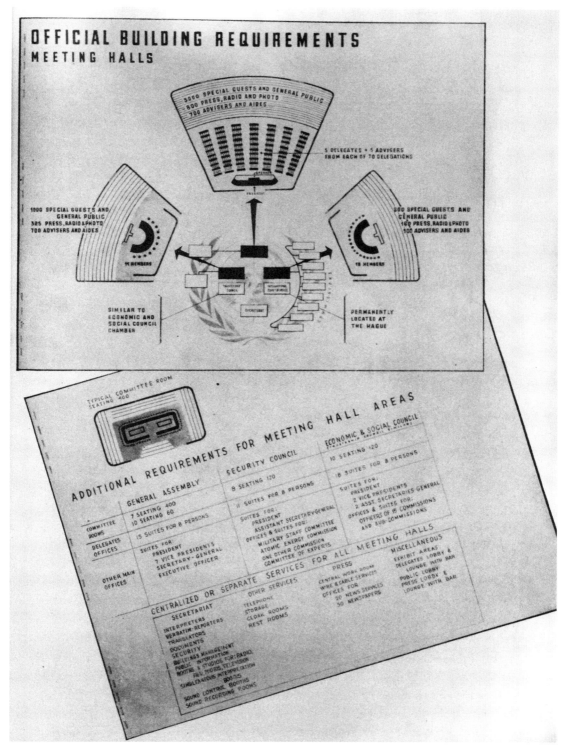

Figure 2.8. Excerpted pages from the official building requirements published in Wallace K. Harrison, "Planning for Peace," *Architectural Record,* April 1947. Courtesy of the United Nations Archives and Records Management.

General Assembly in 1946 did not delineate how different parts of the administration related to one another, or how to organize them in space. Diplomats and UN bureaucrats had ideas about operational affinities and structural connections among organs and divisions, but not a plan for them. Council chambers, meeting halls, conference rooms, plenary halls, office space, and the Secretariat appeared as floating elements in search of an expressive unity. The organization itself, the UN, would be as much a matter of design as it would be a matter of executive planning. Ralph Walker, one of the consulting architects, noted that in the process of resolving the plan, corridors and lounges started gaining an out-of-place prominence, probably the outcome of the board's divided attention between interior arrangements and external form, but also of the stated need for spaces for backstage informal diplomacy.[79] Walker's remark also revealed the growing attention on the physical connections that would allow certain communications while limiting others.

During the four months that the Board of Design convened, its architects debated the placement of principal UN organs.[80] No drawing or proposal survived in its entirety the deliberations of the group; the final project was to be a mash-up of architectural solutions for the international organization. The architects, however, did not think and design in the absence of models. Following the San Francisco Conference, the nascent UN organization, with the help of the United Kingdom's Ministry of Works, had found a first configuration inside the refurbished Central Hall and Church House in London, where it held the first UN General Assembly and Security Council meetings. A semester later local contractors, carpenters, and builders, based on the experience in London, transformed the gymnasium, cafeteria, and Davis Hall at the Bronx branch of Hunter College under the guidance of Ralph Walker.[81] By the time Board of Design members arrived in New York, that UN setup was long gone, but its lessons lived in the paired temporary headquarters at Flushing Meadows and Lake Success, both sites that the architects of the board visited and studied.

The temporary headquarters offered the board architects valuable insights into the new organization and its emerging cultures of assembly and work. Harrison actively sought out the input of UN officials and diplomats, inviting them inside the board's meetings along with consultant engineers and associate architects, setting in dialogue form and social structure. Principal Director for Conference and General Service David B. Vaughan, who had overseen arrangements for the temporary headquarters in NYC, often attended those meetings, describing the delegates' experiences on the ground and possible problems arising from those spaces. Delegates approved the seating arrangement at Flushing Meadows, but recommended that press, radio, and simultaneous interpretation booths be encased within walls rather than hanging over the audience.[82] After the dissolution of the Board of Design, the Headquarters Planning Office conducted an investigation at Lake Success and Flushing Meadows and found that tables constituted a crucial piece of equipment and instrument of the liberal internationalism at work.[83] The Interim Site Committee's specified requirements for the temporary headquarters had designated a hall for the General Assembly, two council chambers (of which one would be dedicated to the Security Council), four committee rooms with tables arranged in a U-shape large enough for fifty-five delegates and a table with verbatim reporters at the center, as well as four to five smaller rooms for committees of fifty people total. For the General Assembly, the same memorandum had asked for accommodation for a "working group" of approximately seven hundred persons, including delegates, alternate delegates, advisers, and UN Secretariat personnel, to be arranged in rows of seating, with space in the back for the public and the press, as well as abundant space for a lobby, check rooms, restrooms, and lounges.[84] The close examination of those temporary headquarters taught the Planning Office that the media infrastructure of booths, broadcast studios, and interpreter stations should be organized along the side walls (neither in the back, as at Lake Success, nor in the corners, as at Hunter College) to optimize filming angles for camerapersons and interpreters.

In a shortwave broadcast, Australian architect and board member G. A. Soilleux, who had worked extensively on theater architecture, recalled the process as "a melting pot" where "ideas, suggestions, schemes . . . are exhaustively culled over, discussed, praised, jeered [sic] at and finally boiled down in a series of joint discussions conducted in a mixture of English, French and the universal language of the pencil."[85] Canadian architect Ernest Cormier similarly noted that the meetings resembled the Tower of Babel. "Every man spoke a different tongue, and with three official languages, French, English and Russian, they had a time pooling ideas."[86] In a press release, the board declared:

> To those outside who question us we can reply: we are united, we are a team; the World Team of the United Nations laying down the plans of a world architecture, world and not international, for therein we shall respect the human, natural and cosmic laws. . . . We are a homogeneous block. There are no names attached to this work. As in any human enterprise, there is simply discipline, which alone is capable of bringing order. Each of us can be legitimately proud at having been called upon to work in this team, and that should be sufficient for us.[87]

Symbolism and Its Discontents

Public and press expected the Board of Design to deliver a symbol of world peace, an architectural signifier of internationalism and global unity. Yet Harrison, who had opened the meetings asking for a "real monument . . . with a feeling that it opens out," systematically steered the board away from conversations on architectural form.[88] In reality, the focus on functions and requirements created the right conditions for a functionalist determination of the headquarters. Soon the Secretariat tower, a variation on the corporate skyscraper, emerged as the most well-defined and monumental in scale component of the UN Headquarters, sparking debates over its orientation, form, and relationship to the rest of the complex. The emphasis on administrative rather than public-facing diplomatic work that the Secretariat building brought about troubled even the most convinced modernists among the board architects. At the same time, the functionalism that had produced a distinctive slab for the organization's bureaucracies was threatening to compromise the General Assembly without delivering the symbol the general public had been asking for. Jonkheer Jan de Ranitz, the Dutch architect who had joined the requirements committee earlier on, had tried to establish a building code that would have solidified the prominence of the General Assembly, prohibiting skyscraper modernism, but Le Corbusier had vehemently and successfully opposed the suggestions out of fear of historicist monumentality gaining a foothold yet again.[89] Every so often, the board architects wondered what would be the appropriate General Assembly form against the towering Secretariat.[90] Some proposals subsumed the General Assembly within larger blocks along with the council chambers, completely disregarding any need to render it legible on the outside. Other proposals obsessively investigated possible architectural symbols capable of rivaling the emerging corporate tower, but those proposals rarely caught on during the meetings.

The intention was for the architectural form to signify the new organization, but opinions varied on what and how to signify. The functionalists among the group resisted conversations on symbols and their value, worrying about opening the door to architectural expressions that had served older institutions such as palaces and churches. But the group also included voices that were critical of de facto architectural modernism, advocating for the new headquarters to deliver a powerful symbol for the world. Ralph Walker, the most vocal among them, had been equating functionalism with the rise of a "mechanistic evangelism" in architectural culture, which he found antithetical to the humanist values that should, according to him, inform any new building following World War II.[91] He had accused the "impersonal, the abstract, the international" of being synonymous with a mass mentality, regretting the celebration of mechanized culture and what he saw as the loss of human values.[92]

The presence of the press during a 1947 mid-April meeting of the board forced architects to revisit the conversation on the value of architectural symbols. This time Harrison, who had been using functionalism as a tactic to avoid debates on form (misleadingly implying that the translation of function to form is causal and direct, leaving no room for interpretation), asked the board to consider the dome as a possible solution for the General Assembly. The opportunity arose with Sven Markelius's proposal and quickly made apparent the ideological nature of

Figure 2.9. Sven Markelius, sketch for UN proposal, 1947. Sven Markelius Papers, ArkDes. Courtesy of ArkDes.

disagreements on forms and symbols (Figure 2.9). For the board, architectural forms were not empty of representational value. They carried political weight that communicated priorities and alliances. Nikolai Bassov, representing the USSR, vehemently criticized domes as symbols of Christianity and religion, a criticism that found the Yugoslav Ernest Weissmann in agreement. It was not that the architects on the board rejected all attempts at visual representation, but rather that they wanted control over it. Symbols opened the door for historical forms to enter the architectural body, a threat that the architects pushed against, proclaiming to the press that symbolism was unnecessary, tradition was dead, and symbols "old."[93] The question at stake was which architectural language the UN Headquarters would make monumental, as the Chinese representative Liang Sicheng noted. Le Corbusier, Maciej Nowicki, and Sven Markelius univocally dismissed the question of monumentality, proclaiming it the end result of "good design." "Radiance," remarked Markelius, would come "from inside," confirming the functionalist imperative at play in designing the Headquarters from the inside out.[94]

After the board settled for scheme 42G—derivative of Oscar Niemeyer's proposal—later in May, Harrison took over, asking the drafting architects to develop a full set of plans and sections to illustrate the proposal for the General Assembly. On September 26, 1947, he presented plans for approval to the Ad Hoc Committee on Headquarters, a committee charged with outlining next steps for the establishment of the headquarters.[95] Contemplating the process, Harrison proclaimed the end result a departure from both the aesthetic monumentality of capitols in Washington and Paris and the "structural monumentality" of modernism where "man is a little dot lost in the great theory." Instead, he argued, the Headquarters that the Board of Design produced was antimonumental in that it centered on the UN delegates and the various publics formed in the council chambers, the assembly, and the lounges. In retrospect, Cormier noted, "We weren't trying to produce an architectural masterpiece, but a tool to do a job."[96] Comparing the design of the Headquarters with railway construction, Harrison proclaimed the process a piecemeal operation from inside out, "one foot at a time."[97]

The UN Headquarters that Harrison presented to the Ad Hoc Committee extended from 42nd to 48th street between 1st Avenue and the East River, without delineating exactly where U.S. territory ended and where UN territory started (Figure 2.10). The shiny slab of the Secretariat skyscraper with its glass curtain wall—a tower that would later accent the Franklin D. Roosevelt Drive views with its white marble cornice—loomed over the curved low silhouette of the General Assembly. Behind the two buildings, the Conference Block that hosted council chambers, conference rooms, and the main lounge would open to the diplomats an expansive view of the East River and Queens but would remain hidden from the general public.

The plans of the future UN Headquarters featured ample low-definition space of lounge areas, exhibition walls, sculptural ramps, and staircases anchored on very well-defined and closed-off spaces—conference rooms and council chambers—additionally buttressed with walls of broadcast and filming studios (Figure 2.11). Two lower levels covered parking needs, while making space as well for the United Nations' printing services, library, and archives.

A monumental lobby with curvaceous balconies gave way to wide low-ceiling passages that led into the upper galleries reserved for the general public in the council chambers and the General Assembly Hall, thence opening up again into the hollowed-out spaces for the convening delegates. But behind this seeming celebration of openness and flexibility lay a rigid understanding of access and diplomatic labor.

Early on, UN representatives had asked the Board of Design architects to separate the publics occupying the Headquarters into four groups with different levels of access and visibility: the general public, Secretariat, delegates, and press. G. A. Soilleux, the board's Australian architect and theater design expert, noted how ordering the social life within the organization and planning for the circulation patterns of four publics had complicated the design process.[98] The architects afforded the four publics distinct experiences of the same building and organization: the general public would enter Headquarters from the foyer behind the auditorium of the General Assembly; the delegates from behind the president's podium; and the press representatives and Secretariat employees from the side of the Secretariat.

The building itself organized how these publics accessed the complex, as well as how they moved inside it, emulating how OSS's Dan Kiley had separated the publics of the Nuremberg Trials earlier in 1945 (chapter 1). By placing the public's entrance on the northern part of the General Assembly building, the board architects limited the general public's access to the open space surrounding the General Assembly Hall and its upper galleries, keeping the public away from the Secretariat building to its south, the delegates' lounges and cafeterias, as well as service areas and office space. A separate entrance on the side guided delegations directly onto the floor of the General Assembly Hall and its seating area, while press representatives entered through the Secretariat, accessing studios, switchboards, messenger services, and telegraphs available to them. Inside the UN, the general public and the press took a seat in the global theater as audience, with the press seating area acting as a buffer zone between the floor and the upper part of the auditorium, a design decision that illustrated programmatic priorities. Meanwhile the Secretariat's international civil servants roamed the entirety of the headquarters but remained invisible to everyone except the delegates.[99] In this sense the architects designed the UN's public sphere as separate from the rest of its publics, although they at times wondered if such a separation was desirable or not. Even the general public, which architects and designers often recalled in their deliberations, and which UN bureaucrats aspired to include within the headquarters, in reality consisted primarily of delegates' personal guests (Figure 2.12).[100]

The preliminary report submitted later that fall to the General Assembly quoted Harrison concluding the Board of Design meetings with a declaration: "The world hopes for a symbol of peace, we gave them a workshop for peace."[101]

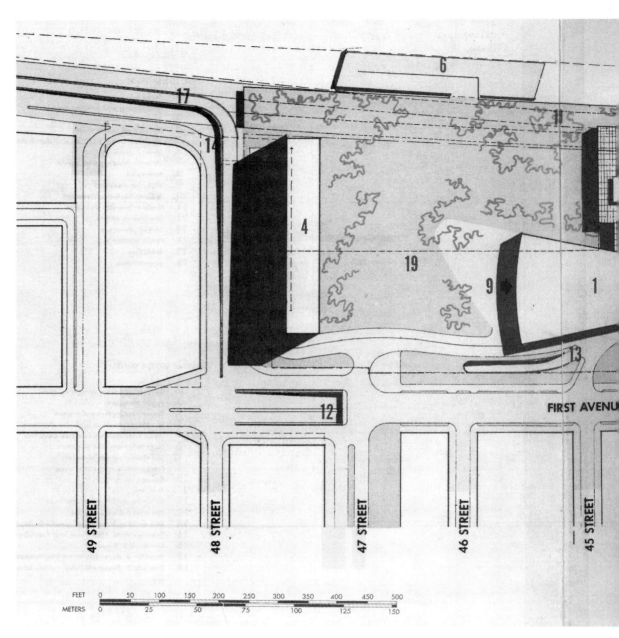

Figure 2.10. Site plan for the Permanent Headquarters before its reduction in size, showing (1) General Assembly; (2) conference area; (3) Secretariat Building; (4) area reserved for delegations and specialized agencies; (5) building of the New York City Housing Authority; (6) pier; (7) Secretariat; (8) delegates' entrance; (9) public entrance; (10) Franklin D. Roosevelt Drive underpass; (11) East River; (12) First Avenue underpass; (13) ramps to garages; (14) entrances to garages; (15) subway vent

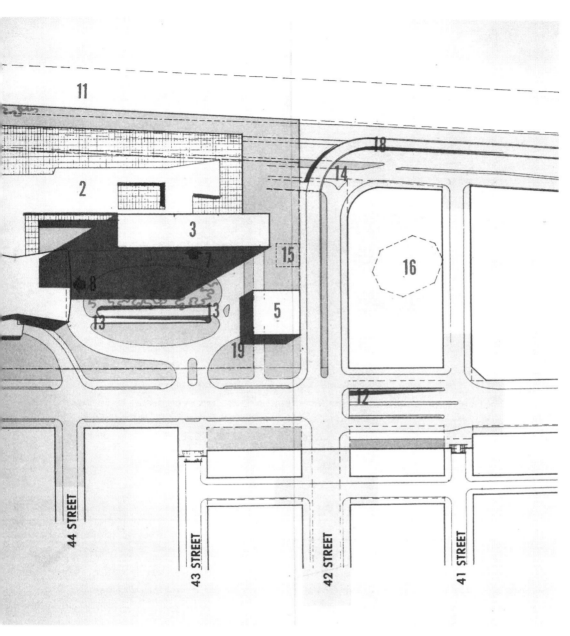

shaft; (16) Queens–Midtown Tunnel vent shaft; (17) northbound ramp to entrance to Franklin D. Roosevelt Drive from E. 48th Street; (18) northbound ramp exit from Franklin D. Roosevelt Drive to E. 42nd Street; (19) parking—lower level. *Report to the General Assembly of the United Nations by the Secretary-General on the Permanent Headquarters of the United Nations* (Lake Success, N.Y.: United Nations Publications, 1947). Courtesy of the United Nations Archives and Records Management.

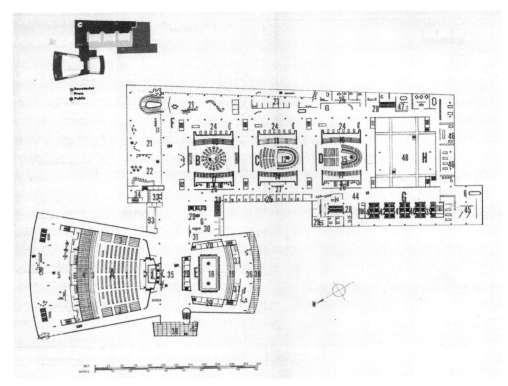

Figure 2.11. Delegates' level plan of the Permanent Headquarters before its reduction in size. The key in the top left corner indicates areas for the Secretariat, press, and public. *Report to the General Assembly of the United Nations by the Secretary-General on the Permanent Headquarters of the United Nations* (Lake Success, N.Y.: United Nations Publications, 1947). Courtesy of the United Nations Archives and Records Management.

The report proclaimed that the Headquarters tied together the various UN organs as "functioning parts of a single coherent organism."[102] The idea of an ever-expanding communications network was still central to the UN's imagination. To that end the Board of Design had visited the Bell Telephone Laboratories, examining the challenges and opportunities telecommunications offered for the headquarters and its design.[103] Communications technologies would provide the "nerves" that tied "together thousands of working units, individuals and groups of individuals within the headquarters and throughout the world," and ultimately, "with the larger world complex of communications between men and nations."[104] But communications, either in the form of telephonic networks or organized movement, structured distinct publics and delivered a tiered system of access, although the planning office wanted the press to believe differently. Within this context, architecture's job was to manage this infrastructure and deliver public spaces that subordinated the technological to the human element, while disguising hierarchies of access and power that the communications systems installed.

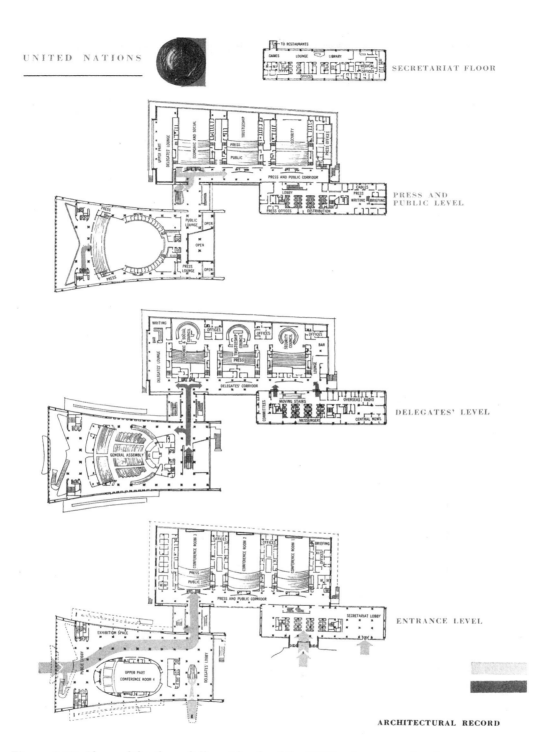

Figure 2.12. Plans of the three different levels of the UN Headquarters showing access for delegates, general public, and press after the reduction of the overall size due to budgetary concerns. Drawings in Henry Stern Churchill, "United Nations: A Description and Appraisal," in *Architectural Record* (July 1952). Courtesy of the United Nations Archives and Records Management.

Tables of Diplomacy

Behind this shift toward a more infrastructural approach to the design of the UN Headquarters lay the political imperative to replace bilateral diplomatic relationships with a system of multilateralism. The UN had reestablished diplomacy as a bureaucratic enterprise, a shift planned at least since the time of the League of Nations Secretariat and its management of colonial interests. Yet the end of World War II placed an impossible task in the hands of diplomats and architects: to produce a space celebrating a liberal understanding of humanity, while architecturally articulating an even bigger bureaucratic organization that would bring order and peace out of the chaos, fear, and paranoia that the war had generated.

Tables emerged as the quintessential objects of liberal internationalism. Most UN committees convened around tables, almost always in rented rooms within office buildings such as the Rockefeller Center or conference venues such as the Church House, in London. Diplomats understood the politics of seating and how tables silently installed hierarchies, entangling their shape and form with discussions on emerging cultures of assembly and the organization of the UN public spheres. Who gets a seat at the table; does the table have a head; how close or far away should the delegates sit; who sits next to whom? These were all questions running through the delegates' minds each time a new committee deployed itself within a room.

This conversation became more apparent with the design of the council chambers, since these were the spaces where UN organs presented themselves to the public as operative institutional structures. Inside the plenary hall of the General Assembly tables demarcated the distinct positions of audience and speaker, but council chamber conversations, where delegates faced and spoke to one another, required that tables created, at least perceptually, a common shared space. Indeed, tables inside meeting halls and council chambers determined the form that the international public sphere would present, and by extension the conversational cultures the organization bestowed on its publics.[105] Diplomats insisted that the new tables should bring all delegates together on equal footing, even if this appearance of equality did not reflect the fiscal realities and political asymmetries among the invited member states.

During the time of the temporary headquarters, table configurations inside meeting halls betrayed lines of institutional continuity that high-ranking officials publicly disavowed. For the Preparatory Commission, for example, the architects borrowed furniture from the London office of the League of Nations, bringing inside the UN the convening structures of the League and ILO (Figure 2.13).[106] In workshops and meetings, national representatives and their advisers sat at oblong tables set against walls, with verbatim reporters and typists often placed in an island at the center—a round-table structure that had been almost religiously observed for meetings of international organizations. For the council chambers

Figure 2.13. First session of the United Nations Security Council, Church House, London, January 17, 1946. Courtesy of the United Nations Photo Library.

administrators even adopted the open round table of the League of Nations Council at the Palais des Nations, a shape that was also used at the temporary headquarters, first at Church House and later at Hunter College and Lake Success, illuminating conspicuously the ties between the two institutions (Figure 2.14). Any future configurations for negotiating colonial and national interests would build on these initial structures.

During the meetings in San Francisco and London, there was a growing impetus to foreground collaborative work and center the new organization on some idealized form of international "cooperation" (Figure 2.15). The mobilizing desire was to install "humans" at the core of a growing anonymous and impersonal technocracy, against the bureaucracies that were taking hold of diplomacy and structures of multilateralism. Those politicians saw in tables the symbolic potential to represent democratic processes centered on conversations, rather than deliberations. Conversations entailed the existence of a central topic or question that brought together different positionalities, hence grounding processes of multilateralism on publics forming around issues of global concern, rather than on singular perspectives and their rhetorical projection toward an audience. These exchanges highlighted the UN bureaucrats' articulation of institutional stewardship as care for the world. In addition, diplomats believed misguidedly that the

Figure 2.14. Ralph T. Walker, Security Council under construction at Hunter College. Ralph T. Walker Papers, Special Collections Research Center, Syracuse University Libraries.

"right" material conditions could elevate international relations into democratic processes around "worldly things" beyond the usual bilateral and multilateral ne-gotiations.[107] World War II and the masses-as-publics of the Third Reich pushed thinkers, politicians, and sociologists at the time to reckon with the dismantling of public life. How publics form and transform became the concern that marked much of the postwar period, along with debates on modes of governance. In *The Human Condition* Hannah Arendt argued that the public realm constituted a space of appearance where citizens deemed equal and free present themselves to one another while coming together to act and speak in concert for a shared political goal. She suggested that the table was a homology of the world we share: "To live together in the world means essentially that a world of things is between those who have it in common, as a table is located between those who sit around it; the world, like every in-between, relates and separates men at the same time. The pub-lic realm, as the common world, gathers us together and yet prevents our falling over each other, so to speak."[108]

THE BUSY MAN'S GUIDE TO THE UNITED NATIONS

U. N. has six 'Principal Organs.' News from Lake Success will be more understandable when you know them by name and how numerous sub-bodies are related to them.

WHAT IT IS

This is "the town-hall meeting of the world." Each member of the United Nations has one vote. A two-third vote is required on all "important questions," otherwise a simple majority suffices. It meets annually in September, but may be convened at the request of a majority of its members or the Security Council.

Five of its 11 members are "permanent"—the so-called Big Five, the U. S., Russia, Britain, China, France. Any seven can rule on "procedural" matters. On all other questions, the Big Five and two other members must vote "yes" to get action; if a Big Five member votes "no" or fails to vote, it "vetoes."

In this body lies much hope for the eventual reduction of causes of war. Its 18 members are elected by the Assembly for three-year terms. It deals with international economic, social, health, educational matters; also human rights and fundamental freedoms. Decisions are reached by a simple majority vote.

Purpose: To promote welfare of peoples in "trust territories" leading to "self-government or independence"—"a sacred trust." Membership: the Big Five, trust administrators, enough more States, elected by the Assembly, to make the number of members not administering the U. N. trusts equal to those having them.

This is a new body—but based on the old Permanent Court of International Justice. Its 15 members hold office nine years and are elected by the Assembly and Security Council. Nine make a quorum for sitting. Official languages are French and English. All judgments are final and without appeal. Its seat is at The Hague.

This comprises the working staff of the United Nations, headed by the Secretary General appointed by the Assembly on recommendation of the Security Council. Appropriate staffs are assigned to the Economic and Social Council and the Trusteeship Council. The Secretariat is temporarily housed at Lake Success, N. Y.

WHAT IT DOES

It may discuss any matters within the scope of the Charter and make recommendations to Security Council —but is limited in dealing with a specific security question. It selects six two-year (nonpermanent) members for Security Council, all 18 members of Economic and Social Council, several Trusteeship Council members.

It has "primary responsibility for the maintenance of international peace and security." It can call for settling disputes by (1) pacific means —e.g. negotiation; (2) "complete or partial" breaking off relations—e.g., diplomatic or economic, etc.; (3) force. The Atomic Energy Commission is associated with the Council.

It makes studies and can recommend to the Assembly or members. Working with or under ESC are 11 Specialized Agencies (ILO—International Labor Organization; UNESCO—U.N. Educational, Scientific, and Cultural Organization; etc.), 11 Commissions (Human Rights, etc.), and non-Governmental bodies (including Rotary).

It plans the report which administering States must make to the Assembly on their trusts. It works with the Assembly in considering reports, studying petitions, and making periodic visits to trust territories. It is to consult with the Economic and Social Council and with its Specialized Agencies whenever it desires.

United Nations members (and other States under specified conditions) MAY accept as compulsory the Court's jurisdiction on international-law questions, treaty interpretations, breaches of international obligations. Recourse to the Security Council is possible when a party fails to follow a judgment issued by the Court.

The Secretary General is chief administrative officer of the United Nations, functioning as such at all meetings of all Principal Organs except the Court. He may call the Security Council's attention to any matter which he thinks may threaten peace and security, and must report annually to the General Assembly.

General Assembly

Security Council

Economic and Social Council

Trusteeship Council

International Court of Justice

Secretariat

Figure 2.15. "The Busy Man's Guide to the United Nations," *The Rotarian*, September 1947. Copyright Rotary International; reprinted with permission.

Arendt was hardly alone. If the League of Nations put forward a global bureaucracy as the response to World War I, then World War II challenged the very idea that reason or technique alone could guarantee individual freedom, let alone the democratic function of a society. In the aftermath of World War II, a group of researchers who had operationalized psychology and the social sciences for military purposes sought to use their wartime work for the cultivation of peacetime democratic reflexes. Social scientists and psychologists did not constrain these efforts to the scale of the state. In fact, the entire world could be addressed as a complex social mechanism that sociologists and psychiatrists could help manage.[109] From Max Horkheimer to Hadley Cantril and Otto Klineberg, researchers proposed that new media frameworks reorganize interpersonal encounters. International organizations were also interested. The United Nations Educational, Scientific, and Cultural Organization (UNESCO) enlisted a wide roster of anthropologists and sociologists for conflict resolution in international relations.[110] The goal was to develop the tools, media, and methods that would shape the future citizens of the world.[111]

Thinking along similar lines in 1945, George de Huszar, a progressivist at the Faculty of European and Asiatic Area Study at the University of Chicago, tied these new frameworks for democratic processes to social and spatial structures. His *Practical Applications of Democracy,* although published while still a graduate student, attracted wide-ranging interest in the fields of political science, international relations, and education. For de Huszar "democratic conduct" took on specific spatial configurations. "Democracy is something you do; not something you talk about. It is more than a form of government, or an attitude, or an opinion. It is participation," he declared. He classified democratic conduct into three different categories: the "talk-democracy" that encouraged dialogue in the form of correspondence; the "consent-democracy" centered on elections; and the "do-democracy" of self-organized publics that mobilize around social or political problems. De Huszar criticized talk-democracy for allowing totalitarian regimes to flourish, and he denounced consent-democracy for infantilizing its citizens. Only do-democracy, according to him, engaged citizens in action, cultivating the democratic reflexes of publics. These small groups (understood as "workshops") set up for questions and issues consisted of no more than twelve people; they shared a "problem" in the center; and they met at a round table. De Huszar believed round tables to be markers of do-democracy collaboration, promoting equal access and participation in problem-solving (Figure 2.17).[112] The method for cultivating democracy deep inside governmental structures and their bureaucracies was to install cooperation as a method to organize work around workshops and roundtables. De Huszar's treatise circulated widely within the UN, convincing delegates and the architects in the Secretariat Division of Public Information who were to advise on settings for UN events that round tables constituted icons of democratic processes, and thus a fitting representation of the institution to the world.

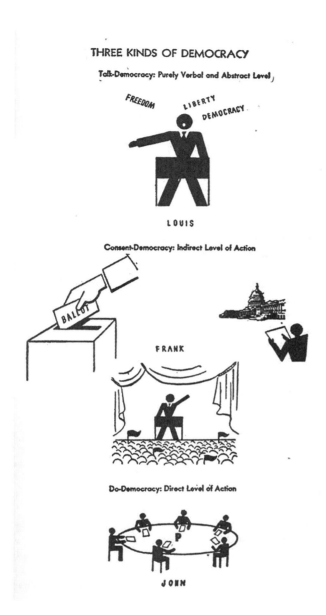

Figure 2.16. Sketch showing the three spatial configurations of "talk-democracy," "consent-democracy," and "do-democracy" in George Bernard de Huszar, *Practical Applications of Democracy* (New York: Harper and Brothers Publishers, 1945).

The UN had inaugurated its existence at a round table, reenacting Arthurian mythologies. At the conferences predating the signing of the charter, the State Department and Executive Offices of the President set up circular tables inside the convening venues at Moscow and Yalta, with cameras and film crews tucked away to cover the events.[113] At the San Francisco Conference on International Organization, the OSS staged the signing of the UN Charter at a perfectly round table, symbolic of the equality that the UN purported to install centrally at the new world order. "The delegates insisted that each man must have an equally important seat around a common table. We have not been able to find any other

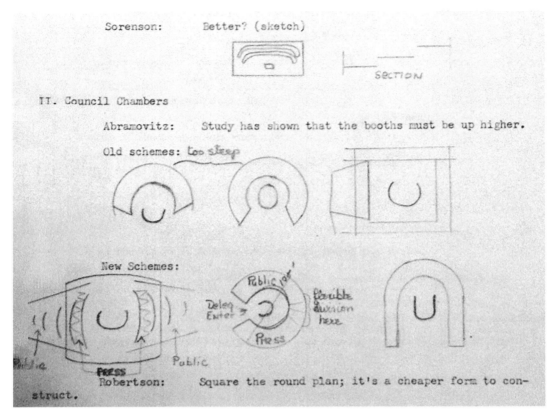

Figure 2.17. Notes from design meeting, March 17, 1947. George A. Dudley Papers, MS 1861, Manuscripts and Archives, Yale University Library.

scheme of keeping equality amongst the delegates," Harrison confessed in a talk before the American Society of Landscape Architects. "I hate to admit it, but we have tried court and auditorium types and this is the only one the various responsible people can agree upon," he noted.[114]

Once the UN moved from the idealized space of the San Francisco Conference to the drawing board, architects and Secretariat diplomats placed round tables firmly inside the council chambers, where cameras and journalists would most likely attend the meetings, and to a lesser degree inside meeting halls and conference rooms. The more removed from the public eye the function of the organ, the less architects adhered to the round form. Ralph Walker, along with Robert Glenn, had prepared the temporary Security Council, placing a semicircular table across the auditorium containing press and public, with yards of pink drapery on the walls dampening reverberation. The Security Council Chamber at Lake Success, most probably modeled on the League of Nations Council, also featured booths for simultaneous interpreters at the very back of the auditorium, and filming and broadcasting booths on the sides.[115]

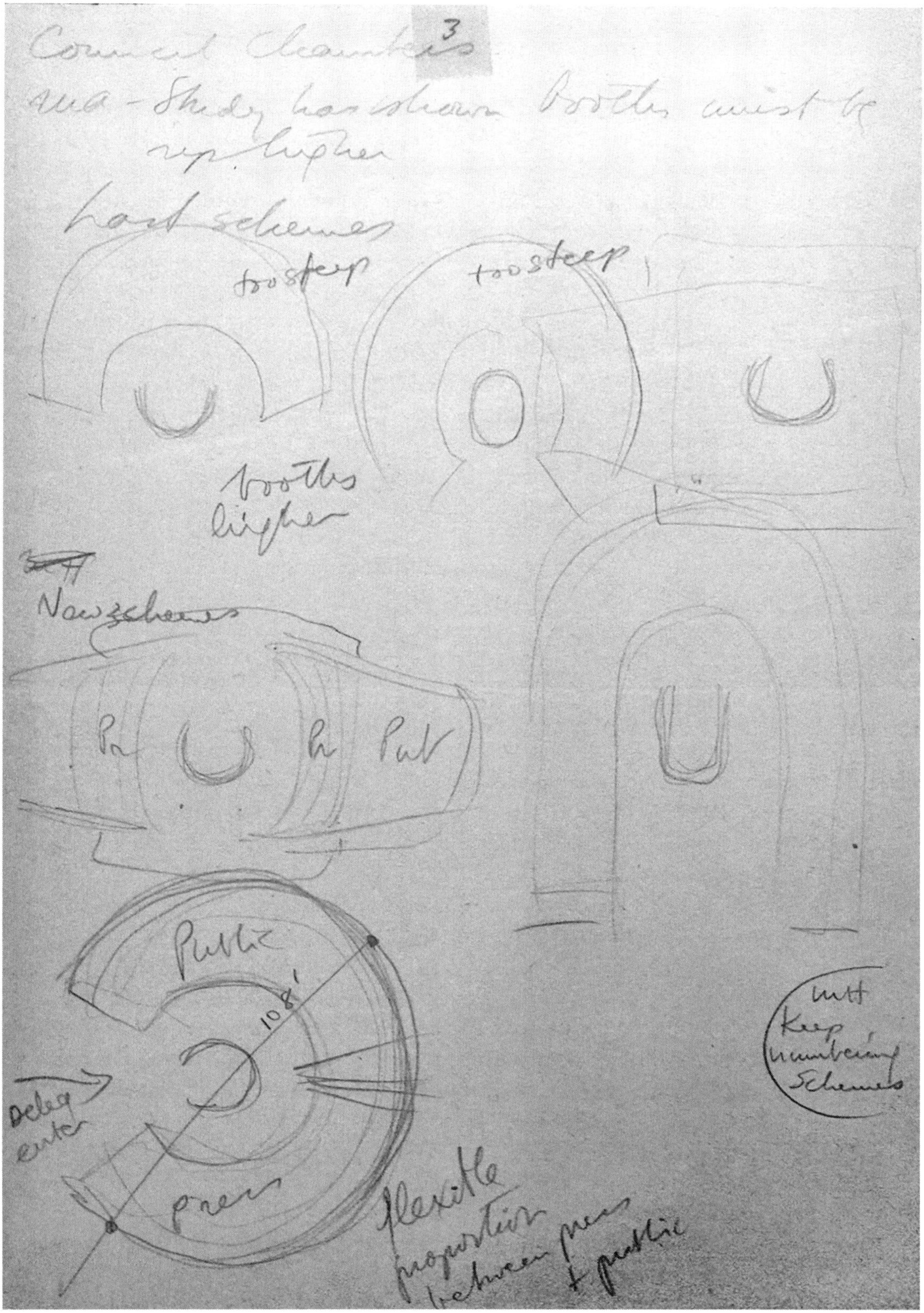

Council Chambers 3

aaa - Study has shown booths must be
up higher

Last schemes
too steep   too steep

booths
higher

New schemes

Pu   h Pub

Public

10'8"

Deleg
enter

press

flexible
proportion
between press
+ public

utt
Keep
numbering
Schemes

The Board of Design architects had also spent a good amount of time thinking about those tables and the relationships they installed while convening in 1947. Round and oval tables required different footage, but also inducted different hierarchies among the delegates, with circular surfaces requiring more space around them and elliptical tabletops unavoidably creating heads among the conveners.[116] Making the symbolic nature of the table clear, Andrew W. Cordier insisted that "the complete circle is best."[117] Tables were to be staged as the symbolic and representational anchors organizing the new public spheres emerging within the council chambers. At the UN temporary headquarters at Hunter College and elsewhere, the presence of mass media had complicated the direct translation of the round table into built form, illuminating the role of camera angles in the design of council chambers. UN official David Vaughn, the Director of Conference and General Services, joined by Cordier, insisted that the press should see the entire floor.[118] The board architects kept wondering if council chambers were rooms or "theaters," a commentary that many architectural publications reiterated after the opening of the headquarters (Figure 2.17).[119] Sicheng noticed that closed-circle round tables did not stage well for television or film; UN representatives reminded the board architects that interpreters would also require eye contact with all delegates speaking, complicating the design. A round table would need broadcasters to televise delegates' backs and would obstruct the view of interpreters in the galleries. Architects also carefully considered how their presence inside council chambers affected the representational value of their form. Experimenting with the layout, they argued that placing public and press on opposite sides of round tables transformed meeting halls and council chambers into gladiatorial spectacles, effectively undoing any of the collaborative spirit the round table was meant to install (Figure 2.18). Nikolai Bassov regretted the affiliations that the plan created with a "circus" or a "ring," and recommended elliptical shapes instead.[120]

The circular form, however, was not adopted universally within the headquarters. Inside the three council chambers, the Board of Design architects adjusted the circular table to accommodate for variable council mandates. The UN Charter bestowed on the Security Council—probably the most asymmetrical UN organ given the veto politics and its two-tier membership system—the authority to manage geopolitical conflict, including taking military action. The Economic and Social Council (ECOSOC) instigated and coordinated research on social and economic issues that at the time ranged from reconstruction to the administration of technical assistance, human rights, economic development, and gender equality. ECOSOC aimed at preparing policies, reaching agreements with specialized agencies, and issuing recommendations for the General Assembly, while taking into consideration the reports of a growing number of regional commissions, internal committees, and conferences. Finally, the Trusteeship Council, consisting of the

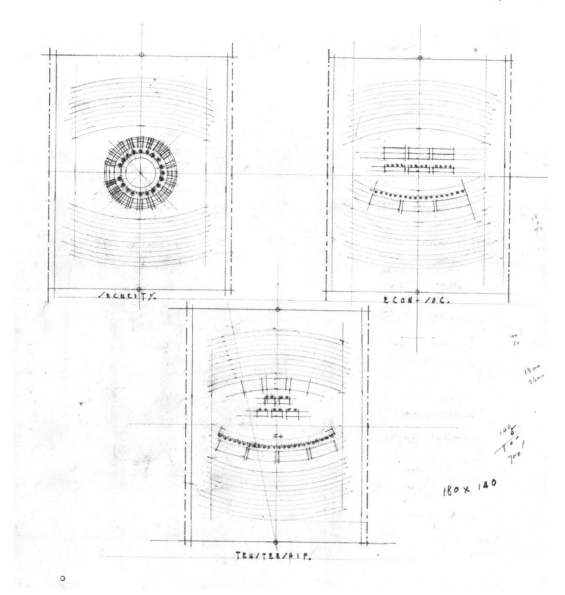

Figure 2.18. Ernest Cormier, plans for the Council Chambers, 1947. Courtesy of Ernest Cormier Fonds and the Canadian Centre for Architecture.

administering authorities (often former colonial powers) and an equal number of non-administering members, oversaw decolonization processes in trust territories and managed colonial interests.

These tables inside the council chambers would have to accommodate administrative support, advisers, typists, and verbatim reporters, impelling the board architects to hollow out the circular table. As a closed form, the circular table implied an organizational finitude that restricted growth and expansion, complicating the institution's aspirations to fold in the entire world. To suggest the openness of those councils while incorporating within their very structure the presence of the press, the architects proposed that the tables remain open toward the audience. Ironically, but maybe precisely because it was the only organ to administer war, and to that end the most exclusive one, the Security Council was given an almost perfectly circular finite table with one side open for its televising. For the Economic and Social Council, the board proposed a horseshoe configuration, and for the Trusteeship Council an open parabolic form, alluding to the evolving work of institutional decolonization in response to anti-colonial movements forcing the hand of the organization. Inside the latter, what was presented to press and public was not delegates convening, but rather decolonizing nations presenting their case to the council, placed along the table (Figure 2.19a). Apart from working on that foundational assumption of national representation that peoples and their governments are one and the same, interchangeable, these tables endowed the organization with institutional platforms that also ordered and formed its public spheres.

This culture of assembling around tables permeated other parts of the organization as well, particularly conference rooms (Figure 2.19b). Inside the Secretariat, meeting rooms with considerably larger and less flexible working tables ended up determining the overall plan. "Everything else serves them," Max Abramovitz declared.[121] To design those rooms, the board consulted with Eero Saarinen, the architect who, during World War II, designed military presentation rooms for the U.S. War Department and the Navy.[122] Julio Vilamajó Echaniz, the Uruguayan architect who had joined the group in late March 1947, had argued for the adoption of the round form inside the General Assembly to signify "working together," a suggestion that did not move forward, but revealed how architects endowed form with representational value. Behind their formal choices there was a surprisingly stagnant understanding of political form. The General Assembly constituted fundamentally an auditorium, a performative space dedicated to public speaking, and council chambers were spaces for debate (chapter 3). A round table seemed more appropriate for council chambers than for plenary halls. Building on the auditorium type, Harrison and team proposed a parabolic plan for the staging of speeches inside the General Assembly, implying an exponential growth representative of the institution's desire for expansion.[123]

Regardless of institutional efforts to present them as such, the three councils were not made equal. UN diplomats and high-ranking officials, along with national representatives from member states, understood well that the Security Council, the only organ approving military sanctions in the name of "peace and security," was to be the heart—and often the biggest obstacle to the democratic processes—of the new organization.[124] Zuleta Ángel, a career diplomat and first

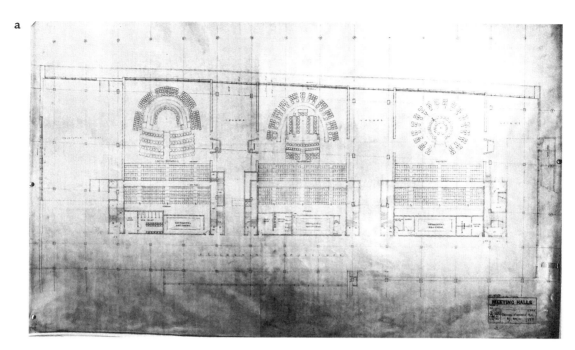

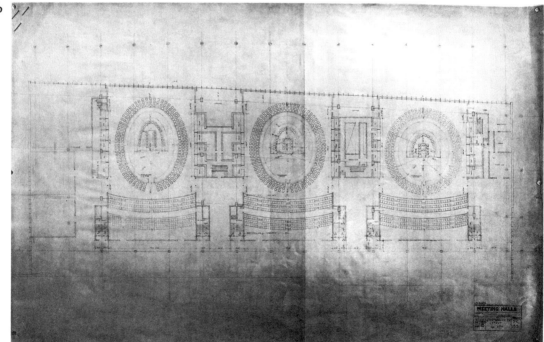

Figure 2.19. Plans with the table layout for the three council chambers (Economic and Social Council Chamber, Trusteeship Council Chamber, and Security Council Chamber) and the three meeting halls on the second floor, 1948. Courtesy of the United Nations Archives and Records Management.

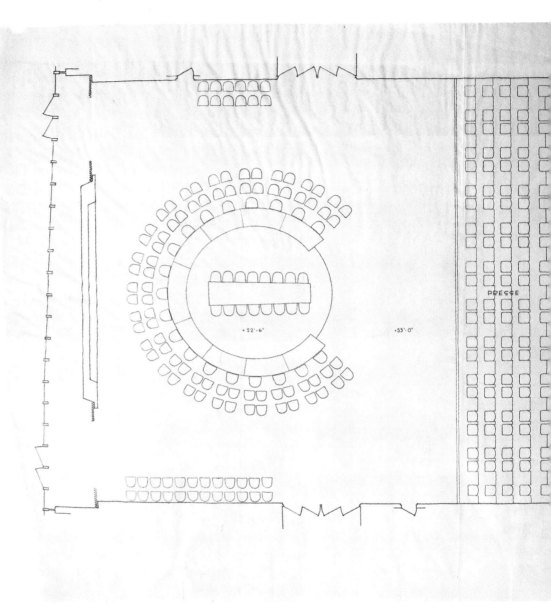

president of the United Nations General Assembly, admitted to the board the structural prominence of the Security Council, contradicting the official directives.[125] Le Corbusier seemed to think that this hierarchy should also be articulated architecturally, proposing a more conspicuous form for the Security Council, but other members of the board, who questioned whether the General Assembly or the Security Council held a more decisive role within the organization, criticized such formal prominence for fixing in space institutional hierarchies.[126] Architects were to build into the headquarters the parity that the institution

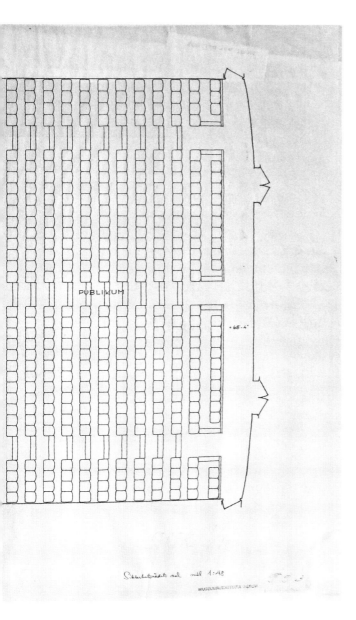

PUBLIKUM

Figure 2.20. Arnstein Arneberg, plan of Security Council, n.d. Arnstein Rynning Arneberg, NAMT.aar621.018. Courtesy of Nasjonalmuseet for kunst, arkitektur og design, Oslo, Norway.

lacked. Although the Security Council operationally ratified the power asymmetries that created it—with five permanent members holding veto power and treating as "guests" the ten nonpermanent members, as Isobel Roele notes—in public its architecture needed to hide them.[127] In this sense the table in the middle of the room installed an illustrative (rather than operative) equality among members.

When, in 1948, Secretary-General Trygve Lie assigned the interior design of the Security Council to his compatriot Arnstein Arneberg, the one element of the room exempted from the design was the table (Figure 2.20).[128] The Headquarters

Planning Office had claimed design purview on the tables, as well as the chairs in the auditorium and, of course, the physical arrangement in space of media, interpreters, secretarial support, and delegates. Abel Sorensen, the Danish architect who had been working for the Headquarters Planning Office overseeing the dressing of the interior, would design and supervise the selection and construction of chairs for press and public, and most importantly the delegates' tables for all council chambers. In the end, all Arneberg had to design was the framing and environment around that table within predetermined plans: walls, ceiling, carpets, curtains, upholstery and delegates' chairs.

Similar directives went out to other Scandinavian architects two years later, when the UN—activating a gift economy to dress its headquarters within budget—invited member states to take over the design of the other two council chambers.[129] The Academy Council of the Royal Danish Academy nominated Finn Juhl to design the Trusteeship Council Chamber,[130] and the Swedish government nominated Sven Markelius for the ECOSOC Council Chamber. The choice of the three designers cemented the position of mid-century Dutch and Scandinavian design as the quintessential expression of modern internationalism. It also helped that Abel Sorensen, under the direction and advice of national export councils and commerce chambers representatives, traveled to Europe in the early summer of 1950 to consult with the three architects and collect information on furniture makers, sampling various national productions for the UN interiors.[131] In short thank-you notes, Sorensen affirmed his loyalties to Scandinavian and Dutch designs, often reassuring officials of their country's representation within the UN.[132]

But the Headquarters Planning Office did not relinquish design control. When Arneberg, working from Oslo, presented Harrison with his proposal for a ceiling fresco and a wall-to-wall mural, the Headquarters Planning Office responded with the creation of yet another committee to set guidelines for the character and placement of art within the Headquarters at large (Plate 6). The architects in the Planning Office found the mural and ceiling fresco disorienting, distracting attention from what they perceived to be the central feature of the room: the round table. Although Harrison managed to talk Arneberg out of the ceiling fresco, he did not prevent the mural, which Arneberg defended not only as part of his own vision, but also as part of the Norwegian gift, effectively turning a debate about aesthetics into a debate about funding. "The Norwegian Government will most likely not be interested in letting the granted amount be used in just any lounge or somewhere," Arneberg remarked.[133]

Withholding funds to push a certain aesthetic language was in perfect alignment with the motives behind the UN's outsourcing of interior design, decoration, and furnishings. The invitation to external architects was part and parcel of a plan to solicit additional financial support for the completion of the UN

Figure 2.21. Sven Markelius, Wallace K. Harrison, Jacques Carlu, and Howard Robertson inspect a model of the Economic and Social Council Chamber, September 2, 1950. Courtesy of the United Nations Photo Library.

Headquarters in the name of cultural internationalism.[134] To maintain control over the present and future of the Headquarters, the Planning Office established a Board of Art Advisers consisting mainly of architects: Howard Robertson, the British architect at the Board of Design; Jacques Carlu, the French architect of the Palais de Chaillot who refurbished the building for the UN General Assembly in 1951 and later designed the NATO Headquarters; and Miguel Covarrubias, the Mexican muralist and art historian.[135] Harrison recruited Irwin Edman, a professor of philosophy at Columbia University, to consult the Board of Art Advisers and help them formulate guidelines. In a long white paper, Edman advised the substitution of narrative symbolism with abstraction and the signification of materiality.[136] The Board of Art Advisers joined Harrison in a second UN Scandinavian trip to discuss the plans for the three council chambers in late August 1950 (Figure 2.21).[137] The goal was to implement this call for modernist abstraction, controlling and directing the design of the council chambers' interiors, so that the focus remained on the tables and the workshop cultures the UN wished to propagate.[138]

Inside the three chambers, Arneberg, Markelius, and Juhl researched ways to embed (and present) collaborative work and its tables within the organization and its media infrastructure. And although Arneberg marched to the beat of his own drum, deploying murals, tapestries, and marble to deliver a room with "character" that was maybe a bit "too conservative" (his words), the other two architects decided to explore what a modern "workshop" would look like.[139] Aino and Alvar Aalto's Finnish Pavilion for the 1939–40 New York World's Fair, with its wooden battens, set an example for both Juhl and Markelius, where the materiality of the room became the ornament.

For the ECOSOC and the Trusteeship Council, Markelius and Juhl respectively exposed mechanical and electrical systems, placing those chambers and their tables in dialogue with the rest of the organization in terms of infrastructure. During the design of the Economic and Social Council Chamber, Markelius negotiated the position of ducts and coils, adding a headache to the engineers' already complicated task of maneuvering the different systems. Along with Bengt Lindroos, he uncovered the air ducts and fans over the auditorium, creating a contrast between the finished delegates' area and the "more or less dissolved volume" of the rest of the chamber (Figure 2.22).[140] In exposing the ducts Markelius obstructed form from emerging, presenting ECOSOC as a work-in-progress and the UN as a networking infrastructure centered on its formed publics (Figure 2.23 and Plate 7).

Juhl, who had been assigned the Trusteeship Council, also engaged in a formal experiment with ventilation ducts and lighting (Plate 8). In his letter to the Planning Office he described the chamber as more of "a 'work-shop' than a formal reception room."[141] Juhl, who had worked on the designs for Vilhelm Lauritzen's Copenhagen Radio House, understood quite well the complexities of broadcast studios, especially in regard to the theatrics involved. Edgar Kaufmann Jr. noted that Juhl's Council Chamber's "clear organization . . . subordinated the spectators to the participants."[142] In a complete reversal of the dynamic that Markelius set up inside ECOSOC, Juhl's coils, ducts, and lighting were organized in trusses and mounted on the ceiling above the delegates' area, while excluding the public from the infrastructure that would regulate the decolonization of Trusteeship territories, which at the time represented a very limited part of the decolonizing world (Plate 9 and Figure 2.24). In doing so, Juhl produced the world public in terms of an audience watching global technocracies at work. In her review of the three council chambers for Interiors, Olga Gueft found them "unquestionably modern," but did not fail to notice the "meeting-hall-theatre" architecture of the room that rendered public and press an audience to the drama on stage, employing theater as a metaphor to describe the three rooms.[143] In doing so, she also revealed the

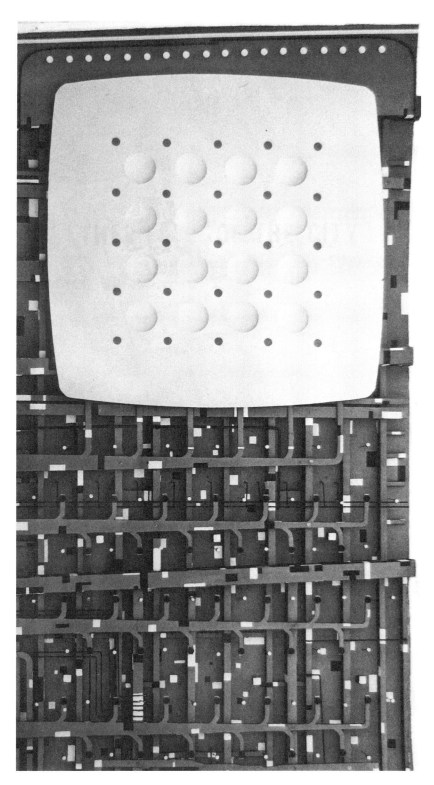

Figure 2.22. Sven Markelius and Bengt Lindroos, model of the ceiling, 1951. Sven Markelius Papers, DesArk, Stockholm, Sweden.

Figure 2.23. The press area and ceiling in Economic and Social Council Chamber, 1952. Sven Markelius Papers, DesArk, Stockholm, Sweden.

Figure 2.24. Trusteeship Council Chamber, 1952. Finn Juhl Papers, Designmuseum Danmark, Copenhagen, Denmark. Courtesy of the United Nations Photo Library.

theatrical nature of the round table that the UN architects had effectively turned into an instrument of diplomacy and an apparatus for multilateralism.

This culture of "workshops" that set out to form publics around issues of global concern in actuality transformed global bureaucracies and defined the work of international institutions in the postwar period. Not everybody was invited to the table—in fact tables, particularly the UN tables, were designed as finite objects. Yet the existence of those tables also made their contestation possible, opening them up to the continuous liberal democratic process of expanding and broadening the publics that get a seat at the table, ultimately transforming the issues that arrive to said table to become matters of concern.

Despite the architects' persistent call to install the Design Board as a permanent feature of the UN, Harrison dismissed all participating architects after four months of convening and asserted control over the rest of the process. In doing so, Harrison decidedly ended architecture's purview in the production of diagrams. Built form would be an entirely different subject matter. But most importantly, he suggestively divorced the architect-as-designer from the construction process—more efficiently carried out, in his opinion, by contractors and architects-as-managers.

The reception of the UN Headquarters among architectural circles was lukewarm. Harrison, who had avoided discussions on symbolism during the board meetings, had caved in, dressing the General Assembly with a sliced dome on the top of its curved ceiling in hopes of securing the loan from the U.S. Congress that would finance the construction of the Headquarters.[144] A sense of deflated monumentality and less than awe-inspiring spaces left both diplomats and designers at a loss for words to describe what it was that the UN architects had delivered. Even as Harrison presented the plans for the new Headquarters to the press, the confusion over the exact nature of the new urban complex persisted, with the popular news magazine *Parade* declaring the UN's new complex simultaneously a "city-within-a-city," a "headquarters," and a "world's capitol."[145]

The anticipation of an architectural symbol for the UN had followed the Headquarters every step of the way, from conversations on the location to debates over the shape of the tables around which national representatives would congregate. Architects blamed the collaborative framework that the architect-in-chief Wallace K. Harrison had adopted for the unresolved monumentality of the United Nations Headquarters. Monuments, or at least the monumentality they were after, could only be the result of a strong individual voice, and not of a collaborative effort and the compromises it entailed. However, UN officials had little interest in monumental scale and more desire for stripped-down technical environments that worked for the new world order and its procedures. By the time the United Nations Headquarters opened its doors to the public, the organization had adopted the term "workshops" to describe its specialized agencies in UN publications, pronouncing FAO and UNESCO "workshops for the world." These "workshops" would be the monuments of UN's liberal and multilateral internationalism, transforming conferences and committees from tools to symbols of the new world order.[146]

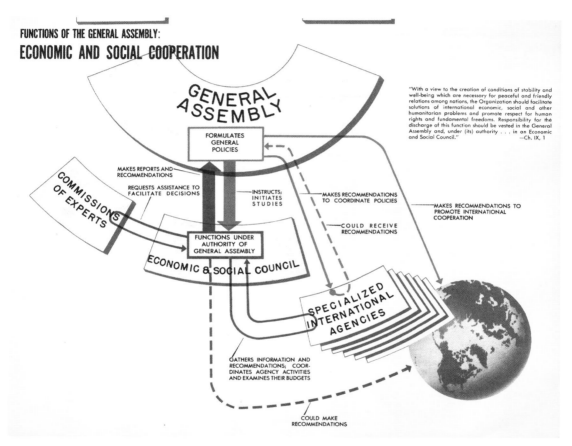

FUNCTIONS OF THE GENERAL ASSEMBLY:
ECONOMIC AND SOCIAL COOPERATION

GENERAL ASSEMBLY

FORMULATES GENERAL POLICIES

"With a view to the creation of conditions of stability and well-being which are necessary for peaceful and friendly relations among nations, the Organization should facilitate solutions of international economic, social and other humanitarian problems and promote respect for human rights and fundamental freedoms. Responsibility for the discharge of this function should be vested in the General Assembly and, under (its) authority . . . in an Economic and Social Council."
—Ch. IX, 1

COMMISSIONS OF EXPERTS

MAKES REPORTS AND RECOMMENDATIONS

REQUESTS ASSISTANCE TO FACILITATE DECISIONS

INSTRUCTS; INITIATES STUDIES

MAKES RECOMMENDATIONS TO COORDINATE POLICIES

MAKES RECOMMENDATIONS TO PROMOTE INTERNATIONAL COOPERATION

COULD RECEIVE RECOMMENDATIONS

FUNCTIONS UNDER AUTHORITY OF GENERAL ASSEMBLY

ECONOMIC & SOCIAL COUNCIL

SPECIALIZED INTERNATIONAL AGENCIES

GATHERS INFORMATION AND RECOMMENDATIONS; COORDINATES AGENCY ACTIVITIES AND EXAMINES THEIR BUDGETS

COULD MAKE RECOMMENDATIONS

Plate 1. Department of State, Proposals for a General International Organization as Developed at Dumbarton Oaks, 1944 (Washington, D.C.: U.S. Government Printing Office, 1945).

Plate 2. Donal McLaughlin, lapel pin for admission to The United Nations Conference on International Organization. McLaughlin's team introduced the laureled globe that became the symbol of the UN. Courtesy of Brian McLaughlin and Donna Firer.

SETTING for SIGNING the UNITED NATIONS CHARTER
San Francisco 1945

Plate 3. Perspectival drawing of Donal McLaughlin's set-up for the signing of the UN Charter, 1945. Courtesy of Brian McLaughlin and Donna Firer.

Plate 4. Prosecution stand with red and yellow lights for the simultaneous interpretation system, 1945. Photograph by Raymond D'Addario. City Archives Nuremberg A 65/II RA-51-D.

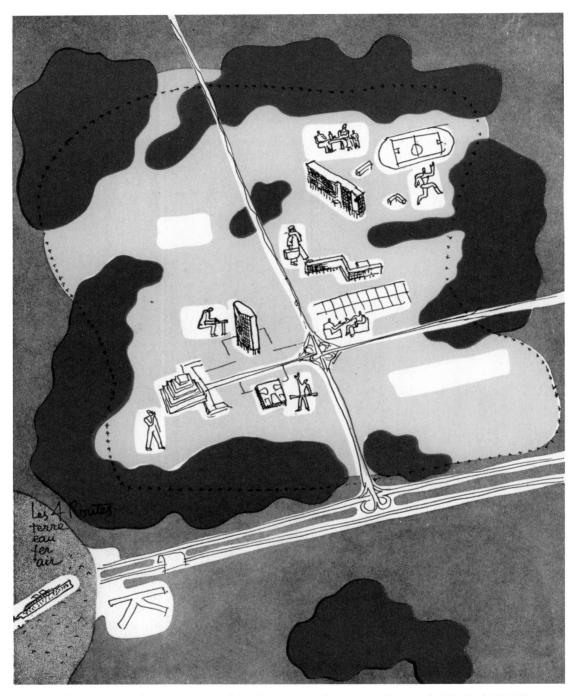

Plate 5. Le Corbusier, proposal for the UN Headquarters. Copyright F.L.C. / ADAGP, Paris / Artists Rights Society (ARS), New York 2023.

Plate 6. Arnstein Arneberg, perspectival drawing of Security Council, n.d. Arnstein Rynning Arneberg, NAMT.aar621.002. Courtesy of the Nasjonalmuseet for kunst, arkitektur og design, Oslo, Norway.

Plate 7. Postcard of the Economic and Social Council Chamber, 1952. Statens centrum för arkitektur och design (ArkDes), Stockholm, Sweden.

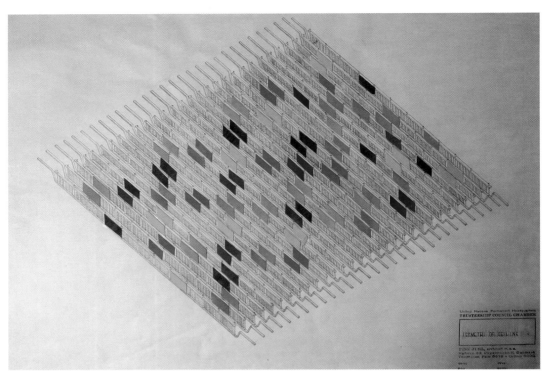

Plate 8. Finn Juhl, axonometric drawing of the ceiling at the Trusteeship Council Chamber, 1951. Courtesy of the Designmuseum Danmark.

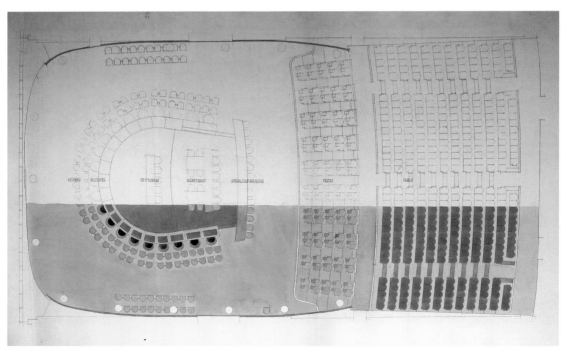

Plate 9. Finn Juhl, plan of the Trusteeship Council Chamber, 1951. Courtesy of the Designmuseum Danmark.

Plate 10. Natalie de Blois, watercolor of the refurbished interior of the New York City Building for the Second Session of the First General Assembly of the United Nations, 1946. Natalie de Blois Architectural Collection, Ms2007–017, Special Collections and University Archives, Virginia Polytechnic Institute, Blacksburg, Virginia.

Plate 11. Photograph showing the exhibition building used for the UN Regional Seminar and International Exhibition in New Delhi, 1954. Photograph by Ernest Weissmann. Courtesy of the Frances Loeb Library, Harvard University Graduate School of Design.

Plate 12. Interior view of the Caracol, showing circular table, wooden slats, and interpretation booths. Courtesy of the Comisión Económica para América Latina y el Caribe (CEPAL), División de Documentos y Publicaciones, Santiago, Chile.

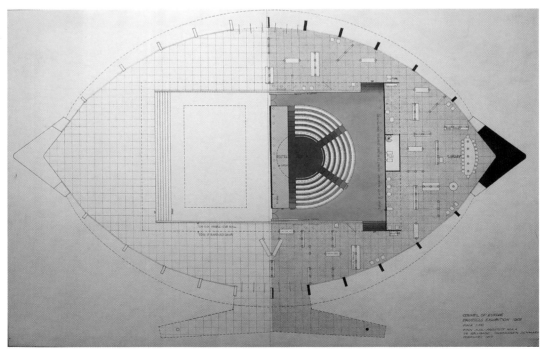

Plate 13. Finn Juhl, plan for the Council of Europe Pavilion, 1958. Courtesy of the Designmuseum Danmark.

3
The Voice of the World

Following the dissolution of the Board of Design, Secretary-General Trygve Lie submitted to the UN General Assembly the official report of the Headquarters Planning Office. Apart from declaring the Headquarters an "architectural organism" that tied all parts of the organization into a comprehensive and continuous whole, the Headquarters Planning Office, led by Wallace K. Harrison, claimed the "human voice" as a vital component in its organization. "The control and regulation of sound, especially the sound of the human voice, is of essential importance to the fundamental operations of the Headquarters of the United Nations," the report read.[1] At the Headquarters, voices activated conduits of diplomacy, but also structured them, connecting diplomats, delegates, national representatives, typists, simultaneous interpreters, and reporters into channels of liberal internationalism. The UN was the space that those conduits created, but also the platform from where delegates expected national concerns over bilateral and multilateral matters to be broadcast and amplified on a global scale. In speaking at the UN, one could aspire to address the world.

The report articulated diplomatic voices as signals within an ever-expanding communication network that set forward the fiction of a continuous frictionless flow of information transubstantiating the spoken word to written record and vice versa. Communication technologies would tie "together thousands of working units, individuals and groups of individuals within the headquarters and throughout the world," and ultimately, "with the larger world complex of communications between men and nations" (Figure 3.1).[2] Intercommunication systems, public address systems, dictaphones, telautographs, teletypes, radio typewriters, and television, as well as microfilm and pneumatic tubes, would actively construct information routes with the ultimate goal of reaching the international community, for "people at home to hear and see events in distant places."[3] In this sense, the United Nations fashioned itself as the voice—and possibly the ear—of the world.

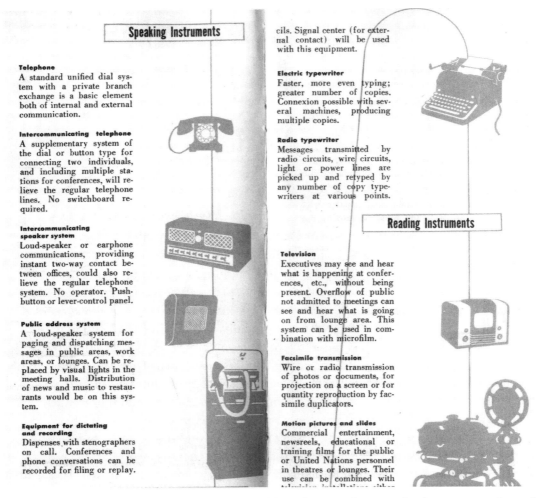

Figure 3.1. *Report to the General Assembly of the United Nations by the Secretary-General on the Permanent Headquarters of the United Nations* (Lake Success, N.Y.: United Nations, 1947).

Broadcasting this diplomatic voice-as-signal was as important to the organization as recording and setting it in motion inside the UN Headquarters. George E. Sokolsky, a McCarthy collaborator and anti-communist columnist at *The New York Sun,* compared the hourglass contour of the UN General Assembly to a loudspeaker (and the Secretariat Tower to a gravestone) in an effort to criticize the institution's political allegiance to internationalism as propaganda.[4] The comparison, reductive as it was, not only underlined Sokolsky's ideological opposition to the internationalist agenda, but also spoke to the postulation of the General Assembly, and the UN at large, as an amplification apparatus that broadcast its message to the world, reaching an audience that exceeded the boundaries of its headquarters.

Yet the voice-as-signal inside the UN Headquarters was also a matter of design that architects needed to address. The global interiors of the UN, in this sense, did not only constitute an architectural but also an acoustic space, making necessary a comprehensive plan for noise reduction and acoustic design of the cacophonous soundscapes of diplomacy. There would be the susurration of journalists, the whispering of advisers, and the murmuring of support staff, a noisy background against which diplomatic voices had to project within plenary halls so as not to lose intelligibility. Sometimes the plan itself created acoustic problems for the assembly. Backstage diplomacy in the lounges and cafeterias of the Headquarters, unless treated, could potentially interrupt the processes inside the formal forums. Which voices mattered to UN's liberal internationalism, and which were noise? Which voices had to remain private, and which were to be admitted in public? The Planning Office, with the help of engineers and acousticians, had to survey and evaluate liberal democracy in terms of acoustics and its communications systems, distinguishing (and hence establishing) meaningful content from noise. Such decisions and plans solidified hierarchies already existing within the diplomatic body and sorted actors along the lines of service, authority, and political representation.

Nowhere was the diplomatic voice given more prominence than in the General Assembly. The continuous criticism toward monumentality detailed in the previous chapter also permeated conversations on acoustics. UN officials warned the Board of Design that reverberant spaces created a sense of distance and formality, asking for acoustics that instigated intimacy without compromising the legibility of the spoken word. This call to preserve a sense of intimacy against reverberant and monumental spaces was at the same time a political and aesthetic project that architects and engineers would articulate in space. The signal architecture and structuring of communication at the Headquarters also defined acts of exclusion and insularity, evident in the decisions that shaped the acoustic design. These acts of exclusion and control stratified the spaces of globalized administration and its public spheres, but also revealed partly the political conundrum of democratic representation within the UN. The voices of the delegates were only mediums for their governments, speaking on behalf of national interests negotiated and formed within national political spheres. This diffusion of responsibility and deferral of authority were structural to the global spaces of international institutions and their politics of liberal multilateralism.

Public Opinion and the World Parliament

Initial plans for the Assembly Hall appeared during the meetings of the Preparatory Commission in London. The first UN General Assembly would convene there on January 10, 1946, while the Inspection Group and the Headquarters Planning Committee were evaluating sites in New York and elsewhere for the temporary headquarters. Delegates expected that the entire world community would follow the inaugural assembly in newsreels or wireless broadcasts. At the first meeting of the Executive Committee, British diplomat Philip Noel-Baker proclaimed public opinion "the life-blood" of the organization. Noel-Baker, who had served as assistant to the Secretary-General of the League of Nations Sir Eric Drummond, believed that the inclusion of the general public (or even a meaningful invitation to the general public) depended on a robust media infrastructure. Mass media would be an invaluable tool in institutional efforts to internationalize the UN's "methods of democracy" and participation.[5] Mass media would stand in for the general public that the organization could not accommodate in its venues, but would also allow the UN to connect directly with local publics around the world, circumventing the governments of sovereign nations—or at least, that was Noel-Baker's ambition.

Diplomats and politicians had been researching the implications of the presence of mass media since the preparation for the Dumbarton Oaks Conference, when Franklin Delano Roosevelt's administration asked writer Groff Conklin, at the time working for OSS intelligence, to draft recommendations. Conklin, studying the approach of Woodrow Wilson's administration to the question of the press in 1919, argued that the "open diplomacy" of U.S. foreign policy that at the time admitted the press inside negotiations without any regulation in actuality opened the doors to the circulation of disinformation. "Absence of secrecy would have meant a free press. A free press would have meant an inordinate amount of press misinformation," he argued. Instead, Conklin suggested that the administration should institutionalize and order the presence of mass media, with crucial conferences (including the Dumbarton Oaks meetings) taking place behind closed doors and press conferences offering structured moments of interaction with press representatives. Intelligence services should be involved, ample communications infrastructures and accommodations should be provided, and a well-organized press protocol should be delineated.[6] The goal was for the U.S. delegation to get control over the circulation of news, and by extension public opinion at large.[7]

In response the 1945 San Francisco Conference further standardized the publicity protocol, appointing "principal" officers for regularized meetings with the press. But the experience on the ground demonstrated that mass media remained a troublesome bedmate: cardinal to the institution, yet invasive and driven by drama and profit.[8] Diplomats feared that the presence of journalists would transform political participation into a spectacle driven by personal vanity, undermining political work on the ground and encouraging populist approaches that accentuated conflict and antagonism. U.S. State Department officials associated the populist language that came with mass media spectacle with the disastrous effects of press coverage during earlier attempts at international organization, and delegates often protested the uneven coverage of speakers, which they found distracting from the issues and negotiations at hand. Noise was another source of complaint, as UN officials sought to establish diplomatic discourse as neutral, tempered, and rational. But there were also political anxieties at play that the presence of mass media accentuated, with national representatives, often upper-class white members of economic elites, trying to maintain their status within the new world order and its media noise. Ultimately, photographers and cameramen in attendance at the opening and signing of the UN Charter distressed officials and politicians, who noted that cameras, flashes, and their continuous chatter were a source of "discomfort and annoyance."[9]

During the first meeting of the UN General Assembly in London the effort to invite yet mitigate the disruptive function of mass media continued. National representatives wanting to reach their domestic audiences back home asked for "speedy, unrestricted and uncensored telegraph, telephone, radio and postal communications with the world at large."[10] Even the Special Advisory Committee on Information that coordinated the collection, archiving, and circulation of information contended that all official organs should meet in public, with the exception of special Security and Trusteeship Council meetings, revealing the tiered publicness of UN organs.[11] A clear protocol would help, but the regulation of mass media's interfacing with the new organization required architectural solutions.

Delegates wondered how photographs, newsreels, and broadcasts would attract the world's investment in the UN's public sphere. For some, media such as film and photography should merely transmit snippets of the UN's structured public appearance, but for others this relay was not enough to bring people in. Noel-Baker argued against the presence of filming crews and photographers, not for their disruptive nature, but for their claims of indexing reality, which to the British diplomat hampered "the imagination of the peoples" and affixed perceptions of diplomatic work. Instead, he professed, wireless broadcasts and articles, with their textual representations of diplomacy, stimulated the work of imagination, allowing for a spectrum of possible interpretations of how global institutions work, but also prompting publics to actively envision themselves there.[12] One's place within this system—visitor, press, delegate, adviser, non-governmental organization representative—also garnered different levels of access to UN platforms. A delegate would both watch and listen to the deliberations, but was the same level of participation desirable also for the larger public? Delegates from the Netherlands and Chile advocated for "pictorial publicity" to be centrally administered, arguing that images were essential for endowing new bodies such as the General Assembly with the authority of a formed presence. Those debates highlighted how the UN as a multilateral organization, in managing the medium—radio, television, film—to control its representation to the public, hoped to also manage operational imaginations of liberal internationalism.

For the first London meeting of the UN General Assembly, there were two main questions at stake. First, the organization needed to determine how the general public would participate within its structured public sphere. Second, it needed to organize and order in space national representatives, civic societies, administration and staff so as to present itself as a formalized public sphere to said general public. National delegations, with diplomatic representatives and their advisers; UN Secretariat staff such as typists, archivists, verbatim reporters, translators, and interpreters; high-ranking Secretariat officials; nongovernmental organizations; press representatives, filming and broadcast crews; and visitors all needed to find their places within the plenary hall and the future permanent Headquarters as well. Determining the place of those publics within UN's assembly architecture was imperative in the launching of the General Assembly as a formalized and legitimate global public sphere in front of the press, and by extension the general public.

In London, the Preparatory Commission experimented with different spatial configurations and the placement of the press, turning the Central Hall at Westminster into a laboratory for the assembling of international bodies.[13] The Commission asked the U.K. Ministry of Works team refurbishing Central Hall to remove the press from the floor, effectively separating journalists, photographers, and reporters from the assembling national representatives and their teams. In placing filming crews and photographers in the open gallery space above the delegates' floor, the construction crew divided the space vertically in tiers of professional affiliation: the ground floor for diplomats and the galleries for the general public and the press. In doing so, the UN also reinforced and expanded the theatrical constitution of the public sphere in the middle. The more engineers, architects, and diplomats removed the journalists from the "floor," the more the operative site of politics and diplomacy transformed into a stage.

Inside the Central Hall, UN officials further explored the visual identity of the institution to communicate structural and institutional coherence in ways that concealed the organization's emergent nature. Optics mattered, especially as officials anticipated that the organization would wander from one temporary setting to the next for at least the immediate future. Concert halls, conference venues, skating rinks, and factories should not come to define the institution, but rather the institution should define them, even in the short time they accommodated the UN. This required the development of a toolkit of visual references that when deployed in space would immediately announce the arrival of the new international organization. The San Francisco Conference offered some initial tools, notably the UN emblem, which designers used on visitor passes, official documents, and even on the walls of the Veterans Building and the Memorial Opera House to mark the presence of the organization. The toolkit also adopted blue-gray hues for its color palette and arrays of national flags to demarcate international space. At the Central Hall in London, the same markers, incorporated into the design of platforms and banisters, signaled the presence of the UN.[14]

To declare the political body modern and distinct from other international organizations, the construction team employed the streamlined aesthetics of inter-war industrial design, evoking a sentiment of frictionless operation for the General Assembly (Figure 3.2). The reception, however, was mixed. Reporting for *The New York Times,* journalist James B. Reston lamented the loss of Central Hall's "Victorian" exterior with the refurbished modernist (at least in his view) interior that resembled "something that Norman Bel Geddes might have designed," adding that Central Hall, with its blue paint and drapes, seemed in between a hall prepared for a "political convention and some monstrous modernistic schoolroom."[15] If the UN was to distinguish itself from past organizations, the architects would have to adopt a bolder approach, as well as prepare to defend modernism to the press as the language of international organization.

In addition to the question of visual identity, the plenary hall also posed acoustic problems. Assembly halls intertwine techniques of listening and speaking with modes of participation and democracy. It is no coincidence that, unlike the three council chambers where the round table became the anchor object for the significations of diplomatic work (see chapter 2), at the General Assembly the Preparatory Commission would look to parliaments for the appropriate architectural type. Considering the etymological roots of the word, a parliament, Mladen Dolar notes, is ultimately "a place reserved for speech."[16] To find oneself in a parliament equates to finding oneself in a place where one voices a problem, a position, or a concern within a public sphere. This political speech as medium carries the weight of its representational function to give voice to—and in this sense to stand in for—its national constituents.

The acoustic problem presented within the UN General Assembly was both performative and constitutive in nature. The General Assembly was to offer the "felicitous conditions" for what J. L. Austin calls "speech acts," the idea that words can do things.[17] The ambition was for the voices of the world to take over the podium so that the speech acts within the General Assembly established the new institution as international in scope and democratic in character. Unlike other sites of global bureaucracies that rationalized the circulation of paper, the UN Headquarters at large and the General Assembly in particular centered in its functions the spoken word and its transmission, without, however, undoing the circuits of the written word woven around it. At Central Hall the importance of acoustics became quickly evident. The public address system that the Ministry of Works technicians had installed to reinforce and amplify the delegates' voices inside the plenary hall and the conference rooms quickly created new—and amplified old—acoustic problems.[18] The space was bigger than needed—"the whole atmosphere is that of mass rallies. . . . It is extremely unlike a meeting place of Governments," an early memorandum stated, revealing anxieties over reverberatory acoustics and their signification. The same memorandum called for a

Figure 3.2. The interior of the Central Hall Westminster during the opening session of the First UN General Assembly, January 10, 1946. Courtesy of the United Nations Photo Library.

concerted effort to "disguise the character of the Hall, and to change its 'atmosphere,'" reducing its size with floor-to-ceiling curtains that also dampened echoes and lowering the podium closer to the floor to bring speakers near the delegates and away from the press and public in the galleries.

Part of the acoustic problem inside Central Hall related to the desire to broadcast the proceedings. The voice-as-signal registering in the microphones had to travel the conduits of the sound system uninterrupted and with clarity, regardless of environmental noise and reverberation. To create this sense of sonic clarity, Ministry of Works technicians, in collaboration with BBC engineers, came up with a soundproofing plan. Soft carpeting and other surgical acoustic treatment would reduce reverberation so that the voice-as-signal projected in space intelligibly.[19] In addition, engineers had to attend to dead spots, interference from the monitoring loudspeaker on the president's table, as well as sound leaks from recording rooms and broadcast studios.[20] The Ministry of Works soundproofed conference rooms and the plenary hall,[21] while installing double doors to insulate the Assembly Hall from any noise emanating from congregating journalists and press in the lobbies.[22]

But soundproofing Central Hall also inhibited the very acoustic function of the space: listening. National representatives attending the Preparatory Commission and the first part of the first session of the General Assembly realized that the overhanging galleries at Central Hall hampered the propagation of sound in the auditorium beneath them, creating acoustically dead zones. This was common knowledge among British delegates, who criticized gallery structures at the House of Commons for creating a depressing atmosphere, limiting their vision and hearing, and hindering their words from reaching the audience. The request to eliminate such space became a matter of "capital importance" in the later design of the Assembly Hall.[23]

In response to the experience at Central Hall, the UN Secretariat issued recommendations for the temporary headquarters under construction in Flushing Meadows, New York, where the General Assembly would hold the second part of its first session later in the fall of 1946. The new memorandum on conference planning covered the full range of UN–related activities, equipping the Flushing Meadows contractors and architects with detailed descriptions of the temporary headquarters. The memorandum recommended that the president's platform be elevated to garner authority and a full view of the delegates; it advised that the speaker's rostrum be placed in front of the president but on a lower plane, clearly denoting hierarchies within the assembly; it noted that interpreters needed direct visual contact with the speaker, an experience confirmed at Hunter College and Lake Success where the Security Council and other UN organs and committees had been convening; and it placed verbatim reporters in a pit in front of the speaker's rostrum. The memorandum also divided delegates, advisers, press, and public, advising a desk configuration guided by the "principle of giving any speaker the feeling of having his audience gathered closely about him" for a "feeling of intimacy from the point of view of the speaker." Barricades would distinguish between the public and the convening body on the ground floor. The memo also formalized the place of the press on the galleries, asking that delegates be separated from the general public, with dedicated entrances.[24]

These suggestions shaped the interior of the New York City Building that Mayor Fiorello LaGuardia, Parks Commissioner Robert Moses, and architect Aymar Embury II had built for the 1939–1940 New York World's Fair at Flushing Meadows, and which at the time served as a skating rink. Inside the New York City Building, Natalie de Blois, a young architect who had just joined the office of Skidmore, Owings & Merrill (SOM) after graduating from Columbia University, converted the ice-skating rink into the plenary hall for the UN General Assembly with the help of John F. O'Brien.[25] De Blois dressed the backdrop of the UN insignia with a large blue drape and placed the interpreters' booths on the sides of the General Assembly, inside built-in booths overlooking the floor (Plate 10). She also tucked away press, filming crews, and broadcast studios behind a temporary wall closing off the second-floor open gallery. In collaboration with the U.S. Signal Corps, the construction crews wired and miked the hall, installing for the first time fully soundproofed studios for radio and film.[26] As a result, the floor

Figure 3.3. Interior view of the Second Session of the United Nations General Assembly during an address by George C. Marshall inside the refurbished New York City Building in Flushing Meadows, September 17, 1947. Courtesy of the United Nations Photo Library.

was cleared of that part of the broadcasting apparatus that fed the UN voice into older systems of communication to reach an international audience beyond its U.S. territory.

From the side galleries, journalists were always presented with a collective, decidedly formed and calibrated public sphere. To render the space equitable and the world malleable, the UN Conference officials instituted a lottery system for seat assignments, preventing delegates from affixing their place in the auditorium and by extension in the world, initially before each session and later weekly.[27] Natalie de Blois and SOM placed cameras, filming crews, and radio broadcasters on the side galleries overlooking the entire floor, not solely the delegate presenting. In other words, these architects and U.S. Signal Corps engineers expanded the stage beyond the locale of the podium to also include the entire assembling body (Figure 3.3). In doing so, they delineated the floor as the site of representation of a world community at work.

By the time that the second part of the first session of the General Assembly was opening at Flushing Meadows, the transformation had registered at least with the U.S. press, which often referred to the UN as "the new world stage."[28] In the following years photographs and newsreels from the temporary headquarters circulated widely in newspapers and movie theaters, establishing the form of the new "world parliament" as a typology for future international institutions— or any institution with claims to globality. But the affinity of theatrical spaces with spectacles alarmed both diplomats and architects. A theater, a space where actors and actresses enact other voices and impersonate rather than represent, complicated and challenged ideas of free will and individualism, placing the diplomat within the context of a larger theater of international affairs. Therefore, the design problem for the permanent General Assembly became how to construct a stage that did not look like one, or put differently, how to obfuscate the theatrical ancestry of the plenary hall and to make space for a tempered and more intimate convening body.

The Acoustic Spaces of Internationalism

The question of plenary hall acoustics was not merely a technicality for acousticians, sound engineers, and architects to deal with. Techniques of listening and speaking determined the diplomatic cultures that the UN aspired to install within its public platforms. Acoustics dictated how a delegate's voice would project onto space, but also how convening diplomats would perceive it: how loud or soft or reverberant that voice would be, as well as how it would reach its intended audience. At the same time, the Headquarters Planning Office had to incorporate simultaneous interpretation systems (see chapter 1) within the larger communications infrastructure to support the convening of an international body. On a certain level those decisions were technological, requiring technical expertise and equipment, but they also carried aesthetic and political implications, deriving from and determining diplomacy and international relations. Defining the acoustic conditions of diplomatic conversations accorded the planning of the General Assembly Hall—and to a certain extent the UN's public platforms at large—an environmental dimension. Members of the Headquarters Planning Office and external consultants debated in terms of atmospheres and environmental aesthetics the selection of sound systems, the placement of broadcast studios, even the choice of simultaneous interpretation system to order the polyglot soundscape of the UN.

Reverberation presented a particularly pesky problem that brought forward the entanglement of aesthetics with politics. Hitler's electoral campaigns had turned high reverberation rates into the sonic hallmark of the Third Reich, associating in the international public's imagination resonant acoustic spaces and public address systems with the presence of undemocratic masses-as-publics. Loudspeakers reverberating in the open field established Hitler's voice, leading his propaganda machine to radio-broadcast his voice echoing in space, rather than using the direct feed from the microphone or a speech reading recorded after the event.[29] Loudspeakers aligned the Third Reich ideology with technological progress. Cornelia Epping-Jäger argues that the triad of sound technologies (microphones, loudspeakers, and amplifiers), ideology, and radiophonic structures of diffusion that made the "dispositive loud/speaker" were integral to the National Socialist propaganda machine, establishing the party's "acoustic presence" by centering Hitler's amplified and resonant voice-as-law.[30]

Yet the UN's "dispositive loud/speaker" (to appropriate Epping-Jäger's term), although not less ideological, aimed for a different affect. Directives against atmospheres that evoked "mass rallies" and calls for ways to reduce reverberation had already appeared during the London preparatory meetings, where officials lamented the choice of the echoing Central Hall.[31] Noel-Baker, channeling the politicians' reluctance regarding public address systems, suggested the replacement of loudspeakers with reflecting sounding boards that centered the Central Hall's soundscape back to the body of the speaker.[32] If resonance lay at the heart of the monumental soundscape of the Third Reich, then the UN should soften the voices of the new international organization, blunting their edges and tempering their differences. The voice on the podium should not be overpowering the delegates gathering inside the General Assembly. In the place of resonant public spheres, the UN called for an intimate atmosphere similar to the one that the "Fireside Chats" evoked during World War II, when FDR's voice was brought inside U.S. households establishing the president as a paternal figure and domestic affairs as housekeeping.[33] Reverberation was necessary for the voice to travel far enough, but needed to be adapted to the new call for clarity and intelligibility, rather than spectacle.

When Harrison formed the Board of Design in early 1947, its architects had to catch up with the acoustic concerns of delegates and UN Secretariat officials. A number of architects already working at the temporary headquarters at Flushing Meadows, Hunter College, and Lake Success (Walker and Skidmore, for example) were aware of the acoustic intricacies, but not all. Some of the Board architects persistently conflated parliaments with concert halls, revealing not only their inability to distinguish but probably also their desire to merge the two programs. The confusion between the two—concert halls and parliaments—had been evident since the time that Harrison, to demonstrate the appropriateness of the Turtle Bay site for the UN Headquarters, scrapped the titles "Metropolitan Opera" and "Philharmonic" from Zeckendorf's X-City and penned in "General Assembly" and "Security Council," sealing on the architectural plan what engineers and bureaucrats had already articulated inside the spaces momentarily hosting the UN: that the convening international body was to be staged in order to be constituted

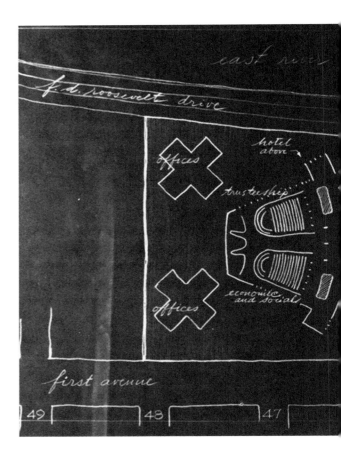

Figure 3.4. Wallace K. Harrison, plan for X-City adapted to illustrate the appropriateness of the Turtle Bay site for the UN Permanent Headquarters, 1946. Wallace K. Harrison architectural drawings and papers, 1913–1986. Courtesy Avery Drawings and Archives.

as a global public sphere (Figure 3.4).[34] The conflation also demonstrated architects' unfamiliarity with the specifics of architectural acoustics. Taking advantage of this inexperience, some Board architects criticized proposals on the grounds of their acoustic design to promote their own plans for the General Assembly, with Le Corbusier pointing to Gustave Lyon's calculations for the League of Nations auditorium that he and Pierre Jeanneret had proposed, along with its architectural predecessor, the Salle Pleyel.[35]

The discussion that ensued revealed persisting anxieties over the capacity of the voice to even survive the large expanses of a monumental interior, but also resistance to the loudspeaker as an anti-acoustic technology.[36] Board architects distinguished between first-order sounds to be amplified, interpreted, and circulated, and second-order sounds that they had to silence and insulate against. The clatter of typists, the rattle of heating and ventilation systems, as well as the throb of the city, were cast as "headquarters noise" against which the voice on the podium had to project.

Ambivalent toward technocratic formulations of the public sphere, Board architects also debated the need for electrical amplification and public address

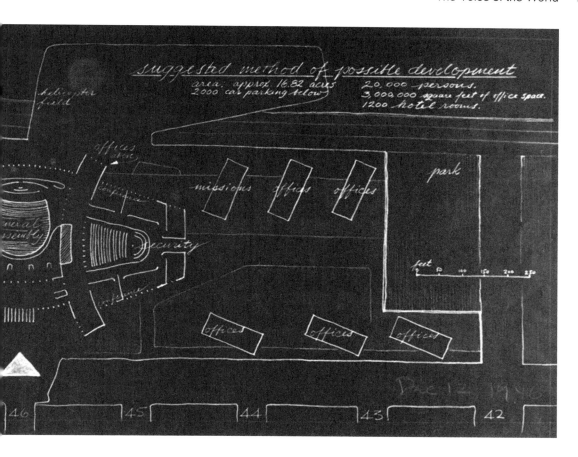

systems, with remarkably little consensus. Despite the fact that loudspeakers and microphones would secure the effective transmission of the voice on the podium to the convening body, they hesitated to admit sound systems into the Assembly Hall. Even the small minority of architects to consider an electroacoustic condition insisted that "good acoustics," meaning architectural acoustics, would only help the scope of the sound system.[37] "Many want [a] natural voice," Harrison noted late in April 1947, echoing the general sentiment among UN officials who, although happy to indulge the machine metaphor when discussing the organization at large, were reluctant to allow it to articulate the UN public sphere.[38] The desire for an unmediated voice of international liberalism to propagate the message of human rights, humanitarian relief, aid programs, and reconstruction was all too evident.

In its essence, the presence of technology undercut the fiction of a human-centric world community. Politicians shared their mistrust of technology in reports and questionnaires, complaining that microphones created noise and confusion. Part of the reason was that electronic amplification often distorted the voice of the speaker. There were also the technological glitches and performance anxiety associated with the use of microphones. Microphones and loudspeakers denaturalized the voice, standing there as a troublesome cue to the technological prosthesis at play. With electronic amplification, it was the loudspeaker that was speaking, or the headphone—not the politician. Sound systems ultimately disassociated speaking bodies from the voices that reached the audience, challenging any sense of control and mastery over one's own voice (and by extension, self). UN delegates reporting to the Planning Office were also skeptical about wires and switches connecting speakers with the Secretariat infrastructural support, suggesting that verbatim reporters and simultaneous interpreters would be placed in physical proximity to the speaker so as to control communications without the interference of wires and cables.[39] But in reality, at stake was the fear that microphones and loudspeakers subjugated the diplomatic body, surrendering its modulation to engineers and technology inside sound control booths, away from the speaking delegate's body.

This was not a new problem in the history of parliamentary spaces. During the 1920s and 1930s, plenary halls and courtrooms from the International Palace of Justice to the Parliament of the United Kingdom had been retrofitted with microphones and loudspeakers in an effort to address inadequate acoustics. Most of the times press and delegates criticized those systems for distorting and alienating the speaking voice. Bidding for wiring the Palais de Chaillot that Jacques Carlu had been retrofitting for the sixth session of the UN General Assembly in 1951, Tannoy Products made a point out of its "natural" sounding sound systems.[40] The company foregrounded its system's ability to create the "illusion that no 'Loudspeakers' were being used," where delegates appeared to talk "in a normal conversational voice," as if "hearing not from an 'Amplifying Loudspeaker,' but from the orator himself with all his naturalness."[41] In short, the naturalness that Tannoy had in mind was normative in the sense that voices and the bodies producing them should coincide in space as if a whole system of wires, modulators, consoles, and in some cases interpreters, did not exist.

Tannoy had tried this approach at the House of Commons and the House of Lords, where the mounted microphones and built-in small loudspeakers promised to facilitate debates without threatening intelligibility or the intimate atmosphere of the two chambers. *Wireless World*, a Marconi publication dedicated to radio, described the House of Commons installation as a "softspeaker system," where all members not only were able to hear, but also to be heard without having to speak from behind a podium (Figure 3.5).[42] To adapt it for Church House, where the UN met in 1945, Tannoy replaced the loudspeaker system with headsets harnessed on the seats and a four-channel switch for simultaneous interpretation. The company reasoned that the headsets brought the speaker closer to listeners, literally bringing the voice on the podium to the ear of the delegate.[43] In reality, however, Tannoy had replaced loudspeakers with headphones

Reprinted from **Wireless World** (OVERSEAS SECTION) *April, 1951*

House of Commons Sound System

Low-Intensity Reinforcing Installation in the New Chamber

THERE has been widespread interest throughout the Commonwealth in the completion and opening of the New Chamber of the House of Commons, replacing the one wrecked by bombs during the War, and overseas readers of *Wireless World* will be especially glad to have this description of the sound reinforcing system installed by Tannoy Products. It differs from the usually accepted *loud*speaker system and could be described more aptly as a *soft*speaker system.

A large number of small low-power reproducing units have been accommodated in the carved woodwork at the rear of the bench type seating—one unit for each two Members' seats. The placing of the reproducers ensures that each Member is within a very restricted range and, therefore, able to hear the reinforced speech free from all reverberations which, if predominant, would destroy intelligibility.

A Parliamentary Debate demands that any Member present should not only be able to hear any, or all other, Members but also should be able to make himself heard by all without leaving his seat. To achieve this, six specially developed uni-directional microphones have been suspended from the ceiling over the front benches, and six—three each side—mounted on bronze cantilever arms over the back benches. A similar microphone has been installed beneath the canopy above the Speaker's Chair, and on the Table of the House is a further microphone on a bronze stand.

To overcome howl caused through acoustic feedback when microphones and loudspeakers are in close proximity, the reproducer units are arranged in zones which are co-related with the pick-up areas of the microphones. Normally, only one microphone is operative at any one time and the reproducer units in

that particular zone are muted, and in some cases the input to those in the adjacent zones attenuated. It is only those zones covering the Floor of the House that are so controlled—the reproducers provided for the Press Gallery and other galleries operate at a constant level.

The selection of the microphones and general supervision of the installation is executed by an intricate remote control system, as the main apparatus is installed beneath the Floor of the House. When a Member rises to speak the operator in his cubicle overlooking the Chamber depresses the switch for the appropriate zone—this connects the microphone and associated pre-amplifier to the power amplifiers and, simultaneously, reduces the amplification of those units feeding the same zone of loudspeakers and partially attenuates the signal to the power amplifiers operating the adjoining zone. The same signal is connected to the remainder of the loudspeaker amplifiers at maximum volume. In order to follow the rapid "cross talk" between Members that arises during debates and, more especially, during "Question

The disposition of the twelve suspended microphones in relation to the seating in the new Chamber of the House of Commons can be seen in this photograph.

Figure 3.5. "House of Commons Sound System," *Wireless World,* April 1951.

to avoid the howling feedback that occurs when microphones pick up sound from loudspeakers.

The call for intimacy constituted the biggest challenge, precisely because it ran against the very presence of loudspeakers. Delegates and diplomats built the UN public forums on the narrative of a shared aspiration and a desire for a new world based on rational and close relationships. Intimacy was central to that fantasy, initially as a response to the instrumentalized masses of the Third Reich, and later as a tool for political liberalism. Intimacy also implied an acoustic space dedicated to listening, to tending to the problems of the world. Dominic Pettman argues that "sonic intimacy," the effort to install an acoustic space for introspection and connection, juxtaposes attempts at instituting a performative and outward-projecting "voice of the world." Yet the UN General Assembly and its conversations on intimacy bid to merge the two to reconstitute the diplomatic sphere as a familial introspective smooth space.[44] The UN, within this context, presents an interesting case, where bureaucrats and diplomats, invested in centering humanism within its platforms, sought to bring intimacy programmatically inside the institution with media and workshops, but ended up producing an aesthetic.

The Headquarters Planning Office insisted on hiding the very act of amplification, not only visually but also aurally. Harrison and Abramovitz thought that the ideal acoustic condition would allow the voice on the podium to reverberate without physical strain throughout the auditorium, avoiding, at the same time, reverberatory cacophony. Echoes, as much as they were a necessary byproduct of acoustic amplification, overlaid spoken words with their acoustic mirrors, ultimately destroying meaning and interfering with the very goal of communication. Rather, the two architects advocated for a relatively silenced General Assembly that could evoke a sense of comfort and warmth, while a loudspeaker system would take over the dissemination of the word on the podium.

The call for intimacy also registered on the visual level. Corridors and dramatic vistas that separated the speaker from the rest of the delegates produced distance and conveyed a stiff sense of decorum that diplomats shuddered at and were not willing to condone. Preparing the requirements for the General Assembly, delegates suggested eliminating side corridors, curving the edges of the auditorium desks, and bringing closer speaker and audience. "The tables should form a curve in front of the Speaker, the wings of which may not reach behind the level of the Speaker. . . . The principle of giving any speaker the feeling of having his audience gathered closely about him is more important than increased freedom of movement on the Assembly floor." Architects would translate this desire for intimacy into lower ceilings, shorter corridors, a preference for carpets and wood, as well as curved walls. In a way, UN bureaucrats anticipated that the architecture of the UN General Assembly would endow the organization with a performative aesthetic of embrace.

The hesitation over electrical amplification revealed an additional tension between the desire for mass media to become conduits for the organization, and the overall distrust toward media. Ernest Weissmann, who at the time was the consultant architect to represent Yugoslavia, recognized the importance of broadcasting within the UN media apparatus, noting that the "architectural motive" behind the "UN Center" should be the public and how "to bring the deliberations of the nations' delegates out of isolation to the people in the street."[45] Similarly, Le Corbusier called the media booths the "mechanical eyes and ears of the world,"[46] a metaphor that he borrowed from Paramount and which Harrison swiftly adopted to press upon the Board the representational value those spaces would carry. The whole world would be watching the public platforms the architects designed for the UN.[47]

During Board meetings, visiting UN diplomats reminded architects that part of their job was to frame the perspective of mass media. "The press should see the entire floor," Vaughan proclaimed.[48] Following the recommendation of sound engineers and broadcast specialists, the Headquarters Planning Office asked architects to consider sightlines in their placement of the press booths in all council chambers and meeting halls.[49] Officials requested a booth for "long shots" to dramatically cover the proceedings of the General Assembly.[50]

Dimitri Manouilsky, a Ukrainian diplomat in the USSR's delegation, urged UN officials to adopt the IBM system at the time installed at Courtroom 600 for the Nuremberg Trials, a proposal that raised concerns among delegates and interpreters alike. The Board architects also had opinions about the interpretation system. Le Corbusier condemned the coupling of orators with microphones and the replacement of the "human voice" with the "mechanical interpreter" for disrupting what he perceived to be an intimate connection between speaker and audience. In his mind, the interpreters' exemption from the plenary field denied them humanity and rendered them machines. "But no, gentlemen, a mechanical voice speaks to a field of dead people," he claimed, appealing to the architects' conflicting sentiments toward the electrification of the human voice.[51]

The press, on the other hand, celebrated the simultaneous interpretation system as a big technological aid to international diplomacy. *The Binghamton Sun* proclaimed the wireless radio simultaneous interpretation headset that IBM installed at Lake Success and Flushing Meadows a most impactful "little gadget" for "international understanding," especially for paying timely attention to "the force of many arguments" that otherwise would be lost in translation within the "babble of tongues" (Figure 3.6). In arguing so, the newspaper obliterated the interpreters and celebrated the device as the system itself.[52] The initial proposal to

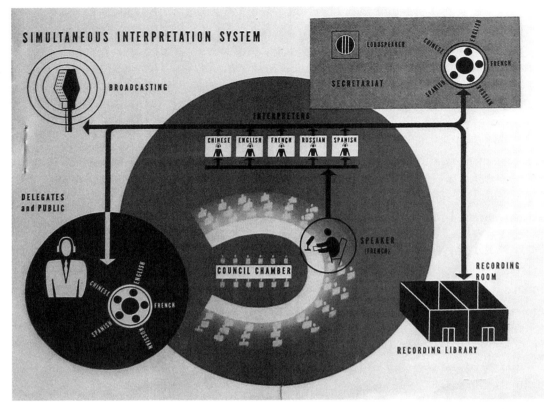

Figure 3.6. Diagram of Simultaneous Interpretation System in a council chamber. Similar systems were deployed at the General Assembly, the Security Council, the Trusteeship Council, and the Economic and Social Council. James E. Payne, "United It Stands," *Steelways* (January 1950): 1–5; reprinted with permission from the American Iron and Steel Institute.

recycle the same units for the permanent headquarters caused protest from competing companies.[53] As a result, the Headquarters Planning Office allowed IBM to bid only for the channel selectors, the cables, and some of the headphones, which opened the door to more competitors including Siemens, Philips, and Telex.[54]

The booths for the interpreters placed additional demands on the Board architects. The Nuremberg Trials setup next to the witness stand was inconvenient for prohibiting eye contact with each speaker on the podium. The open glass booths at the rear side of the temporary headquarters in Lake Success admitted environmental noise inside the booth, interfering with the interpreters' listening. Architects decided to place those booths, along with the rest of the media infrastructures, inside galleries behind a unifying double glass, ultimately embedding them on the walls and having them overlook the entire floor.[55]

With the simultaneous interpreters removed from the floor and placed alongside the rest of infrastructural support—journalists, cameramen, and radio producers—the UN demonstrated its desire to produce the convening public as an uninterrupted functioning whole. All interpretations would reach delegates via wires and headphones. Everything else would be background noise, rendering the existence of loudspeakers superfluous to the operations of the General Assembly. Delegates could tune in and out of speeches, choosing the language channel of their preference. The global polity congregating at the center did not share the same acoustic space, but rather acquired an atomized experience of the assembly. In this sense, the acoustic space they inhabited was built around the individual, creating, nonetheless, an intimate acoustic relationship with the interpreter at work. Each member related directly with the larger communication organism and not to one another, illuminating the organization's aspiration to insert itself as the interfacing system. Amplification was purely ornamental, enveloping the convening body in the voice projecting into space.

Architectures of Sound Control

Following the conclusion of the Board of Design meetings, the Headquarters Planning Office set out to identify acousticians to work on the headquarters. The Office initially offered the project to UCLA professor Vern O. Knudsen, co-founder of the Acoustical Society of America and a prominent acoustician in the United States.[56] Knudsen, who had been researching speech in auditoriums, believed acoustic design to be the management of variables and argued that plenary halls and spaces designed for the spoken word required a lower reverberation rate and the elimination of noise to render speech intelligible.[57]

For the UN, Knudsen compiled a comprehensive study of assembly halls and courtrooms in Europe, creating a map of auditory conditions. He visited the Palais des Nations, the International Court of Justice, and the Palais de Chaillot, where the General Assembly was temporarily convening at the time, and declared the acoustics of all three rooms substandard: the Palais des Nations had "frightfully reverberant" lobbies, with echoes fluttering inside the General Assembly Hall; the International Court of Justice was "excessively reverberant and noisy" with the installed Philips amplification system helping, but not remedying, the room acoustics; and the Palais de Chaillot, although satisfying acoustically given its refurbishment by Jacques Carlu, had a defective simultaneous interpretation system that did not insulate the interpreters against environmental noise.[58] In the report Knudsen noted that apart from interfering with speech intelligibility, high reverberation created a sense of monumentality. To control both, he recommended that the Headquarters Planning Office additionally insulate the General Assembly and any broadcast booths adjacent to the main plenary hall.

When Knudsen resigned from the UN project on account of his teaching responsibilities at UCLA, he recommended one of his students for the job: the much younger acoustics researcher and architect Richard Bolt.[59] Bolt, who at the time was teaching at MIT, invited his colleague Leo L. Beranek to work with him on the UN Headquarters early in October 1948. Beranek, who had just moved from Harvard to MIT to teach communication engineering and oversee the interdepartmental Acoustics Laboratory, was awestruck.[60] "I hate to say it but we really didn't know anything. The first time Bolt unrolled those blueprints for the U.N. headquarters that had already been developed, they covered the whole floor of the room. . . . It was frightening," he recalled in his autobiography.[61] From 1948 to 1951, Bolt and Beranek reviewed the acoustic design of the headquarters, with Beranek planning in addition the sound system for the General Assembly. Young architect Robert B. Newman joined the team later in 1948, eventually becoming a partner. The project spurred them to form the acoustic consultancy Bolt, Beranek and Newman (BBN), a consultancy that later pioneered time-sharing systems, research on machine-human symbiosis, and eventually the computer network known as ARPANET, a progenitor of the Internet.[62]

Hired for their background in architectural acoustics (Bolt had a BA in architecture), Bolt and Beranek did not fail to notice immediately that intelligibility was the main acoustic problem they would have to address. In other words, the two engineers, like Knudsen earlier, noted that for the diplomatic voice-as-signal to be deployed within the UN, acoustic design had to ensure its intelligibility to all listeners regardless of medium of transmission (wires and air). The screech of audio feedback, distortion, muffled sound, or even jumbled signals made apparent the presence of an electroacoustic system that organized the voice of the world, albeit disrupting ideas of organic unity and frictionless communication within the international community. The completion of the communication loop depended on the environmental conditions against which the projected sound traveled. Cafeterias, lounges, corridors, as well as meeting rooms and chambers presented plenty of threats to the intelligibility of diplomatic exchanges. In this sense, the potential failure of the UN communication apparatus was as much a technological as it was a political question.

The idea of noise as a threat to communication has a military past. Bolt, and especially Beranek, had been steeped in research on telecommunication systems and speech intelligibility since early in World War II, when noise complaints from the Air Corps reached the U.S. National Defense Committee (NDC). Signals were failing to reach their targets; pilots were reporting noise fatigue; and signalmen could hardly comprehend commands amid action. Convinced that noise was the source of the problem, the U.S. National Defense Research Committee (NDRC) launched a research initiative on the soundproofing of long-range bombardments, examining noise as both a mechanical and psychological problem.[63] Noise did not only affect aircraft, but also tank, submarine, and ship communications systems—in short, a much wider variety of combat vehicles. Two Harvard laboratories, one centered around Beranek and dedicated to the "quieting" of aircraft noise, the Electro-Acoustic Laboratory (EAL), and the other centered around psychologist Stanley S. Stevens and Medical School physiologist Hallowell Davis and researching psychological factors in communications, the Psycho-Acoustic Laboratory (PAL), set out to study human performance under "intense sound fields."[64] The two labs, operating from the basement of Memorial Hall (PAL) and the Cruft Laboratory (EAL), decidedly placed military communications at the intersection of acoustics, electrical engineering, and psychology.[65] But most importantly, the two laboratories reframed communications as a question of "sound control," rather than acoustics, with Philip Morse pronouncing them a core research center for work on communications at large, equal in significance to Bell Labs.[66]

Initial experiments inside the highly reverberant boiler room of the Memorial Hall basement at Harvard had conscientious objectors coordinating, targeting, sorting, and coding in noise and quiet.[67] The experiments showed that noise, contrary to popular belief, did not fatigue the pilots, but rather interfered with communications—the ability to receive, comprehend, and deliver information—thus impairing ground, air, and sea operations.[68] The discovery recentered aircraft research around sound control and the articulation of the spoken word. The two laboratories tested and calibrated communications systems for the U.S. Signal Corps, the Air Corps, and the Navy. Articulation tests helped the labs to test communication systems, while research on microphones and headsets showed that silence and low reverberation rates promoted speech intelligibility and noise impaired it.

To calibrate military communication systems, the young engineers developed a "dead room," a new type of laboratory architecture to measure instruments and test articulation. "Dead rooms" had been the foundational facility for any research on noise and sound control since the mid-1930s, although they tended to come in a variety of shapes and forms. As Henning Schmidgen explains, the *camera silenta*, often presenting as a box within a box, an insulated room within a larger institutional infrastructure, emerged in the early twentieth century as a research medium for psychologists who looked for ways to isolate their subjects from distracting noise. Yet those acoustically dead rooms depended on a web of telecommunications that reconstructed tested subjects as flows of information connected via telephones or clocks.[69]

EAL was working with some models in mind.[70] By the time Beranek set out to equip Harvard with one, Bell Telephone Laboratories had already built a "dead room" and Erwin Meyer had pioneered the use of wedges to wide acclaim within the acoustics community.[71] Meyer's solution impressed Beranek for its acoustic properties and high absorbance, but also for its dramatic appearance. The "acoustical stalagmites and stalactites projecting from the walls, ceiling and

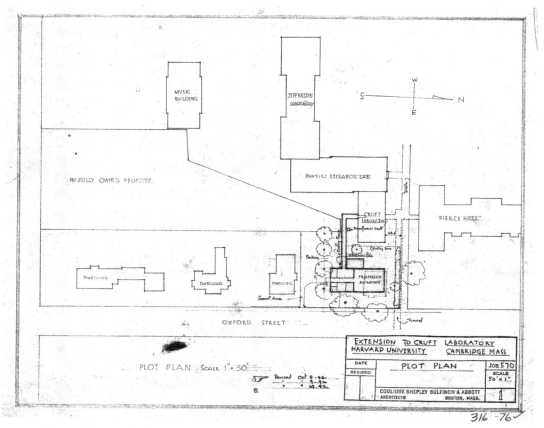

Figure 3.7. Coolidge Shepley Bulfinch & Abbott, plot plan, 1942. Courtesy of Shepley Bulfinch.

floor" offered Meyer's dead room the presentation of a subterranean cave, distinctive enough to become an iconic laboratory space.[72] To that end, Beranek rebranded Meyer's room as his own invention, baptizing the new laboratory space that Coolidge Shepley Bulfinch & Abbott built for EAL an "anechoic chamber"—meaning a room so absorptive that no echoes or reverberation could exist (Figures 3.7 and 3.8).[73] The chamber photographed well and quickly became an iconic space for communications systems and modern acoustics that nonetheless was demolished to make space for the Science Center, which opened its doors in 1972. Visitors at the anechoic chamber felt profoundly disoriented, with their words and the sounds of their moving bodies being absorbed by the wedged walls. Inside an anechoic chamber there was no echo to reassure visitors of their own existence and standing in the world. "People speak with lifeless voices" and "talking demands a conscious effort," noted the *Boston Sunday Post*.[74]

Beranek's anechoic chamber illustrated the complexity of acoustic control in

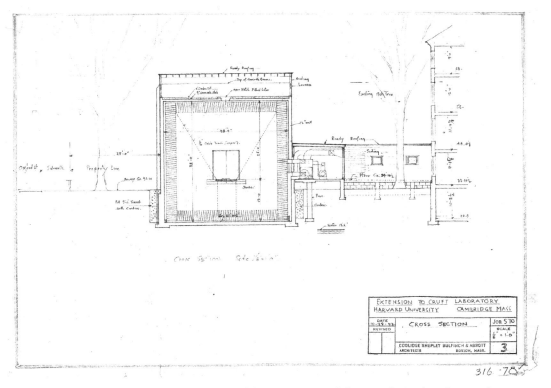

Figure 3.8. Coolidge Shepley Bulfinch & Abbott, section of the anechoic chamber and the air-conditioning plant, 1942. Courtesy of Shepley Bulfinch.

interior spaces (Figure 3.9). To eliminate echoes, a condition found at open fields, the chamber had to be completely sealed. Yet, to admit humans inside the anechoic chamber required the renewal of air, with a continuous or intermittent airflow. To completely seal the chamber against both exterior and interior noise, contractors removed any mechanical support systems and any sound control rooms outside the chamber. The team also engineered two soundproofed doors to act as a "sound lock" against exterior noise, concocting a plug made of fiberglass wedges to isolate the AC unit when not in use.[75]

For the design of the General Assembly, Beranek brought this military understanding of the space of communications within the headquarters. Similarly to the cockpits he was researching for the Air Force, the General Assembly would become a completely controlled environment, an insulated box within a box, connected to an ever-expanding network of institutions and field stations. The first report that Bolt issued in collaboration with Beranek practically reconstituted the General Assembly as an anechoic chamber. Bolt argued that soundproofing was the foundational condition of communication and advised the Headquarters

Figure 3.9. Harvard Anechoic Chamber with Leo L. Beranek and unidentified individual on the acoustically transparent bridge, circa 1945. UAV 713.9013 Harvard University Archives.

Planning Office to plan "based on the assumption that all the functions can best be carried on in a very quiet and highly deadened space," especially for the General Assembly, where speeches were to be recorded, interpreted, transcribed, transmitted, and projected in space.[76] In this sense, the General Assembly would need to be deadened to communicate with its audiences.

The two acousticians put forward a silencing plan. Subway vibrations, sprinklers, typewriters, noisy lobbies, plumbing, and air-conditioning systems potentially threatened the acoustic sanctity of the plenary hall and the rest of the forums within the headquarters.[77] "We potentially had noise between rooms which required noise reduction. We had ventilating system noise. We had rooms that were shaped impossibly. The whole project was scary as the dickens," Beranek recalled.[78] To achieve the controlled environment of the anechoic chamber, they soundproofed the General Assembly against the mechanical infrastructure and ventilation systems, but the air conditioning systems continued undermining the acoustic seal. "In the first place, we didn't know how much noise fans made, and we didn't know what the criteria were that you design against; how quiet did the room have to be? So, how much did you have to cut the noise down? The only thing that was known was if you used ducts and lined them, you'd get so many decibels reduction per length of lined duct," noted Beranek.[79] Regardless of BBN's surprise, the noise of mechanical systems had been a known problem in the entertainment industry since the introduction of air-conditioning systems in film production plants and broadcast studios. As Joseph Siry demonstrates, those environments required relative silence to control the signals picked up by microphones.[80] To solve the problem, Bolt and Beranek measured the sound levels of ventilation systems at the General Motors Laboratories and the Sears, Roebuck and Company store, evaluating their performance for noise.[81]

But mechanical noise was not the only problem. Systems of continuous airflow often resulted in cross-talking and sound transmission, which undermined the purported sound control inside the UN's platforms. To reduce unwanted transmission, BBN designed sound traps for ducts, nozzles, and fans.[82] Insulating against the air-conditioning system proved a nightmare and Bolt and Beranek strongly opposed Sven Markelius's and Finn Juhl's plans to expose council chamber ductwork in any structural way, suggesting the complete encasement of the whole infrastructure out of sight.[83] In addition, two sets of double doors on the rear side of the auditorium further insulated the General Assembly from the surrounding corridors, especially the noise of the foyer; celotex and cork absorbed the steps and voices of the advisers in the auditorium; and soundproofing around ventilation ducts eliminated vibrations and noise from the air-conditioning system. Bolt and Beranek insulated the interpretation booths against noise, as well as the booths for radio broadcasters and film crews, and suggested the installation of floating desks to reduce traveling vibrations.

But the two engineers did not limit their work to soundproofing. They noted that parallel walls resulted in flutter echoes and standing waves, creating dead spots and limiting the distribution of the projecting voice. They proposed the installation of "echo rooms" with double splayed windows, sloped walls, and curved surfaces, all solutions found in architectural acoustics treatises.[84] However, any suggestions that the Headquarters Planning Office deemed architectural met with unyielding opposition. A "straight wall not only looks better but would be simpler to build if it is acceptable to you," wrote architect and Headquarters Planning Office assistant director Michael M. Harris in an effort to dissuade them from architectural solutions.[85] The Office maintained that all visual matters fell under the supervision of architects and designers, not acousticians.

For BBN the main problem with the acoustic design of the General Assembly auditorium was its constitution as an open field. "The character of this space . . .

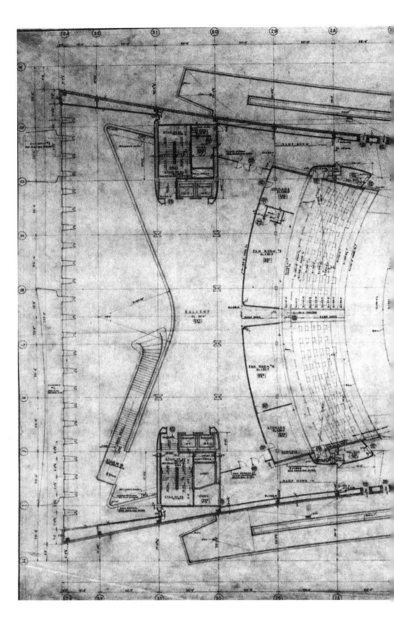

Figure 3.10. Plan of the General Assembly at the UN Headquarters, circa 1950. Wallace K. Harrison architectural drawings and papers, 1913–1986. Courtesy Avery Drawings and Archives.

poses a problem which is more nearly one of outdoor acoustics than one of enclosed auditorium acoustics," they noted. In their mind, regardless of architects' efforts to institute the General Assembly as an intimate sphere, the space was acoustically "monumental," and only a public address system would solve the problem of scale. Meanwhile Harrison was asking BBN to undo acoustically the scale of the interior (Figure 3.10).[86] Since architectural acoustic solutions were not on the table, the three engineers turned to sound control, effectively transform-

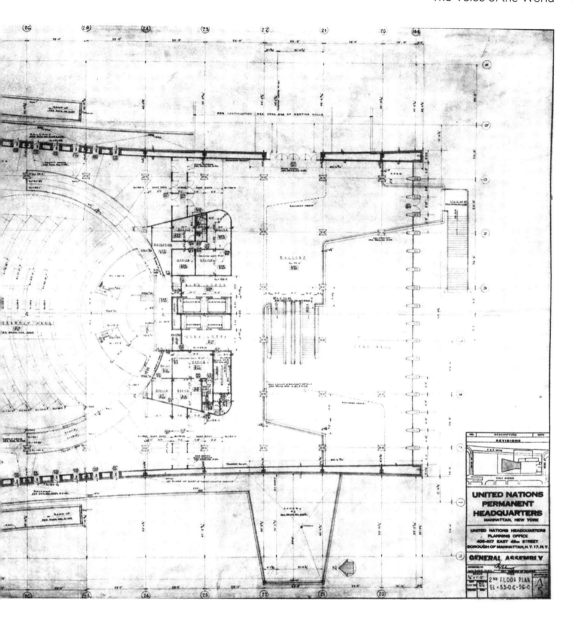

ing the General Assembly into a "cockpit" from which to connect and order the world. Within this context, the General Assembly should be silenced so that sound would reach loudspeakers, headphones, interpretation booths, recording stations and broadcasting studios without noise. The additional benefit to this thorough soundproofing was the overall reduction of reverberation to acoustically disguise the scale of the plenary hall. In this process of diffusion, architectural amplification was superfluous.

With loudspeakers being the de facto means of amplification, the engineers shifted their attention to placement, determining the spatial relationship of the delegate speaking to the sound emanating from the loudspeakers. BBN wanted to celebrate the presence of loudspeakers, initially proposing mounting a set from the ceiling within an acoustically transparent globe speaking back to the delegates as the voice of the world.[87] Harrison opposed the proposal for reconstructing the spoken word of international politics as a transcendental experience and the voice of the delegates as almost divine. Amplification, the endowment of the body with tools to exceed its own limitations, was not to be evidently celebrated in an organization recentering publics around a new humanism. Instead, and to the horror of BBN, Harrison asked for more realism, suggesting a loudspeaker placement found at the time in movie theaters, with the voice emanating from the direction of the podium and toward the convening body, a suggestion that the team was pushed to follow (Figure 3.11).

To naturalize the presence of technology requires additional technique. Pairing microphones with loudspeakers facing one another was a recipe for a distorting feedback loop. In response, BBN placed the main loudspeaker in a soundproof container filled with fiberglass wedges, similar to those developed for the anechoic chamber.[88] They recommended a highly directional microphone that could separate the voice of the speaker from the background noise, a technology that Altec Lansing, a company specializing in high-fidelity sound systems, had been advertising (Figure 3.12).[89] Regardless of calls for a multipurpose use of the plenary hall as a concert hall, BBN advised against it, arguing that the two programs carried fundamentally different acoustic requirements: optimum concert hall acoustics demanded higher reverberation rates and the diffusion of sound, while parliament and plenary hall acoustics required sound absorption and accentuation of the directionality of speech.

The position of the main loudspeaker group, however, carried symbolic value. "The speaker's voice should appear to come from the region in which the speaker is standing," a memorandum noted.[90] To maintain the directionality of speech, the team would have to place the loudspeaker behind the podium and rostrum, on a wall that the Headquarters Planning Office had imagined adorned with seals of the member states framing the speaker (Figure 3.13). In the middle of this rostrum the UN emblem provided a focal point (Figure 3.14). Covering landmasses with wire mesh and oceans with fabric, BBN transformed the emblem into the point of projection, the core of the UN soundscape, from which the voice of the delegates would emanate as the voice of the world.[91] To reinforce the feeling of immediacy, the team furnished the podium with an additional loudspeaker to accentuate the directionality and reaffirm that the voice was actually originating from the speaking body present in front of the rostrum. The sound system completed the simulacrum of media transparency, realism, and global democracy. The

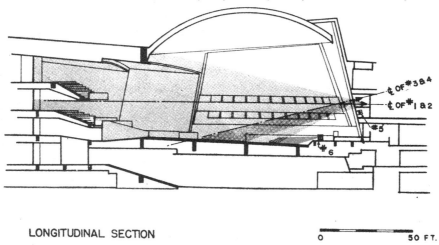

LONGITUDINAL SECTION

0   50 FT.

Figure 4.—*Longitudinal section of the hall showing, by the shading, the regions served by the three principal groups of the main loudspeakers. Loudspeakers 1 and 2 serve the rear two-thirds of the hall. Loudspeakers 3 and 4 serve the front one-third of the hall, except for a few seats directly in front of the lectern that are served by loudspeaker 6.*

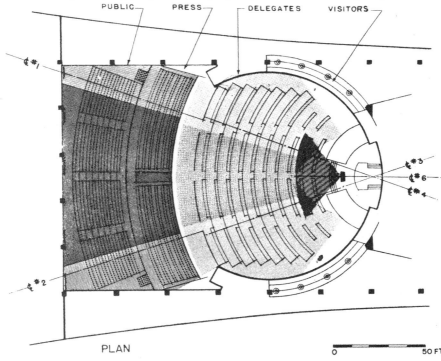

PLAN

0   50 FT

Figure 5.—*Plan view of the hall showing, by the shading, the regions served by the various loudspeakers. The visitors' sections are served by eight low-level overhead loudspeakers indicated by the double circles.*

Figure 3.11. Section and plan of the General Assembly, 1955. H. D. G. Goyder and Leo L. Beranek, "Sound System for Plenary Hall of UN General Assembly," Proceedings of the IRE Australia (February 1955). Courtesy of Leo L. Beranek.

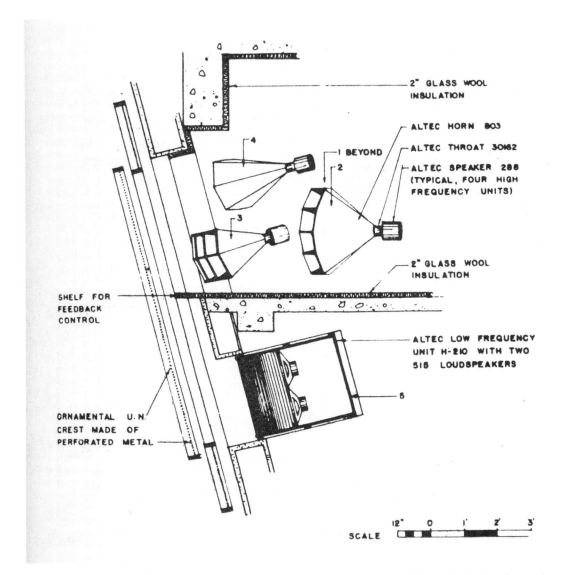

Figure 3.12. Drawing showing loudspeakers in the cage, 1955. H. D. G. Goyder and Leo L. Beranek, "Sound System for Plenary Hall of UN General Assembly," Proceedings of the IRE Australia (February 1955). Courtesy of Leo L. Beranek.

"intimate public" that UN officials asked for would be the product of thorough soundproofing and the tight assembling of delegates, with headsets, microphones, interpreters, and control rooms. The "natural" voice of the speaking delegate, once it traveled through the wires and mouths of interpreters, would project onto space through an icon of the new world system and its hegemonic structures. The public forum was to be a modulated and modulating space.

Figure 3.13. Wallace K. Harrison in front of the open loudspeaker cage in the General Assembly, 1952. Wallace K. Harrison architectural drawings and papers, 1913–1986. Courtesy Avery Drawings and Archives.

UN Broadcasts

Meanwhile, the audiences that the plenary hall could not include, mass media would reach. The Headquarters Planning Office expected that the voices projected within the headquarters would feed—either in the form of recordings or text, and at times in the company of visuals—a larger communication infrastructure reaching publics around the world, hence transforming any localized concern into a matter of global interest. At least since San Francisco, the developing organization had aspired to have mass media perform a political function that would enlarge the UN's audience, based on a belief that the circulation of information alone would bring about an internationalist spirit. Architecture would need to formalize in space these media expectations.

The United Nations Information Organization (UNIO), the Allied powers' press clearinghouse for news on different war fronts that had helped build bridges among the various national media conglomerates, had already set the tone for the possible institutional forms that such an information division could take. The

Figure 3.14. General Assembly Hall, 1952. Wallace K. Harrison architectural drawings and papers, 1913–1986. Courtesy Avery Drawings and Archives.

League of Nations, the precursor to the UN, had featured an Information Section that facilitated the dissemination of policies and recommendations decided in Geneva directly to the governments of member states. Following this path, the United Nations Headquarters offered a new opportunity to determine the organization's broadcast architecture.

Information and broadcasting had been thoroughly discussed during the meetings of the Preparatory Commission, which had appointed a Technical Advisory Committee on Information to present recommendations to the first General Assembly in London. Adriaan Pelt, the Dutch journalist who had served as Director of the Information Section at the League of Nations and had led the Netherlands' Information Bureau, proposed a distinct Information Section to organize

the distribution of news and the organization's public relations, at the same time that he also advocated for more robust radio, film, and exhibition departments.[92] "It is difficult to imagine an international organization without a radio station of its own," he noted, and added that a "modern information section should have, as already pointed out, a less official and formal character than did the League."[93] The General Assembly ratified the recommendation for a new Department of Public Information (DPI) in its first session and launched a Committee on Communications that brought together Signal Corps engineers, television and radio technicians, directors, acousticians, and communication engineers to plan the United Nations' communications infrastructure and its outreach.[94]

In many ways, the DPI followed the institutional structure of its immediate predecessor, UNIO. Housed within the UN Secretariat, DPI was tasked with advertising the work of the organization, educating the public (as official press releases claimed) and, at the same time, providing access to critical information for journalists and other UN missions, a mandate that, according to Barbara Crossette, compromised the integrity of the division, since the charge to propagandize and the charge for informational transparency were in essence antithetical.[95] New publications, in particular the *United Nations Review* and the *United Nations Yearbook,* would both archive and circulate news about the organization.[96] Documentary films and exhibitions could circumvent the problem of language, with the goal of making "the Organization real to large segments of the public."[97] Its film and visual information division would produce, often in collaboration with the film industry, newsreels and documentaries to feed in cinemas around the world. In addition, DPI featured a "public relations" division to actively cultivate relationships with distributors and national press representatives, but also to explicitly target schools, colleges, churches, clubs, women's group, as well as nongovernmental organizations and media networks.[98] There was also the metaphorical "broadcasting" of the organization itself, seeding the world with regional field offices that served as its ears and mouth. By 1968 there were forty-nine United Nations Information Centers covering more than a hundred countries, with a special focus on regions with scarce communications infrastructure, and the directive to collect and report back to the headquarters information about them as well.[99] By producing and promoting its own programming, DPI allowed the UN to control the message and image of the organization, as well as its representation.

To secure the UN's positive disposition toward communications technologies and mass media, crucial institutional positions went to high-ranking officials with experience either in the League of Nations Information Section or with American broadcast networks. For example, Byron Price, former member of both United Press and the Associated Press, Vice President of the Motion Picture Association of America, and later Assistant to the Secretary-General at the United Nations, took over the Department of Administrative and Financial Services that managed budgets. Price, who had helped Roosevelt negotiate wartime censorship against the constitutional freedom of the press, oversaw budgetary concerns particularly with an eye toward the organization's public relations, which proved invaluable as the need for budgetary reform often endangered DPI and its operations.[100]

DPI officials doubled down on broadcasting the work of the organization, hoping that the dissemination of information and news from different parts of the world would create a sense of community with shared values and goals, but also that radio first (and television later) would allow the UN to circumvent national governments and build a "direct" international audience (Figure 3.15). The first Assistant Secretary-General to lead DPI, Benjamin Cohen, confirmed the instrumental role of radio emphatically:

Figure 3.15. Members of the United Nations Radio Division within DPI pose while listening to a radio broadcast from Geneva in the temporary Secretariat headquarters at Lake Success, 1947. From left to right: General Frank E. Stoner, Chief Communications Engineer, Hugh Williams, Chief Liaison Officer, and Sanford Major, Chief Technical Supervisor. Courtesy of the United Nations Photo Library.

But it is essential for the United Nations to build up a direct audience. It is a collectivity, not merely a group of fifty-one separate nations. As a collectivity, it has its own responsibility to make its voice heard throughout the world. Unless it can develop and maintain permanent contact with world opinion it will be powerless in time of crisis.[101]

In order to achieve world coverage, the UN sought out radio and telecommunications engineers who had set up and maintained Radio Nations, the League of Nations broadcasting station. In most cases, those engineers had acquired their expertise installing colonial telecommunications infrastructures that tied peripheries to metropolises. Gijsbert Frans van Dissel, the Dutch engineer who was heading the efforts to determine requirements for a UN Radio, had served as Head Manager of the Government Radio Service in the Dutch East Indies and later on as a member of the League of Nations Communications and Transit Section.[102] In his general recommendations, Van Dissel proposed a "broadcasting service of a world wide character" that would cover the territories of member states, as well as offer point-to-point services among the permanent members of the Security Council (in his draft initially referred to as the "four big Powers") and another point-to-point service with national broadcasters so as to secure the further dissemination of footage produced at the Headquarters.[103]

Setting up an operative radio station in the Headquarters would not be a problem, but broadcasting was, particularly since it required a technical infrastructure that spanned different countries' legal systems and national telecommunications networks. Conditions of sovereignty extended to the airwaves, making any attempt to acquire a dedicated bandwidth a matter of intergovernmental negotiations. Before World War II, national radio stations could register the wavelengths of their choice with the International Telecommunication Union, an organization invited to partake in the UN assembly as an invested regulatory body. As a result, by the time that the UN petitioned certain wavelengths for its own stations, there was no airwave space left for use. The Transport and Communications Commission of the Economic and Social Council suggested that the International Telecommunication Union hold a conference on the system for distributing frequencies. As part of the negotiations with the United States on the extraterritorial status of the headquarters site, they also asked for the right to use airwaves that were originally assigned to U.S. radio broadcasters.[104]

Engineers debated the structure of radio broadcasting as well, particularly in terms of outreach. For shortwave broadcasting, the UN acquired the frequencies originally registered with the Bern Bureau for Radio Nations, but shortwave broadcasting offered lower sound clarity and was less appealing to general audiences.[105] FM radio guaranteed better sound but required a relay system of transmitters and the cooperation of national networks, and neither the United States nor any other member country were willing to make space for it on their airwaves. In addition, one single transmitter would not solve the problem of global broadcast. In fact, General Frank E. Stoner, who suggested a system of relay broadcasting and close collaboration with local FM radio stations, advised the UN toward more flexibility and less focus on infrastructure.[106] By early September 1946, an interdepartmental unit for radio communications headed by Pelt, Stoner, and Van Dissel came up with a redistribution of frequencies plan for "une veritable ceinture mondiale," a suggestion that did not, however, materialize.[107] The only viable solution was to delegate broadcasting to national and private networks until at some later point the economic and political conditions would allow for an independent global radio network. The decision to delegate broadcasting turned DPI's attention to programming and production. The UN Headquarters would produce content that national net-

Figure 3.16. Gottscho-Schleisner, Inc., photograph of broadcast in studio with public at the National Broadcasting Company, 30 Rockefeller Plaza, New York City, 1945. Library of Congress, Prints and Photographs Division, Gottscho-Schleisner Collection LC-G613- 48380.

works could then use, hence disseminating recommendations or news about the UN.

To determine the spatial and technical needs of radio and film production, the Headquarters Planning Office looked into the design and construction of broadcasting and filming studios, at the time celebrated for their modernist typology (Figure 3.16). The first session of the General Assembly in London offered some insights. In London, the BBC had equipped Central Hall with staff, equipment, and studio space, broadcasting the proceedings far and wide with the hopes of enabling a global participation of "the peoples" (at least as "listeners").[108] Building on the World Service's growing reach that, under the name "Empire Service," had once connected deployed settlers, expats, and local elites against anti-colonial upheavals across the British Empire,[109] the UN hoped to similarly fabricate its own imagined world community with UN Radio.[110] BBC engineers and technicians built broadcasting facilities that they rented out to commercial and national broadcasting companies, setting the standards for technical needs and global coverage.[111]

Figure 3.17. View from the United Nations Radio booth at the Security Council in the temporary headquarters at Lake Success, N.Y., 1947. Courtesy of the United Nations Photo Library.

At Hunter College later in spring of 1946, a two-story tower of stacked broadcast studios behind soundproof glass appeared at the corner of the old gym where the UN Security Council convened in front of an acoustic splayed wall, not only emulating the control rooms in the corners of soundstages overlooking the filming of talkies, but also demonstrating the transformation of Council Chambers and Assembly Halls into studios for recording and diffusing conversations. Similarly, a year later at Lake Success, Ralph Walker furnished the new location of the Security Council with soundproofed studio booths for filming and radio (Figure 3.17). Radio was instrumental in broadening the UN's audience beyond a very limited governing elite, scaling up and widening the territories and communities that DPI covered.[112] Film, and in particular the Hollywood film industry, contrived to shape public opinion around the role of the UN in the international scene.[113] But television would eventually become the main medium through which the UN would establish the image of its public forums.

Figure 3.18. United Nations Recording Studio in the temporary General Assembly in Flushing Meadows, 1947. Courtesy of the United Nations Photo Library.

The seeds for globally televising UN meetings had been planted at Flushing Meadows when the Conference Division introduced television sets into an overflow lounge space (Figure 3.18).[114] Within the UN, television provided a convenient transmission technology and allowed for a vision of televised proceedings to linger a bit longer, regardless of earlier hesitations that images hindered the public's imagination. Maybe resonating with what Doron Galili identifies to be the vested interest of broadcast networks in technologies of moving image transmission, DPI placed the responsibility for television under broadcast and not film.[115] On October 10, 1946, the Television Broadcasters Association Convention presented Secretary-General Trygve Lie with a scroll pledging the entertainment industry's support of the United Nations in its outreach programs.[116] Instead, the UN proposed to supply recordings and kinescopes (filmed televised images) for distribution through media networks. In equipping these halls for broadcasts by both radio and television (even if initially for internal use), the UN reconfigured its public platforms as production sets. Equipment and furniture loans—the seats inside the Flushing Meadows site were dispatched from the Paramount Theater—solidified the constitution of those spaces as studios.

The Board architects perceived studios as essential components of the apparatus they were setting up for the UN. Photographs and articles on the architecture of broadcast studios, presenting detailed equipment and architectural requirements, as well as design problems and possible solutions, had been circulating the architectural press since the 1930s.[117] NBC's broadcasting studios often appeared as models in journals such as *Architectural Forum* and *Architectural Record,* introducing architects to the radio program and building type.[118] In fact, the Board of Design had been convening in proximity to the Radio City broadcasting studios that Corbett Harrison and MacMurray, along with J. André Fouilhoux and Raymond Hood, had designed for the Rockefeller Center, visiting them to comprehend the programmatic needs of such spaces. The air-conditioned NBC studios had opened their doors to wide acclaim, presenting a useful example of how to negotiate the technical requirements of broadcasting with the spatial demands for the admittance of audiences.[119] The moving panels that isolated NBC audiences from the stage allowed studios to remain flexible to the shifting demands of radio programming. Acoustics was particularly important to this new architecture that centered on the spoken word and the voice-as-signal. Emily Thompson shows how intelligibility within the world of broadcast studios and soundstages prompted sound engineers to develop methods of insulating so as to reduce reverberation times, even structurally isolating soundstages and control rooms to avoid the travel of vibrations.[120] For example, lighting consultant Henry L. Logan of the Holophane Company had designed embedded lighting fixtures for the ceilings to allow for the additional acoustic control of the studios.

The Headquarters Planning Office actively sought out the expertise of network representatives and engineers, as well as the National Broadcasting Company (NBC), the Columbia Broadcasting System (CBS), and the American Broadcasting Company (ABC), but it also consulted smaller independent stations such as WNEW. The goal was to determine how the introduction of studios and broadcasting technology would transform the UN's Headquarters at large.[121] Board architects also visited the studios set up inside Flushing Meadows and Lake Success, where the CBC and BBC shared booths for the coverage of the General Assembly and the Security Council respectively (an experience that led the two national broadcast companies to ask for separate accommodations in the permanent headquarters, to no avail).[122] Laboring to distinguish the formalized public sphere of diplomats on the floor from its support systems of media, they found Natalie de Blois's Flushing Meadows configuration to be a useful model for the design of the permanent General Assembly.[123] During visits to Lake Success, the Planning Office criticized the booths around the Security Council for not offering a full view of the

delegates at the table, while finding the radio booths sufficient.[124] While final-
izing the plans, the architects channeled the lesson of broadcast studios in their
configuration of the General Assembly and the Security Council Chamber as
broadcasting studios.[125] In the end, the interiors of Council Chambers and the
General Assembly more and more resembled the studios of broadcast and television networks, with booths arranged on the sides to produce and transmit
what was happening on stage.

UN broadcasts, however, encountered an aggregation of obstacles, from local
networks burying UN programming in off-peak slots to technical issues such as
poor signal quality.[126] An effort to establish an amateur radio station—a proposal pioneered by General Stoner—did not take off. Without a transmitter of
its own, UN Radio relied on the "Voice of America" and other networks and
agencies, limiting reception in many parts of the world. An Expert Committee
suggested in response the production of fifteen-minute broadcasts during the
annual meetings of the General Assembly (when demand was guaranteed) and
weekly programs the rest of the year. When later, on account of low demand and
budgetary restructuring, the committee suggested that the UN should relay only
on demand, DPI rebelled against the recommendation, arguing that a market-
driven definition of programming would curtail the main goal of the organization:
to reach an international collective despite the disposition of local governments
and their media. Some of the committee members recommended the termina-
tion of live broadcasts, but the other half resisted, arguing that they allowed the
international community to "share in the proceedings," enabling journalists and
officials to follow the deliberations and conversations.[127]

Although the UN anticipated that television would enter the headquarters
eventually, committee after committee abandoned the plan for an independent
television station, especially since kinescoped newsreels and radio broadcasting seemed to satisfy the demand for news. After 1957, amid a push for financial reform of the organization, the Expert Committee assigned with the task of
evaluating DPI (at that time called the Office of Public Information) proposed
that the UN refocus its energies on programming, rather than infrastructure.[128]
The focus of the Radio Division shifted from the dissemination of information at
large to broadcasting to the decolonizing world. As a result, DPI encouraged UN
officials to invest in developing media content, solidifying the institution's de-
pendence on national and private broadcast companies and telecommunications
organizations.[129]

In its official publications, the UN Department of Public Information reiterated
the central role that mass media would play for the organization. "The rooms are
stages on which—by means of all the mass media of communication such as television, radio, motion pictures and the press—the Public may view the activities of

its representatives," explained the journal *Your United Nations*.[130] This interfacing of mass media and international organization prompted conversations on media systems for global coverage. Walter Duschinsky, who worked on the telecommunications systems at the headquarters, anticipated a "global television system" to address national and international territories. He declared television a "tremendous medium" capable of being utilized to bring "good will in world relations,"[131] while claiming that "communication centers [were] expressions of the character of the age" and architecture the instrument to organize these neocolonial aspirations of media technologies.[132] That being said, television would take on, and in this sense continue, the work of newsreels in presenting images of the UN's formed publics to the world.

Radio, however, centered the voice and its materiality in the planning for the headquarters (and any subsequent platforms the UN would engineer). In assembling humans and machines in networks circulating information, the UN opened its public spheres to the workings of communications, introducing communication engineering to the political configuration of the postwar global community. To address the voice-as-signal that claimed from the podium to be of and for the world, the Board architects turned to communications engineering, ultimately transforming the UN's global interiors into broadcast studios for global diplomacy. Acousticians reconfigured acoustic problems to questions of electroacoustic communications, bringing inside the space of international organization war epistemologies that intertwined diplomacy with military engineering.

Following the inauguration of the UN, MIT Professor Karl W. Deutsch argued that government is not just a political problem but rather a problem of "steering" in the cybernetics sense, hence belonging to discussions of "communication and decision." In his book *The Nerves of Government: Models of Political Communication and Control,* Deutsch, previously a member of OSS and a participant in the San Francisco Conference, attempted a cybernetic political theory that claimed the "governing of human organizations" to be similar to the governing of machines.[133] His assertion resonated with a general effort to re-culture the cybernetic program that had emerged from military research for the post–World War II political and social realms. But also, as the planning of the United Nations Headquarters shows, the grounds for such an epistemic transference never quite constituted a straightforward affair. The presence of interpreters at the General Assembly, for example, problematized the idea of prosthesis as an exclusively technological one. The prosthetic part in the UN's interpretation system was not a machine, but rather a human being. As Deutsch noted, communication was "social" before becoming "technological." Actually, it was the "division of intellectual labor" that preceded and even produced the division between "human minds and an ever growing array of electronic or other communications."[134]

To counterbalance endemic machine metaphors, fears of technological take-over, and allusions to totalitarian regimes, UN delegates urged the Planning Office to foreground intimacy in the planning of its public spaces. In this sense, the UN delegates appeared to believe what architects already understood very well: that the habitus of this new multilateral organization, the way its space was organized and experienced, was as central to the appearance of the new world order as any other legal and bureaucratic framework. The simulacrum of global governance as an intimate and informal affair was as much an architectural business as it was an engineering and acoustic one. Intimacy, or at least its architectural and acoustic illusion, promised to shape, if not transform, the new public spheres of internationalism and present them as global and democratic. At the same time, this illusion of intimacy proved instrumental for the organization, particularly for claiming a direct relationship with the people who comprised its publics outside its immediate environments, while reproducing economic and political asymmetries on the background.

4

The Headquarters and the Field

The completion of the UN Headquarters in New York City modeled the organization's visual and architectural language of institutional internationalism, proposing an architecture of multilateralism for the post–World War II order. In parallel to building this architecture of multilateralism inside the Headquarters, the organization had started considering ways to reach and install its platforms and cultures of assembly outside its principal seat. Yes, the proceedings would be televised and broadcast to the world, but the UN also needed a different set of platforms that would allow parts of the organization to engage directly with people and problems on the ground. Apart from being a complicated legal and political project, the UN's communications organism could only partially help the organization's outreach efforts. To cultivate internationalist sensibilities on the ground, bureaucrats of the UN Secretariat would have to find ways to install UN platforms in the field. That metaphorical global interior, rather than offering brick-and-mortar bound space for the organization, created platform opportunities where international publics formed around UN events to rehearse relationships structured back in the United Nations itself.

Central to this enterprise was a distinction between the Headquarters—the site where national representatives, civic society, and diplomats convened—and the field, where the UN hoped to install its operations. In the early years of the organization there was no stable definition of what constituted the field or how to approach it. Rather, the UN and its field of operations were co-constitutive, in the sense that efforts to break down and order the postwar world into zones had a direct impact on the structure of the organization itself. A regional organization of the field slowly emerged as the alternative unit to a nation-based system of order. This ordering system grouped together otherwise culturally, religiously, and historically diverse communities, thus producing geographic regions as coherent cultural and economic networks of nation-states. The regional system infiltrated the larger UN organization and its organs, defining and structuring its field of intervention, as well as later planning efforts beyond the UN.[1] This was especially visible in the UN's developmentalist activities that the Economic and Social Council administered. As early as 1947 ECOSOC, the main council to recommend policies for social matters within the UN, began launching regional commissions to oversee reconstruction and development activities in Asia (Economic and Social Commission for Asia and the Far East—ECAFE, 1947), Europe (Economic Commission for Europe—ECE, 1947), and Latin America (Economic Commission for Latin America—ECLA, 1948). Down the road they added Africa (Economic Commission for Africa—ECA, 1958), and much later the Middle East (Economic and Social Commission for Western Asia—ESCWA, 1973). Within this construction of world order North America and the USSR were incorporated within the ECE, a fact that spoke to the Cold War mentality that shaped aid politics to Europe and beyond, but effectively they both stood outside regional commissions. Effectively, the United States demarcated its separate status not as a zone of development but rather as a model and resource for expertise, illuminating structural inequalities within the UN's world.[2]

One of the biggest challenges that United Nations diplomats faced was shepherding the world's passage from late colonialism—where the extraction politics and racial capitalism of empires ordered continents and managed internal geopolitical dynamics—into a world of postcolonial multilateralism, where institutions regulated platforms of exchange among nation-states. Decolonization presented a complicated political process that entailed diplomatic and communicational maneuvers to reach local communities formerly connected to imperial networks. To do so UN delegates had agreed on a system of trusteeship that put non-self-governing territories—former colonial territories—under the overview of the organization following bilateral agreements with those member states that had formerly managed them, mostly colonial powers: France, the United Kingdom, Belgium, Australia, New Zealand, the United States, and Italy. The Trusteeship Council, which held its first session in 1947, administered territories still under League of Nations–issued mandates by offering a platform for their transition to sovereign statehood and the discharge of colonial rulers. Basically, to use UN parlance, the Council consisted of the permanent member states of the Security Council, the administering former colonial powers, and an equal number of non-administering member states. This configuration was meant to balance out colonial interests and create the condition for new alliances to emerge, while promoting the interests of the non-self-governing territories. But the project of decolonization was larger than the charge that the Trusteeship Council had received over territories in Africa and Oceania. What the UN as an organization needed was to entangle itself within the national interiors of the decolonizing world.

To reach those publics, UN bureaucrats needed to reconsider what participation in the organizational processes would mean for them, and how to achieve that outside the Headquarters. The UN's mass media could only reach a limited number of households based on access to radio, television, and newspapers, and the cost of traveling made access to the New York Headquarters prohibitive for the large majority. Decolonization processes offered the UN the opportunity to develop a new relationship with its publics in the field, interpellating itself in the role of the facilitator. Political and institutional structures organized within the Headquarters would travel to permeate and order multilateralism in the field upon the invitation of member states. It was within this context of a decolonizing world and an organization that aspired to project itself as a global manager of crisis and conflict that regional seminars emerged as answers and media to entangle the UN with national processes, while installing its public sphere in the field by exporting the physical and metaphorical structures that the UN's "global interior" created inside its Headquarters.

Expertise Networks and Communication Channels

Expertise constituted a cornerstone of the UN, permeating the organization and its organs, as Lucia Allais has argued.[3] Legal consultants, career diplomats, and League of Nations veterans participated in committees negotiating the institutional frameworks of the UN organs. Architects, planners, engineers, construction companies, but also military technicians and acousticians, advised the Headquarters Planning Office on the building of their spaces. ECOSOC, the council that sought to address social issues, considered expertise a resource for resolving global economic and social inequalities. ECOSOC frameworks divided the globe into a developed industrialized world with access to expertise and technical knowledge and an underdeveloped decolonizing world in need of said technique and expertise to manage national resources, production, and administration. Following the signing of the UN Charter, ECOSOC officials started investigating possible ways to create and manage a network of vetted experts that enmeshed the institution with the field, organizing its geographies of development.

Professional organizations, anxious to see their advocacy organs partaking in the reconfiguration of the political and economic world order, also started organizing on the ground. In conferences and symposia, engineers, scientists, and scholars advocated openly for a new scientific internationalism centered on the circulation of expertise. These efforts built on earlier attempts to circulate and share scientific discovery on a global scale, while claiming a professionalized class of experts as its leading force.[4] The idea was that scientific internationalism— the making and sharing of scientific inquiry—was world-making, in the sense that it required (and in fact created) community around the circulation of knowledge, regardless of national boundaries. Those experts, who had seen their professional organizations expanding and reconfiguring their networks in international meetings and congresses, promoted a view of the world where expertise and technical knowledge traveled globally as equalizers of political and economic inequities.

These parallel efforts came to a head in 1946 when the International Technical Congress (ITC) critically shifted the conversation toward the global problem of the built environment. Taking place at the Centre Marcelin-Berthelot in the governmental heart of Paris (the National Assembly was just minutes away), the ITC elevated housing and the built environment to a major aspect of its development agenda, while placing engineering and expertise at the core of the solution. Architects and planners, who had been closely following the discussions around reconstruction and economic development in war-affected European and decolonizing countries, were among those professional groups that hoped for a permanent position within the UN and its networks. If the UN opened its own platforms (construed inside and outside the organization's and its specialized agencies' headquarters) to these experts' organizations, then these architects, civil engineers, planners, and structural engineers would set in motion the entire project of institutional internationalism, along with its governmental technocracies, liberal ideologies, and global bureaucracies. To that end, they agreed on a positivist plan for a battalion of associations wherein engineers and experts (among them architects and planners) would have the opportunity to meet and build international professional networks: a World Engineering Federation, a UN Technical Staff, an administration for housing and community planning, an International Institution of Scientific Management, and International Technical Schools.[5]

Presenting technocracy as the way forward for the UN, the engineers and technicians in attendance insisted that technique—unlike other means of internationalism such as diplomacy, or legislation, or even culture—did not involve politics. Focusing on technique, they argued, would allow the UN to move beyond political interests, economic hurdles, and national boundaries to reach and establish a presence inside other countries' interiors. Technique could be the vehicle of internationalism that culture could not be. The ultimate goal of the Technical Congress was to forge an operative channel within the United Nations and its specialized agencies that would effectively bring engineers, architects, and planners within the organization. The more immediate concern was to locate which UN organs and specialized agencies would take on the organization of technical intervention in the decolonizing world. Participants' answer was that ECOSOC should establish a center for the study of housing and town planning, devising a more permanent place for planners and architects in the organization. The Housing and Town and Country Planning (HTCP) Section of the UN Secretariat Department of Social Affairs was in many ways a response to this call. Representatives from CIAM and the International Federation for Town and Country Planning (IFTCP), who had been hoping for a more robust participation within the United Nations, were excited to see engineers and technical experts advocating for a concerted

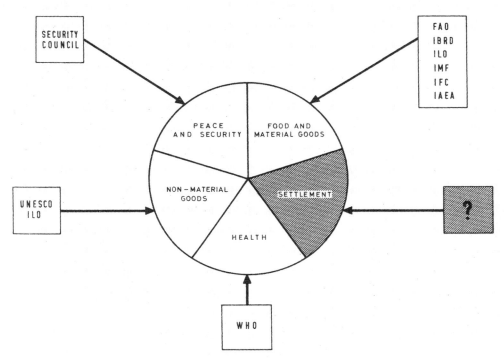

Figure 4.1. Pie chart by C. A. Doxiadis on human needs and corresponding U.N. agencies, from *Ekistics* 17, no. 101 (April 1964): 225. Copyright Constantinos and Emma Doxiadis Foundation.

effort to address the built environment.[6] Individual planners and architects, such as Constantinos Doxiadis, also supported such claims (Figure 4.1).

Yet the focus on North American and Western European expertise, especially within the Technical Congress in Paris, told a different story, revealing how ingrained in colonial projects the professional development of experts was. The Congress's almost 130 presentations and reports on engineering, management of resources, scientific management of labor, standardization, planning, and public works, as well as telecommunications, transportation, and power grids, revered the state of engineering and technical expertise in France, the United Kingdom, and the United States. The knowledge circulation the Congress articulated was mostly unidirectional, describing technical transfers from North America and Western Europe to the decolonizing world and rarely vice versa. Arturo Escobar points to this very asymmetry, arguing that development rhetoric interpellated

North American and Western European economies to be the models after which the world should be reconstructed and organized, actively producing the "Third World" as a category and a region awaiting development.[7] In this sense, the focus on expertise and technical knowledge replicated the power imbalances already built into the institution, regardless of the presentation of equality.

The UN's response to questions of the built environment and its infrastructures was initially uneven and only partially addressed by the United Nations Relief and Rehabilitation Administration (UNRRA), the aid agency administering relief predominantly in Europe. UNRRA, however, offered an organizational roadmap for development projects that United Nations bureaucrats decided to follow, with the caveat that any expectations of financial and material support would be eliminated as unsustainable for the organization.[8] Instead, setting aside questions of capital and equality, UN officials foregrounded the role of technical knowledge over the management of resources in development projects, in a sense presenting technique itself as a resource. This emphasis on expertise as the cornerstone of UN development projects, but also the UN edifice at large, resonated with a wish to base the new world order on research, rationality, technique, and a global circulation of knowledge, with the organization and its specialized agencies as clearinghouses at the center.

To explore the tools and systems that the organization needed to discuss the built environment on a multinational scale, the UN Secretariat invited American planner Jacob Crane to compile a study for international action; he responded with a robust program for expertise transfer and technical exchange. Crane, who served as housing consultant for the UN in its efforts to formalize a technical assistance program, proposed that the Secretariat install a "team of experts" on the built environment to guide any requests from policy to "construction and management."[9] He argued that the UN's approach to development should focus on establishing a communications infrastructure and not on offering financial support. Building new "channels of communication," as Crane referred to them, constituted the first step toward an effective and economically feasible assistance project. These communication channels included research projects, dedicated periodicals, manuals, and of course conferences and seminars, always with the goal of educating publics.[10]

In reports and memoranda, UN bureaucrats and external consultants articulated a similar desire for expert networks, referring, like Crane, to "channels of communication," either as the main objective or as a foundational step in the organization's outreach and development projects. One important channel was that between the UN and national governments.[11] The goal was to ensure that the positionalities of new states and their governments shifted toward development and modernity. In all cases, there was a differential—a difference in power, resources, and knowledge—that activated each channel. There was a part of the world that in the mind of UN bureaucrats was lacking and a part of the world ready to provide. This differential logic enabled the project of development and forged a place for the UN, endowing the organization with authority while addressing territories and publics.

The figure of the network quickly emerged as a form of social and organizational structure that would help UN officials to connect the physical headquarters with strategic nodes of expertise exchange in the postcolonial world, namely field offices and conference sites. In this sense networks—systems of connections across space, disciplinary divisions, and professional institutions—became the lifeblood of the organization. Apart from potentially advancing public causes, the UN's networks could also bring more work and connections back to the UN. And in becoming the organizational hub through which connections are made, the UN also further legitimized itself and its operations outside the Headquarters.

But the work of the network, as political theorists and sociologists show, is more complex than its schematic abstraction suggests.[12] "Nodes" and "hubs," Manuel Castells argues, organize the "network society" and the space of flows of capital and knowledge, accessed largely by "dominant, managerial elites."[13] Driven by a two-fold desire to diffuse and centralize the operations that drive their growth, human, institutional, and telecommunications networks are all foundationally uneven. Not all connections are equally valuable to members, and not all hubs hold the same significance within those networks. As Michael Hardt and Antonio Negri note, networks—and in particular institutional networks of expertise—require a power differential to set in motion the movement from one hub to the next (in the case of the UN, from the Headquarters to field offices). They claim that this recuperation of difference is foundational to supranational agencies that step in to manage and negotiate the movement of expertise and capital. They argue that the communication networks springing from international institutions, apart from being necessary to "the movement of globalization," ultimately legitimize and authorize the global institutions managing those interconnections.[14] In this sense, communication networks and global institutions were interconnected and codependent in ways that the physical, political, and social design of the Headquarters anticipated.

To manage those channels of communication, in 1949 ECOSOC and the UN General Assembly launched a new agency, the Technical Assistance Administration (TAA), with the charge to coordinate research on economic development and public administration across the globe. Unlike former structures of colonial planning, the TAA guidelines required formal requests from member states for the UN to initiate technical assistance projects. After invitation, the TAA would send experts to consult with local agencies on the right course of action.[15] By officially taking space within the UN Secretariat Tower, TAA officials would be part of both the UN's physical and metaphorical global interior, mobilizing resources and

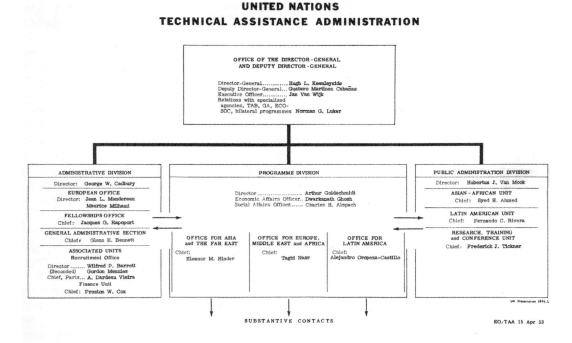

Figure 4.2. Diagram of United Nations Technical Assistance Administration, April 15, 1953 (File 34705). Copyright Constantinos and Emma Doxiadis Foundation.

expert networks to effectively reach the field. TAA administrators at the central Headquarters oversaw and instigated projects in member states' interiors, actively establishing communication channels in the form of experts and reports moving back and forth. Bringing citizens from the decolonizing world into the UN's publics expanded the cultures of assembly from inside the Headquarters into the world outside it. The TAA, firmly grounded in the UN's physical global interior, would become an agent in the creation and expansion of the UN's networks of expertise (Figure 4.2).[16]

UN administrators used the TAA to refine and strengthen relationships between the UN and its specialized agencies, nongovernmental associations, and private foundations, recalibrating the organization's family of networks. Following resolutions that the General Assembly passed to support development in "war devastated areas," "developing countries," and "dependent" territories, the UN Secretariat invited specialized agencies such as the World Health Organization (WHO) and the Food and Agriculture Organization (FAO) into diagnostic conversations to determine their involvement and contribution to TAA activities.[17] The stated goal was to handle operational overlaps in the production of an institutional network dealing with the administrative problems, destabilized economies, crumbling infrastructures, and housing shortages in the areas of the world the TAA would address.

Comments by Hugh Llewellyn Keenleyside, a career diplomat and the TAA's Director-General, show how technical diplomacy was an effective but also risky tool for the UN:

> International technical assistance is a new form of diplomacy, compli-cated by three factors: established usages do not exist; most of the tech-nical problems involved are inextricably intertwined with political and social problems; and many envoys are not schooled in the techniques of diplomacy while at the same time they have to interfere more directly in the affairs of the recipient countries than did the old-time diplomats.[18]

The pretext for the TAA's mingling with internal national affairs was of course the "people"—or the "welfare of the peoples," as Keenleyside claimed, even when the agency intervened with administrative and governmental structures.[19] However, the TAA did not directly reach publics and local communities. Similarly to the UN General Assembly, the agency aimed for connecting the professional class with the organization, hoping these professionals would transmit technique to the general public. In this sense, the TAA was a diffusion mechanism mobilized by the idea that the world community awaited the UN's intervention to find its place within the new world order—a fantasy that drove the expansion of the organization.

Yet there were cultural and social differences to tend. Margaret Mead, who at the time consulted for UNESCO, proposed the management of those differ-ences in terms of communication systems.[20] For Mead, these differentials called for the establishment of feedback loops for intellectual exchanges. Similarly to Jacob Crane, she advocated for "channels of communication" between the "East" and the "West" to enlarge the "enlightenment" of both and bring the two into an equilibrium—an argument that she would also make at the Macy Conferences in the 1950s.[21] This orientalist analysis of cultural difference in terms of East and West resonated with earlier colonial orderings of the world, but Mead, unlike her predecessors, envisioned a syncretic future.[22] She stipulated rural representation in international organizations, as well as calling for the "institutions of the city" to "be extended deep into the life of the village."[23] In many ways, diagnosing the difference between urbanity and rurality activated developmentalist projects and the network-building they required.

Mead was not alone in that. UN and UNESCO officials targeted villages not only as primary sites in need of technical assistance and fundamental educa-tion, but also as the sites where international organizations would install their physical and metaphorical platforms. In 1951, the Preparatory Commission of UNESCO opened its first physical regional center in Patzcuaro, Mexico. *Courier,* UNESCO's main publication, called Patzcuaro "the world's most unusual social experiments," a "laboratory" for "rural educators" that sought to "help them to do things themselves."[24] For a bit over a year, UN experts taught fifty-two "students" from Bolivia, Costa Rica, Ecuador and other countries in South and Central America the techniques of training villagers back home in what the organization understood to be a better version of village life. Students practiced fundamentals and demonstrated agricultural techniques for populations in a network of neighboring villages, emulating the teaching methods to bring back to their countries later on. Once back home, the students would reinscribe UNESCO's methods on the ground as expert carriers of change (Figure 4.3).[25] In the erasure of eidetic difference between the "laboratory" and the site of implementation, UNESCO was actually entangling global models with local actors, and in doing so turning the world community into its pupils. But the students would not only learn technique, but also how to enter those international spaces as appointed national representatives of their countries and how to interact with one another—in short, they would learn how to form an international social space with UN programs at its center. The students of this new global reality would play a twofold role: first, to carry change beyond the temporal and spatial realities of UN–organized seminars; and second, to naturalize imports of expertise and technology as already local. It was people who would travel and forge the UN's new paths, translating and infusing standardized methods for everyday life and building with local traditions. And while participating in the UN's vision for the future of the postcolonial world, those very students of development would enact the UN's cultures of assembly directly in these field sites, forming part of a metaphorical, expanded global interior.

Early technical reports targeted rural sites for technical assistance. In 1951, a group of experts reached South Asia to survey housing conditions for low-income families in the "humid tropics." The three-month expedition traveled to India, Pakistan, Thailand, Singapore and Malaya (the Philippines were included in the report without the experts visiting). In the eyes of planners Jacob Crane, Jacobus Thijsse, and the rest of the team the trip confirmed the rural—which they registered as "underdeveloped"—status of much of South Asia, but also produced South and Southeast Asia as a cohesive region with similar planning problems, requiring, or so the team hoped, analogous solutions. The results echoed reports reaching the TAA from missions in Latin America. The problem of housing, the advisers observed, extended beyond the sites of major cities to include villages where the vast majority lived in "substandard quarters" without "proper" infrastructure for food storage and personal hygiene. But more importantly, the report urged the UN to prioritize rural populations and their built environments within

AT THE CENTRE

...AND OUTSIDE

An instructor explains the use of the cine-camera.

Health education is fun when it's a puppet show.

Discussing future posters in art studio.

Tarascan women learn fine points of needlework.

Filmstrips are produced to meet local needs.

It's easy to enlarge that window, student explains.

Figure 4.3. The laboratories of Patzcuaro, from Tidor Mende, "Report on Patzcuaro: One of the World's Most Unusual Social Experiments," *Courier: Publication of the United Nations Educational, Scientific and Cultural Organization* V. 5, no. 2 (February 1952): 3–4. Copyright UNESCO.

its development agenda, outlining two main lines of interrogation for future seminars and exhibitions: villages and self-help programs. The built environment gave the UN a reason to activate channels of communication that would permit the TAA to reach South Asian countries and their interiors. These networks, although predominantly concerning development and education projects, extended the media architectures installed at the UN's physical Headquarters, but this time with experts carrying the organization outwards, and seminars inviting international participants to enact the modalities of UN's global publics.

The Seminar as Medium

Once the TAA was established and its mission outlined, scientists, technical experts, and architects set out to convene conferences for the reception of the UN's mission outside its Headquarters. As historians of international relations discuss, conferences and congresses offered rich sites where industrialists, diplomats, and scientists tested and figured out the contours of an operative global community.[26] These conferences often used the visual vocabulary that the UN had developed for its Headquarters: gray-blue banners, the UN logo, flags. But in reality, these platforms—often in the form of workshops, seminars, and conferences—did not emulate the Headquarters' global interiors to the letter. What was exported instead were the cultures of assembly and spatial structures that architects had helped build within the organization.

In 1951, the *UN Bulletin* called for new "international channels of information" for a "fundamental education" in South and Southeast Asia, arguing that the presence of more experts would support rural areas in their emancipation from colonial rule and the dependencies it had installed.[27] Yet these fights for sovereignty were coming to fruition during the Cold War. So it was fortuitous that in 1952 the Indian government reached out to the UN for assistance in organizing an exhibition for its growing building sector.

Following independence and partition, the Indian government under the guidance of Prime Minister Jawaharlal Nehru had embarked on an ambitious plan to modernize the economy and infrastructure. Nehru's "development planning," as Partha Chatterjee shows, invested in technique so as to claim a place "outside politics," and hence more easily become "an instrument of politics," especially in relationship to Nehru's nationalist anti-colonial plan for India's self-determination.[28] Community planning was one of these strategies that allowed the Indian government to implement larger reforms in the economy, as well as to work toward a welfare state. Nehru, of course, was not the first to implicate Indian statehood with infrastructure and technique. In fact, Gyan Prakash reminds us, the British colonial presence had invested in modern technique and science to seize territory and govern its peoples (he refers in particular to railways).[29] What

was new about Nehru's technocracy was the intertwining of technique with national anti-colonial governmentality.[30] For Nehru, however, a collaboration with
the UN's TAA would validate his development plan and present it on a global
stage.

The executive secretary of ECAFE, Palamadai S. Lokanathan, saw in the TAA
a well of resources for South Asia at large and brought the Indian government's
request to the UN Department of Social Affairs. The TAA and the Indian government reached an agreement to co-organize a conference in 1952 that soon
transformed into a more robust event with workshops, seminars, and an exhibition component to take place in 1954 in New Delhi.[31] Advocating for the proposal, Ernest Weissmann mobilized TAA funds for an International Exhibition
on Low-Cost Housing and a United Nations Regional Seminar on Housing and
Community Improvement in New Delhi.[32] Weissmann's ambition was to amplify
HTCP's presence in Asia by helping bring to fruition a regional nongovernmental
organization for housing that would attract interested regional authorities and
planning departments, while encouraging contact with the UN.[33] The Regional
Seminar and International Exhibition in India offered an opportunity for the
UN–affiliated TAA to sort out administrative procedures and protocols, although,
as Ijlal Muzaffar notes, TAA projects continued to exist in a state of "perpetual
management" that asked the advisers to coproduce its administration.[34] Most
importantly, the seminar and exhibition enabled the UN's TAA and ECAFE to
build bridges, cultivate connections, and establish a presence in the political and
economic scene of South and Southeast Asia.

Seminars differed from exhibitions, however, in that they operated as zones
of exchange. Building on the outcomes of the Progressive Education Association,
a U.S. educational reform group, and its Committee on Workshops that had published reports on effective training, UNESCO launched a research program on
"techniques" of convening.[35] "An international seminar is an intensive short
study course . . . aimed towards an exchange of experiences and knowledge of
techniques on a strictly defined subject," a UN observer of UNESCO seminars
reported. Although similar to a "workshop," the observer continued, an "international seminar" was not a conference or a cycle of lectures. Seminars worked
toward defining "directives for further action and progress." They outlined "plans
to be carried out," after an intense focus of "trained minds" and "exchange of
opinions."[36]

Guidelines for "regional seminars" delineated the financial responsibility
of each part, with the UN covering costs for international experts and the host
country costs for national representatives and facilities. The UN guidelines also
indicated space requirements, necessary equipment and personnel—translators,
interpreters, typists—to support seminars on the ground.[37] In fact, such was
the conflation between the global spaces inside and outside the UN's physical

Headquarters that seminar participants often anticipated the treatment and amenities of the UN Headquarters. The perceived informality of seminars took after the "study groups" and committee meetings that the UN and its organs had been setting up.[38] The same "cultures of assembly" that ordered the workings of the physical Headquarters, then, also organized the structures of these international platforms.

At the same time that the UN aspired to organize the postcolonial world via regional seminars, particularly within the context of technical assistance,[39] the Indian government was striving to become a political and economic hub for South Asia. The suggestion of using a regional seminar to network India with other South and Southeast Asian countries could not have arrived at a better time: Jawaharlal Nehru's plan for a strong Indian presence within an Asian coalition required the building of regional networks. But presenting India as the regional center of South Asia was only one part of the equation; the other part was to bring the UN in immediate contact with Indian projects in front of a South Asian audience of administrators, politicians, and planners, to open the possibility of a different set of alliances.

To direct the UN's Regional Seminar and to advise the Indian government on the International Exhibition, Weissmann suggested Jaqueline Tyrwhitt, who at the time was looking for ways into the UN's housing and planning work. Born in South Africa, raised in England, educated in Germany, well-traveled and cosmopolitan, Tyrwhitt not only had the capacity to traverse informational networks, but also to expand them.[40] She was a teacher (she led a war correspondence course in the United Kingdom and taught in a number of Canadian and U.S. institutions), and as such she understood the UN's educational imperative. Being entangled with the main professional associations for architecture and planning of her time (CIAM and the Association for Planning and Regional Reconstruction are just two examples), Tyrwhitt could also bring modernist debates on planning and architecture into contact with conversations on development and internationalism, important qualities for a UN technical adviser on a mission to connect developing peripheries with world organizational centers.[41] Intrigued by her work, Weissmann had first recruited Tyrwhitt for a seminar and exhibition on housing and community improvement to tentatively take place in Morocco, cohosted by CIAM and the UN.[42] When funding fell through, he redirected her to the seminar and exhibition in New Delhi, India.[43]

Similarly to other technical advisers, Tyrwhitt started the preparation work for her role as director of the 1954 UN Seminar and Exhibition by weaving a network of experts and planners, while reinforcing the centrality of institutional hubs of internationalism on the way. Unlike UN administrators at the Headquarters, technical advisers like Tyrwhitt actively produced the links and edges of the network, introducing new centers of activity and their institutions to the stratified world order that the UN Secretariat was undertaking. From Toronto to New Delhi, Tyrwhitt roamed the administrative and metropolitan centers of old and new world orders, gathering institutional knowledge and contacts.

UN–appointed directors of TAA projects addressing the built environment often tapped into IFTCP and CIAM networks of planners and architects, but also pursued connections with UN officials, building relations with local experts. In the temporary headquarters in New York, Tyrwhitt acclimated to the organizational realities of the UN, while sketching a possible roster of speakers and collaborators. In London, she mapped out the political and planning scene of newly independent India with the help of architects and planners, while pooling imperial knowledge on South Asian housing and planning for the UN. In Geneva, where UN officials were appropriating League of Nations infrastructure, she met with representatives of specialized agencies and discussed ways of opening the platforms of the seminar and exhibition to them.

During those initial conversations, Tyrwhitt, who understood how networks spring from and expand through conferences and seminars since her involvement at the organization of CIAM congresses, used the Regional Seminar to plan the networks she hoped it would reinforce within the UN.[44] By the time she set foot in India in early June 1953, she had an outline for a regional seminar with international experts and some thoughts for an exhibition. She organized the seminar discussions around three themes, each headed by UN technical advisers and discussion leaders: Jacob Crane, with Rafael Picó and Constantinos Doxiadis, led the conversation on Housing and Community Improvement; Charles Abrams, with Frederick Adams and Arieh Sharon (who replaced the Tennessee Valley Authority's David Lilienthal), led the panels on Physical Planning; and Robert Fitzmaurice, with Jacobus Thijsse and Anthony Atkinson, led the discussion on Building Materials and Techniques.[45] The decision to invite those and not other architects and planners to chair each section spoke to the UN's practice of having Western experts frame the conversation. Even the few seeming exceptions—Puerto Rican geographer Picó, Israeli architect Sharon, and Greek planner Doxiadis—represented national elites. The UN asked the session leaders to frame mostly regional conversations, for which the Indian government had solicited papers and participation from "governments in the region."[46] In this sense, the Regional Seminar followed the workshop structure implemented at the UN Headquarters, with experts arriving from different member states to head conversations meant to inform local development plans. It created a platform for the diffusion of the UN's organizational structures in the same way that television networks allowed the UN to diffuse resolutions of the General Assembly.

In India Tyrwhitt continued her network-building, this time primarily as an adviser to the Indian government. She embarked on an exhaustive trip around South Asia, identifying possible collaborators in urban planning and the building industry, ultimately producing the regional network that UN Secretariat officials would tap into and of which the Indian government would be the center. Her job was to make the UN's presence known, as much as to mobilize local governments and ignite interest in technical assistance.[47] To actively construct the Economic and Security Council's regional classification of South Asia and to establish the ECAFE region as a coherent cultural, economic, and political reality, she solicited participation from local governments, preserving old and building new connections with other architects and planners later to be invited to the seminar.[48] Tyrwhitt's networking practices promised to bring about development and connections to resources and institutions. For example, Minnette de Silva warmly welcomed Tyrwhitt's seminar, hoping that this would propel the transformation of Marg, CIAM's regional group in India, into a solid institution of architectural modernism in the area.[49]

But in order for the seminar and workshop to create a discursive space for intellectual exchanges and collaborations, the organization needed to divest experts from politics. The truth was that UN administrators saw politics as an obstacle to—rather than the foundation of—their expanding network. UN employees, the "international servants" of the organization, were expected to fuel and operate the "vast and complicated machine" as mute channels that could "be seen but not heard."[50] TAA advisers, similarly to other technical experts hired in UN missions and seminars, came with a promise of transparency and objectivity that in reality enabled them to dissociate their proposals from the politics that these proposals (and future interventions) carried. This dissociation allowed UN consultants to argue that their presence was not part of a political act and that the UN, although a political and diplomatic organization, prioritized objective knowledge over political interests. Neutralizing the TAA's work benefited the organization, which rushed to insert its platforms in the field.

In preparation for the TAA event in India, Doxiadis compiled a manual of instructions for the future UN expert (understood as a man throughout the report), outlining UN expectations and guidelines regarding reimbursement, protocol, rules of contact, and procedures of intelligence collection. The technical adviser, Constantinos Doxiadis noted, "*is* the United Nations," carrying the weight of representation for the entire organization. The most important quality in outside experts, he argued, was their capacity to serve the international organization regardless of personal and political views. To be a valuable expert in the eyes of the organization, the technical adviser needed to remain transparent and shed any "prejudice or bias" in the face of internationalism, as if those were easily discarded. International meetings often involved people from different "nationalities, religions and cultures," and a UN representative (for Doxiadis, technical advisers in particular) should carry the content produced on the ground back to the physical Headquarters and vice versa without, however, attaching to the information personal judgment and bias.[51]

Figure 4.4. Example of United Nations seminar configuration, showing refurbished hall for the United Nations Seminar on Apartheid, Racial Discrimination, and Colonialism in Southern Africa, Zambia, with the UN emblem on the wall, interpreter booths, and tables in U-shape formation for the delegates, 1967. Courtesy of the United Nations Photo Library.

Part of the role of the technical adviser was to divest these channels that connected the field with the Headquarters—and by extension the concept of international aid at large—from any financial expectation. As mentioned previously, TAA administrators centered the agency on "technical assistance" and the circulation of expertise, rather than financial support, in their efforts. The technical adviser's job was to distinguish this circulation of expertise from the circulation of resources, or, even better, to articulate expertise as a resource equal in value to manual labor, materials, and equipment. As the UN TAA's mouthpiece, Tyrwhitt tirelessly reminded Indian authorities of the UN's limitations regarding funding.[52] She stated that housing, the Indian government's main concern for the seminar, constituted for the UN a local problem regardless of its global scale.[53] Therefore the TAA asked experts for final reports that would give applicable and actionable recommendations within a member state's internal budget and technical limitations.[54] Similarly to the public sphere articulated within the UN Headquarters, direct participation was structured and limited to professional and governmental representatives the same way that only officially appointed national representatives and their advisers would participate inside the UN's global interiors back at the Headquarters. And in both cases the public outside would receive UN technique either through literal media—radio, television, and so on—or metaphorical media, as was the case with the technical advisers in the various fields of operation. Inside the seminar venues, the invited experts, activating the channel infrastructure that they were installing, would network the seminar with the UN Headquarters and even project outwards, to new seminars and workshops (Figure 4.4). The space of the seminar, in this sense, formed the public interior that fed this metaphorical architecture of expertise exchange, a generative node in the UN's network of technical expertise.

Exhibiting Worlds

If the space of seminars and small-scale workshops transferred the UN's architectures of assembly from the Headquarters into the field, then exhibitions forged a place for the sharing of ideas and expertise, demonstrating, at the same time, how an active connection with the UN's technocratic networks would order those exchanges to transform life on the ground. Not all exhibitions, of course, addressed the same audience. The UN Department of Public Information, following the model of the U.S. State Department, had frequently used exhibitions to illustrate the organization's scope, its growing membership, and its initiatives, aiming at educating North American and Western European audiences. With statistical tables, photographs, charts, and drawings, exhibitions outlined the work of the organization, rendering graspable the institutional framework within which delegates, politicians, and consultants operated. But when the exhibitions turned to postcolonial publics, the tone changed to cultivate a positive disposition toward the organization on the ground, while visualizing what a relationship with the institution and its techniques could mean for publics at large.

For the international audience of planners, regional industries, local professionals and politicians from South and Southeast Asia, globetrotting experts, and governmental officials of the 1954 UN Regional Seminar, Tyrwhitt proposed two distinct exhibitions, both taking place on the fairgrounds outside the Red Fort in New Delhi. Building on the UN's exhibition strategies deployed in the United

States and Europe, Tyrwhitt mounted inside the permanent fair buildings a display of models and drawings from around the world, with plans and mock-ups of housing and community development creating an international "trading zone" of ideas exchange (Plate 11). Following Tyrwhitt's invitation to member states participating in the Seminar, models from Ceylon and Thailand arrived, as well as architectural drawings and plans from community planning projects in Europe, constructing the landscape of development that national representatives, Indian politicians, and Seminar participants visited. This first display built on CIAM approaches to conference exhibitions, hoping to organize and rationalize development outcomes and practices that grounded the Seminar exchanges in comparison and then circulated both regional and international networks.

The second exhibition, more ambitious in scale and scope, created a demonstration center with life-size replicas of low-cost housing and public buildings, exemplifying how the UN's networks of expertise circulation would transform rural life and its platforms (Figure 4.5). Indian officials invited governmental and private companies to build these low-cost housing replicas and place the growing Indian building industry at the center of South and Southeast Asian networks.[55] But this second exhibition would also show how the reception of UN technique turned villages into central hubs of regional networks. During her earlier trip in South and Southeast Asia, Tyrwhitt had assembled the parts of her life-size exhibition that would cast the potential of the rural as the pragmatic and future agent of global networks.[56] In villages around Punjab, but also outside New Delhi, she captured scenes from village life, turning the "village" into a kit of parts: "A Village Well," a "Village Carpenter," a "Village Cart," read the captions of photographs she mailed to former CIAM secretary-general Sigfried Giedion late in October (Figure 4.6).[57] Channeling the TAA's program, Tyrwhitt would reassemble this kit of parts on the exhibition grounds to show how technique alone, especially when vetted and cleared by an international institution such as the UN, improved conditions on the ground, as if financial support and politics did not play any role in development. In doing so, she also installed a village center for the reception and diffusion of UN technique in the form of community functions. In other words, the organization interpellated the village as a broadcast medium for UN messages, similarly to how North American and Western European world citizens received news via the radio or the television at home.

If the exhibition on low-cost housing showed how the state could make housing a public concern, the "village centre," demonstrating "the social aspects of community development . . . in a practical manner," showcased the UN's assistance plans for the decolonizing part of the world.[58] For UN TAA officials, the exhibition, especially within the context of the international body of expertise invited, would transform development projects from "purely local projects to wider territorial schemes," this time under the purview of an international organization.[59] In addition, the village exhibition would advertise the merits of technical assistance,

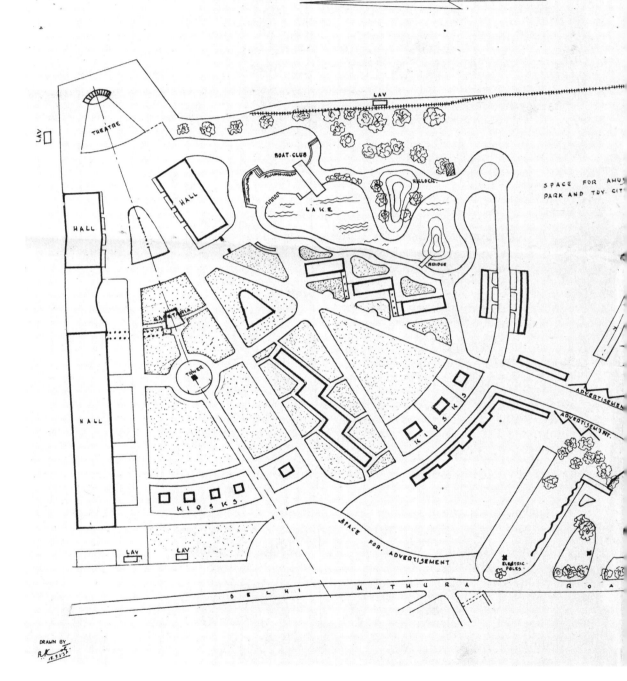

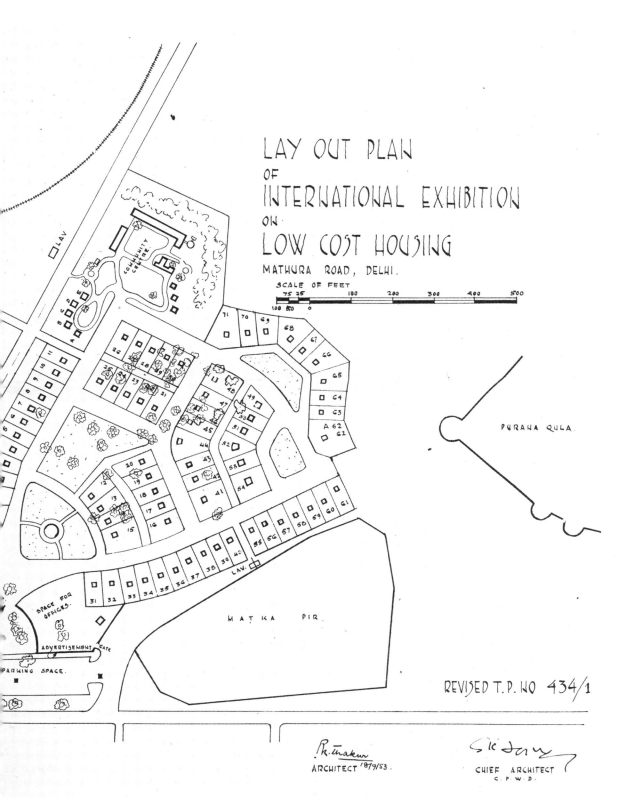

Figure 4.5. Plan of the Seminar and Exhibition Grounds in New Delhi, 1954. Courtesy of the RIBA Archives.

Figure 4.6. Tyrwhitt's photograph of village cart and well in Punjab, India, 1953. Courtesy of the gta Archives, ETH.

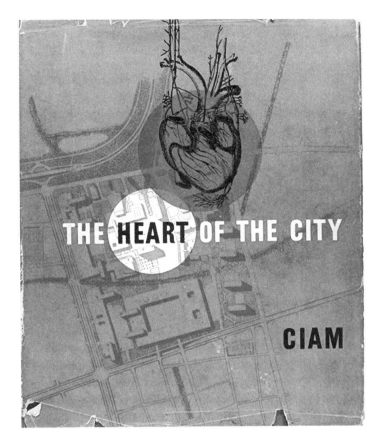

Figure 4.7. Cover of Jaqueline Tyrwhitt, Josep Lluís Sert, and Ernesto N. Rogers, eds., *CIAM 8: The Heart of the City: Towards the Humanisation of Urban Life* (London: Lund Humphries, 1952).

putting on display the built environment that technique and expertise improved without using words. But, also, the exhibition placed emphasis on village planning for the rest of South and Southeast Asia, setting an example of institutional internationalism at work for the postcolonial world.

Tyrwhitt had been developing her idea for a community center (later renamed village center) on the fringes of CIAM debates about "urban cores."[60] When appointed as director of the 1954 Regional Seminar, Tyrwhitt had just finished editing *The Heart of the City,* where a group of CIAM modernists, faced with the problem of post–World War II reconstruction, revisited the question of public space in terms of "cores" (Figure 4.7). The book was the result of the CIAM meeting at Hoddesdon that claimed "cores" as part of an essential grammar to organize communities across scales, from villages and neighborhoods to metropolitan areas.[61] The presentations (and later the published essays) divorced those centers from the economic infrastructures that supported them—the home, the colonies, the church—and the histories that produced them, presenting them as universal ideals and models.[62] The discussion mostly evoked earlier conversations on monumentality and community centers that, as Daniel Abramson notes, Giedion used to legitimize and naturalize a Western idealization of "cores" for an urban elite.[63] This way CIAM planners and architects promoted the idea that cores— civic centers with public platforms and institutions—could travel and define urban and rural spaces beyond the jurisdiction of North American and Western European cities.

Without using the language of networks, CIAM participants addressed cores as nodal points that concentrated and diffused people, commodities, and ideas, hence presenting them as part of a network architecture. Speaking to this articulation of cores as nodes in the UN's network of technical assistance, Josep Lluís Sert proposed media centers with television screens and loudspeakers for the decolonizing world, transforming the civic centers (and along with them villages as well) into interiors of an expanding global network that tied anew the periphery to centers of global power.[64] Tyrwhitt insisted, however, that unlike "civic centers" that interfaced governments with the body politic, "cores" concerned people.[65] "The Civic Center—that monumental group of buildings standing in isolated grandeur—is not what is meant by the Core. The Core is not the seat of civic dignity: the Core is the gathering place of the people," she noted in her own contribution.[66] She continued implicating CIAM with the New Delhi Seminar and Exhibition not only on a conceptual level, but also on the organizational level, as a constitutive presence in the events. Tyrwhitt even recruited CIAM members for the Seminar and solicited the presentation panels on urban cores for the New Delhi International Exhibition, an initiative that fell through when the panels remained in Boston with Sert and only photographs of a smaller selection of visual material was dispatched to Tyrwhitt at the end of December.[67]

At the village exhibition, Tyrwhitt used CIAM's idealization of the "core" to make room for new rural institutions built from sun-dried bricks and rammed earth—the Education Centre, the Health Clinic, the Grain Storage, and the Craftsmen's Sheds. These institutions defined an open platform, a "microcosm of village culture," illustrating "certain fundamental principles of community living" for the entirety of the village to partake in (Figure 4.8).[68] Tyrwhitt, who claimed that the organization and structure of the village center held more gravity than its outward appearance, placed the school and the assembly under the same roof, insinuating that the education and reorganization of rural citizenry also started there, in the village. Designed to replace the cultural and political centers of the past, Tyrwhitt's village center acted both as an extension of the state (in the sense that the exhibition proposed those centers as platforms for launching national policies) and a hub in the UN's network that promised to educate local villagers according to standards and procedures developed at the promised heart of this new world order. The exhibition modeled not only structures of village planning and building, but also ways of life: a large tree to mark a public open space, the correct placement of drinking-water wells, kitchen gardens with separate pits for

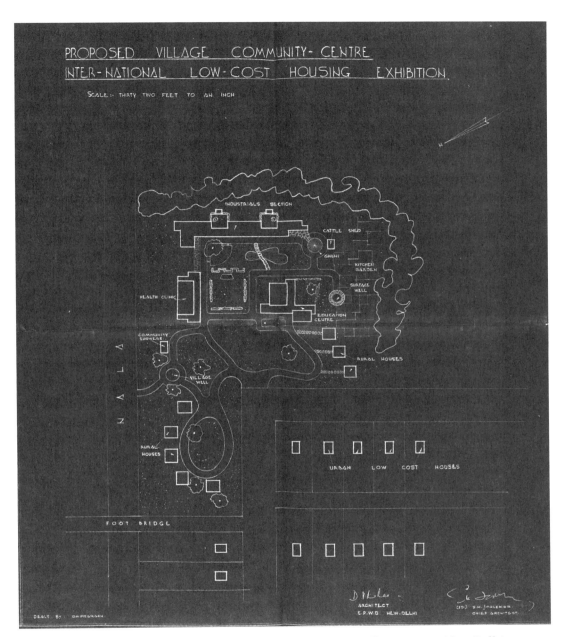

Figure 4.8. S. K. Joglekar and D. V. Rao (CPWD), plan of the Village Centre, New Delhi, 1954. Courtesy of the RIBA Archives.

manure and smokeless *chulas,* cattle dip and compost, workshops for crafts, open drains, and a rationalized waste management system:

> As far as possible this village centre should be made to come alive. That is there should be real children in the school, a nurse should be in attendance at the health centre, and people should be working in the craft workshops.

The impression should be given that this is the focus of active and friendly village life—simple but not drab, down to earth but full of vitality.[69]

Echoing colonial exhibitions of the early twentieth century, the village center staged the new roles it proposed for architects, villagers, and the state in India's development. The labor on display did not produce any surplus value but sustained the life of the village in a constant recycling feedback loop. Manual labor reinscribed within development the body of the villager as a catalyst and agent of progress: a Punjabi potter making cottage tiles, a blacksmith for bolts and hooks, a carpenter, and a weaver were all parts of the exhibit for international and local visitors (Figure 4.9).[70]

The village that Tyrwhitt conceived of as a platform for modernist planning ideals and UN institutions was the same that Indian authorities had been articulating as a springboard for independence and sovereignty. The village constituted a powerful engine in Gandhian utopianism and its claims to an essential Indian identity.[71] Gandhi's craft-based economy called forth villages to be the central sites and vehicles for home rule. "If the village perishes, India will perish too," he wrote.[72] Later Prime Minister Jawaharlal Nehru, who diverged from Gandhi to emphasize development, likewise reclaimed villages as sites of governmental intervention. Villages enabled the Indian government to mobilize precolonial predilections and to give "a national sense of direction" to Nehru's plan that distanced itself from centralized colonial practices of urban planning.[73] The goal was to make the state anew the "ultimate owner" of land and transfer power to a decentralized but networked form of self-government that directly connected villages to Nehru's government, circumventing any forms of preindependence local governance that were blocking the Nehruvian top-down technocratic project of development.[74] Within this context, the Indian government had already understood the importance of villages as reception and projection nodes in networks of state control.

By 1953 the Community Projects Administration (CPA), an Indian government initiative to recenter village networks around agrarian reform and refugee integration, had launched a growing program of development projects that targeted villages as both physical and administrative entities. Building on the Pilot Project that the American planner Albert Mayer had launched in the Etawah region of Uttar Pradesh, CPA aimed to organize larger constellations of villages around training centers that connected villagers to expertise, therefore enacting Nehru's project of modernization.[75] The sixty-four villages that Mayer chose in 1948 formed the foundation for CPA's efforts to recalibrate the networks of rural economies and refugee influx around Nehru's state.[76] Mayer used training centers to transform villages into the hubs of an outward-looking network of rural communities, where experts would "funnel" technique and development to villag-

Figure 4.9. Workers build the Health Clinic at the Village Centre, 1953. Courtesy of the United Nations Photo Library.

ers, not so much through abstract teaching and lecturing, as through engagement and demonstration on the ground. The idea was that sustained change could only happen from within, and that all the state would do is build a knowledge infrastructure. The locals, and not the experts, would be the media to diffuse the new knowledge and enact agricultural reform (Figure 4.10).[77] In doing so, Mayer and CPA established villages as nodes in a network of expertise transfer, ripe for the UN to plug into.

Tyrwhitt convinced the UN that her village center would bring the organization to the very heart of the social change already underway in rural India. Farhan S. Karim details how the village exhibition shaped ideas around postcolonial Indian modernity, as well as brought CIAM conversations to New Delhi.[78] Tyrwhitt willingly appropriated the postcolonial rural networks that CPA put together for TAA's developmentalist discourse, making the case for their utility in reaching rural publics. This view of Indian villages was already evident in her edited anthology of reports that the Scottish planner and sociologist Patrick Geddes had compiled during his time in India. There Tyrwhitt put together a view of Indian villages as the product of social and economic networks particular in scale and scope to rural economies.[79] The exhibition, though, entangled those rural publics with UN networks of expertise. In forming a village out of the low-cost housing exhibition

Figure 4.10. Albert Mayer, *Pilot Project, India: The Story of Rural Development at Etawah, Uttar Pradesh* (Berkeley: University of California Press, 1958).

and claiming for the UN a place at its heart—regardless of how inconspicuous—Tyrwhitt spoke to the organization's desire to intervene and restructure the very networks spanning from the village center to the postcolonial countryside.

At the village exhibition, Tyrwhitt made room for UN specialized agencies to inhabit and structure the very space of informality and communal living. The intention was that the village center would serve as "a valuable field demonstration centre for the Agencies involved," while also promoting CPA's work.[80] A health center, an industrial center for craftsmanship, an educational center, and an open area with cattle and well would serve as footholds for the World Health Organization, the Food and Agriculture Organization, the International Labor Organization, and UNESCO respectively, which would provide for equipment proving that, rather than decentralizing in a Gandhian fashion of self-sufficiency, these villages were designed to hook the rural into other networks of the distribution of modernity.[81] The Village Center, in this sense, connected "learning and responsibility" behind dried brick and rammed earth, embedding and naturalizing the UN as an administrative structure for India's interior.[82] In contrast to Nehru's technological vision of progress and modernist aesthetics that disrupted the colonial past, UN programs proposed a return to a reformed tradition, whereby it would undertake the rationalization and organization of local expertise and technique to produce a traditional form, hence sustaining the differential that instigated the arrival of international experts in the first place.

Strikingly, although the exhibition posited tradition as the path toward postcolonial India, the model village itself lacked any religious center. The TAA made no space for a shrine, or temple, or mosque in the village to model development. In place of a shrine, the UN, in collaboration with Indian architects and engineers, built a replica of Gandhi's hut, proclaiming it a site of spiritual commemoration.[83] Leaving out the question of religion erased the difficulty of dealing with caste by pretending that somehow the problem would magically disappear. A major side benefit of this structural shift in the organization of the village for the UN would be a condition in which caste hierarchies could be discarded, and along with them caste-oriented networks, making space for institutional networks, both national and international, to step in.

Nehru and the UN hoped that the exhibition would ignite "enthusiasm to introduce certain aspects of this demonstration into their own home villages."[84] UNESCO encouraged Tyrwhitt to dress her village center with "fundamental education" programming, turning the core of the village into a training center for technical expertise.[85] Similarly to Gandhi's imagined villages and Nehru's rural networks, the UN's village center served also as a school introducing the villagers-pupils to the UN's world of technique, fundamental education, and administrative culture. The village center was where villagers would learn how to be villagers in postindependence times, with the UN's guiding hand and in connection to other hubs in the UN's expanding network of headquarters, seminar rooms, and field offices. The idea was that the exhibition would teach administrators and rural communities how to produce the village—both in terms of the operations necessary for its construction and maintenance, and the organization of rural economies and the communities around them. And more so, the exhibition, in placing the UN at the very center of the village, also constructed the rural population as its constituents.

CPA representative R. B. Gupta applauded the self-help approach to village improvements.[86] Central Public Works Department's N. Krishnaswami embraced the focus on village development that Tyrwhitt's center enabled.[87] The same agency also stressed the importance of model villages for the "settling" of "displaced persons," calling for the emulation of the UN's village center in the creation of a model core for all surrounding villages.[88] Israeli architect Joseph M. Neufeld, who had been thinking about the design of hospitals at the time, noted during the 1954 Delhi Seminar that a "community core is not only an important part of the community plan, but is itself a tool for planning."[89] He saw community cores as "ideal planning center[s]" for the larger region surrounding them.

But the purpose of the village exhibition was not only to entangle rural life with the UN's technical assistance programs, but also to become a lesson in UN world-making. To circulate the village exhibition beyond the fairgrounds, the UN solicited the help of media, ultimately creating a reverberant space with radio announcements, drawings, reports, photographs, and films. Kodachrome rolls, cameras, and filming equipment documented photographically both the exhibition and the seminars.[90] In New Delhi, G. F. Middleton, who was invited to build a rammed-earth house using the mold he had been perfecting in Israel, filmed the UN exhibition.[91] The Indian Films Division produced a short documentary on the Village Centre, creating a permanent record for the Indian government.[92] Radio was also essential in creating an imagined community around this ideation of the village and the UN's presence in South Asia. The publics that films and photographs could not reach, radio would, announcing to the world the reordering that was taking place in New Delhi and the folding of India deeper into the UN's techniques. The remnant of a previous fair that celebrated railways, a relay antenna on the fairground in New Delhi, became an evocative celebration of connectivity, marking the desire to plug the exhibition into larger networks. It offered the UN an opportunity not only to make the seminar a nodal point, but also to denote the immediate connection with other nodal points and practices of development, particularly the physical Headquarters back in New York City. The idea was that media would carry this instance of platform-making as content for other experts and their networks to learn from, while reports and clippings, mainly meant for the libraries of specialized agencies and experts involved in similar development

Figure 4.11. Technical experts and planners attend the UN Regional Seminar during a field trip, 1954. Copyright Constantinos and Emma Doxiadis Foundation.

projects, became the record of reference.[93] Apart from mediating UN's cultures of assembly and techniques of expertise transfer, the Village Center—and alongside it the Seminar—needed physical media, spools of film, and radio, to reach the UN's publics back in the UN Headquarters and beyond, wherever the UN sought to install its operations.

As with other UN workshops and conferences around the world, the 1954 New Delhi seminar and exhibition enlarged and strengthened the UN network of professionals working to diffuse the modernity of this new world order. The village center tied planners, administrators, and experts—both local and foreign—into a network of learning that expanded beyond the site of the seminar and exhibition itself. As a strategy, the regional seminar and exhibition invited participants to engage in conversations that moved beyond the space of the nation, ultimately creating what McLuhan later called the "global village," the experience of the world as a space of collapsed distances.[94] In New Delhi, Tyrwhitt was introduced to Doxiadis at the same time that Doxiadis and other UN consultants–such as Charles Abrams and Jacob Crane—were introduced to the developing world (Figure 4.11). *Ekistics,* the journal around which Doxiadis built a community of planners, started in 1954 as an annotated bibliography—*Tropical Housing & Planning Monthly Bulletin*—responding to the UN event in Delhi that identified a gap in print media actively producing the common ground between development and planning.[95] The 1954

Seminar and Exhibition modeled relationships between the UN and urban plan-ners, who as technical advisers could now shape and contain the world of tomor-row, reconfiguring the network of urban planning actors in the post–World War II period as CIAM was heading toward its resolution. And in truth, the ramifications of the Regional Seminar were larger than the very moment that it happened, not only for the planning of the built environment and the circulation of expertise, but also for the UN and its proliferating publics.

If at the signing of the UN Charter the organization invited mass media inside its workings to connect with a public outside, if at the Nuremberg Trials it used architecture to fabricate its perspective, and if at the UN Headquarters it further elaborated the stratification of the international polity and produced the general public as an audience to the theatrics of multilateralism, then the UN Seminar at New Delhi turned the global interior into a strategy for creating UN publics anchored outside of the Headquarters. Although the seminar did not explicitly target the general public—quite to the contrary, the seminar was exclusively de-signed for experts—the village center exhibition did. Architects, planners, and administrators, as well as local communities, entered the space of the village ex-hibition as students of development. The UN invited them to learn and teach each other methods and techniques of planning and building in the Global South, ulti-mately instituting a platform, a metaphorical public interior that expanded (and to some extend informed) the organization's global interior.

Jaqueline Tyrwhitt returned to the role of a UN technical consultant three more times, establishing programs on town and regional planning in universities around the world, from Toronto to Bandung and from the United Kingdom to Mumbai. The UN Seminar and Exhibition in New Delhi set up a cascade of other UN seminars, workshops and exhibitions that intensified activity on planning and housing as a matter of technique and its circulation. Those exhibitions and seminars that extended the work of the UN outside its headquarters aimed at a controlled and self-managed implementation that, in the end, rendered net-works of expertise invisible to the general public. UN Seminars offered the illu-sion that a global village of experts, contracting and retracting, convening, and then diffusing the lessons of their meetings throughout the world, could act as UN ambassadors.

From the headquarters to the field, the UN rearticulated the workshop, once imagined taking place within the rooms of its New York City Headquarters, as a technique of internationalism at large. It is not that international meetings did not exist before the advent of the UN. The UN's innovation was to place work-shops and conferences within its larger architecture of expertise networks as the public interiors to expand, and in certain ways globalize, the relationships and publics that the physical headquarters structured. The physical Headquarters in New York would determine the social and political space of multilateralism, as well as the media representations of its global publics of diplomats, politicians, and civic society. The metaphorical public interior that traveled outside that space would further allow new publics to form around the practices already established at the center. It will come as no surprise, then, that the 1954 UN representatives at the Regional Seminar and International Exhibition requested the institutionalization of periodic seminars for experts, declaring such forums important sites of internationalism.[96]

The UN, and UNESCO in particular, invested resources and time in investigating different conference structures. When in 1968 Margaret Mead published her research on the "small conference," a "new and powerful communication form," she critically shifted from discussing proceedings as the place of knowledge production, to examining the platforms themselves.[97] Mead understood very well that the purpose of the "small conference" was not really to produce a publication but rather to allow for the participants to build "rapport," to form a public and by extension a discourse.[98] Mead was not only referring to her experience at the Josiah Macy Jr. Foundation conferences, but also the UNESCO, WHO, and UN seminars and conferences in which she had participated. For her, the atmosphere of "temporary parity" that these seminars created was the necessary condition for the formation of active publics around problems.[99] She noted that the form of the "small conference"—what UN officials called the "seminar"—could help institutions to internationalize their platforms while channeling "historical forms" of gathering, such as the classroom or the parliament. "Within the United Nations the struggle between the demands for representativeness and authoritative materials, and the need to keep face-to-face groups small enough to do any work, is reflected in the variety of devices, ranging from world conferences to small working parties and task forces which are continuing features of its activities," she explained.[100]

Most importantly, these platforms created the conditions for new organizations and alliances, both professional and political, to form and multiply. Although situated within the institution and designed to be contained by the organization, the spaces of seminars framed a different experience of internationalism, demonstrating the potential to create different structures and networks around platforms. These seminar spaces, in a way, proposed their appropriation for purposes outside the scope of United Nations operations. In fact, when the Non-Aligned Movement sought to organize their constituents in a series of meetings, it used these same techniques to critique and move beyond the limitations of the UN's institutional platforms. In multiple ways, to address and sustain the relationship between headquarters and the field, the UN turned its forums into itinerant platforms that traveled and organized publics around the world, proliferating and disseminating the ways of the organization as the habitus of liberal internationalism on the ground.

Epilogue
Itinerant Platforms

In a footnote on the design history of the headquarters of the United Nations Educational, Scientific, and Cultural Organization (UNESCO) in Paris, Chris Pearson refers to an unusual incident. The UNESCO House, as it was known at the time, was the second UN–affiliated building to open after the completion of the UN Headquarters in New York City, and maybe the first to absorb the lessons of its construction and management. Tired of how ill-lit the Executive Board Room was, UNESCO officials asked Marcel Breuer and Bernard Zehrfuss to find a solution and bring more natural light in. Zehrfuss and Breuer were hesitant to puncture solid walls to install windows, but Philip Johnson, whose office had undertaken the interior design, shrugged nonchalantly in response: "It makes no difference to me, it is entirely up to you. Good luck!"[1] Maybe this is an all-too-common exchange between an architect and a client for a small private project, but for an international institution, whose recently completed headquarters carried the weight and promise of global and infinite scientific and cultural exchange, the architect's indifference was surprising. It is possible that Johnson's office was focusing on other projects at the time, or that Johnson was disinterested in the project of cultural internationalism, and therefore ascribed little value to his office's contribution. But maybe at play was a much more complex give-and-take between architectural claims to authorship and the making of global interiors for international institutions.

The Executive Board Room was one of eight chambers that member states had donated to UNESCO. Gifting interiors to international institutions was at the time an established practice and a smart budgetary tool that allowed member states to appear in the global space of the headquarters and claim to frame its public spheres in exchange for funding the completion of the project. Following the example of the Scandinavian gifts that had furnished the three council chambers at the UN Headquarters, the U.S. government, with the help of the International Council at the Museum of Modern Art, had sponsored the Executive Board Room and commissioned its design to Philip Johnson Associates (Figure E.1).[2] But, in

Figure E.1. R. Lesage, interior of the Executive Board Room, 1964. Copyright UNESCO.

the same way that the setting of tables, media booths, auditoriums, and chairs inside the UN's council chambers had already been determined in the master plan of the UN Headquarters, those rooms had been pre-decided outside the architectural office (Figure E.2, E.3). In actuality, the structural relationships of the UNESCO House rooms had been resolved back in New York City, where architects, engineers, and acousticians had given the UN's cultures of assembly architectural form, which then was carried to UNESCO in plans and guidelines as the set habitus of institutional internationalism.[3]

The broadcast configuration of the global interior—with its stratified publics, media galleries, and global polity wired in interpretation systems inside dampened halls—opened institutional spaces to a wider public. From San Francisco to the completion of the UN Headquarters, architects imagined, designed, built, and calibrated platforms for political multilateralism. In doing so, they also shaped institutional relationships in an emergent multimodal world, while delineating the place of media and communications within it. In certain ways those global platforms reflected the political aspirations of midcentury liberalism and its core

Figure E.2. Marc Laloux, interior of Committee Room V, gift of the government of Switzerland, 1958. Copyright UNESCO.

values of representational democracy, human rights, aid, security rhetoric and development politics; and in other ways, they signaled institutional shortcomings and the failure to uphold those promises. In their itinerant deployment outside the New York Headquarters, global interiors delivered platforms for diplomatic continuity among international bureaucracies (think here the North Atlantic Treaty Organization).

The UNESCO House that opened its doors to the public in 1958 offered an opportunity to further finesse architectural types for global institutions. The design and construction had been undertaken by an international team of architects and engineers—Breuer, Zehrfuss, and Pier Luigi Nervi—overseen by another international team of consulting architects—Walter Gropius, Sven Markelius, Lucio Costa, Ernesto Rogers, and Le Corbusier. In addition, individual artists and designers, such as Joan Miró, Pablo Picasso, Eero Saarinen, and Isamu Noguchi, had contributed murals, sculptures and furniture for the interior.[4] There was an evident turn toward formal and symbolic considerations, found in the team's

Figure E.3. R. Lesage, interior of Committee Room VII during meeting, with decorations and furnishing donated by the government of Italy, 1958. Copyright UNESCO.

attention to engineered forms, conversations on the architectural expression of UNESCO's cultural diplomacy, and discussions of how the complex would be located on its site. But regardless of this turn to architectural form and the symbols that the complex would deliver to the city, the overall plan and the interior structures deviated only slightly from the program back in New York. In other words, this concern with how built form would appear in public space was possible precisely because the UN Headquarters had already worked out the interior of the building.

If the completion of the UN Headquarters delivered a model, then the UNESCO House started turning the model into a type. For a plan to become a type that then iteratively circulates as directives for future buildings with similar functions, there needs to be a sustained demand that mobilizes (and produces) it. In fact, the United Nations Headquarters was only the first in a series of headquarters that the organization and its specialized agencies launched around the world. Following the opening of the New York Headquarters, an ambitious and expansive building program for affiliated specialized agencies and regional field offices unfolded. Plans for the design of the UNESCO Headquarters had already been underway since 1952. In 1956, the UN announced an architectural competition for the Place des Nations, eventually won by André Gutton. The International Telecommunication Union commissioned André Bordigoni to build its headquarters overlooking the yet-to-be-built Place des Nations in 1956.[5] Swiss architect Jean Tschumi, who had just designed the Nestlé Headquarters, won the 1960 international competition for the World Health Organization building, a complex completed by Pierre Bonnard in Pregny in 1966.[6] The International Labor Organization acquired its own monumental curved wall of offices in Geneva's Grand Morillon in 1974.[7] Many more headquarters and building complexes followed; ironically, the majority stood in the same city that the UN had rejected as its seat in 1945.[8] It helped that the United Nations had repurposed the Palais des Nations for its operations in Europe, as well as its library and archive, and that an invested city administration offered incentives for more UN building projects. These buildings, often in need of conference rooms and plenary halls for international meetings, looked back to the UN Headquarters for models, gradually reifying them as architectural types for global institutions.

A growing network of consulting and chief architects transposed plans from one building to the next, and along with plans, their understanding of international bureaucracies and their needs, as well as any previous lessons they gathered. For example, Wallace K. Harrison, who had served as head of the UN Headquarters Planning Office, co-supervised the design of the International Labor Organization Headquarters with Robert H. Matthew and Carlos Raúl Villanueva. The project was commissioned to French architect Eugène Beaudouin (whose proposal for the UNESCO House had been rejected), Swiss architect Alberto Camenzind, and Nervi, UNESCO's head engineer. Eero Saarinen, who had consulted with the UN Headquarters and whose proposal for the World Health Organization failed to win that competition, designed furniture for UNESCO. Markelius and Le Corbusier, who had worked together at the UN Board of Design, consulted for UNESCO. In this sense, architects repurposed UN Headquarters architectures, carrying plans and ideas from one institution to the next.

It is not a coincidence that those transfers mostly concerned interiors. For every new building, the UN Headquarters offered a working model that defined the spaces where international publics formed around problems. Think here of the council chamber that Jean Tschumi designed for the World Health Organization and placed in a separate marble cube outside the main building, or the UNESCO Assembly Hall. Similarly, efforts to house temporary or smaller scale UN–related operations inside preexisting buildings found in the plans that the

UN Headquarters circulated a way of signifying that they partook the larger UN system of international institutions. This was especially true for field offices and regional UN branches that often took over vacant buildings or leased spaces inside larger governmental complexes. In part an economical solution, refurbishment was possible because the interiors carried more political and diplomatic value for the UN than the external form of the building infrastructure the organization was using.

The transformation of the UN's global interior into a type that could then travel the conduits of international diplomacy helped globalize the organization's platforms. Outside Geneva and New York, the UN regional commissions established their headquarters at times by renting out space and at other times by investing in new buildings. The headquarters for the Economic Commission for Latin America (ECLA) that UN Secretary-General U Thant inaugurated in Santiago, Chile, in 1966 constitutes an example.[9] The winning entry, which Chilean architect Emilio Duhart designed in collaboration with Christian de Groote, Roberto Goycoolea, and Oscar Santelices, detached the assembly hall (Diamante) and main conference room (Caracol) from the rest of the building, placing them inside a courtyard surrounded by a wall of office spaces (Anillo).[10] Although the goal was to present architecturally regional multilateral institutions as distinct and situated, the architects again repurposed the interior spatial configurations of the UN Headquarters. The Caracol, with its cedar slats and central circular table on the floor, brought inside ECLA some of the aesthetics and cultures of assembly that the UN had launched a decade earlier in its headquarters (Plate 12). Serving as the main assembly hall after plans for a separate assembly hall were abandoned, Caracol's principal conference hall formed a spiral that denoted a "future pattern of development" while "enfolding the round table for the delegates of the ECLA member countries."[11] Similarly, the Economic and Social Commission for Asia and the Far East's headquarters, located first inside Sala Santitham (1954) and later rehomed in a modernist extension for the Secretariat (1975) in Bangkok, used the types of platforms developed in New York.

Architecture schools, especially in the northeastern United States, introduced the UN Headquarters as a studio brief, asking students to imagine and design complexes for world assemblies and global governance. Others used the Headquarters as a "classroom," particularly during its construction phase. The site quickly peaked in popularity for architectural field trips, regardless (or even because of) its incomplete state. A surge of requests for field visits reached the Secretariat: Edgar Kaufmann Jr. asked to take his NYU class to visit the site,[12] as did Columbia's art history professor George R. Collins,[13] Syracuse's architecture professor D. Kenneth "Doc" Sargent,[14] and the University of Pennsylvania's architecture professor Leon Clemmer.[15] At the same time, its open guts attracted national delegations of engineers and architects, who hoped to encounter the engineering forefront of construction techniques and materials during their vis-its.[16] There was an imagination of technique attached to the construction site that architects found intriguing and that marked the culture of an entire generation of practitioners, particularly with regard to how architectural modernism could build governance and bureaucracies.

This was not by accident. The post–World War II period brought about a deep entanglement of American corporate capitalism with international institutions. U.S. corporations were particularly interested in patronizing and milking those associations. Chase Manhattan Bank, which issued the check to fund the pur-chase of the Turtle Bay site, borrowed and put on display the signed and canceled check at its Museum of the Moneys of the World at the Rockefeller Center for years to come.[17] IBM, as I discussed in chapter 1, equipped the headquarters with its interpretation systems. MoMA saw an opportunity to promote modernist aes-thetics in this intertwining of corporate capitalism with liberal internationalism. When Mary Barnes and Toshiko Mori worked on the interiors of the new IBM Tower that would replace the old-world headquarters on Madison Avenue, the boardroom took the form of a complete round table. Arthur Drexler, the curator of the exhibition *Buildings for Business and Government,* which opened its doors to the public in 1957, attributed this surge of architectural production to the emer-gence of the United States as the new global power to reckon with. "Emboldened perhaps by its present role in world affairs," the curator noted, "the United States no longer demands that major government commissions be executed in antique styles." He instead proclaimed that architects have finally given the United States what it needed: "modern American buildings."[18] Most of the offices represented in the exhibition were related one way or another to the production of global spaces, either on the level of institutions or corporations. In fact, some of those offices, such as Skidmore, Owings & Merrill (SOM), had participated in the planning and construction of the UN Headquarters. What the exhibition diagnosed as an af-finity between corporate America and governmental buildings was in reality the quite conscious and willful production of government as business and of business as government, and to that end globalized as well.

UN delegates and officials, who participated in council and committee meet-ings, realized very quickly that these physical interiors organized much more than just diplomatic work. They actively produced an internationalist imagination of a world society. To walk in the UN's Babelesque corridors and sit in the conference rooms along with journalists and publics following debates unfolding around the table, transposed the visitors within the world of international relations, trig-gering an imagination of participation in this world community of policymakers, media, and politicians. There was no other medium as impactful as architecture itself. UN Department of Public Information officials, who comprehended well the potential value the building carried for the organization, organized tours that opened up the Headquarters to visitors as the building was nearing completion. They declared that the most effective way to illustrate the work of the UN was to visit the Headquarters and experience firsthand the collectives forming inside the three council chambers and the General Assembly. The External Relations Division even instituted scripted guided tours as part of the organization's public relations toolkit, ensuring a uniform message about the organization.[19]

By the early 1950s, the UN's distinct visual and architectural language came to define more widely institutional spaces of multilateralism. Political and diplomatic attempts at multilateralism outside the UN used those same spaces as representations of cooperation in their inaugural presentations to the world. At Expo 58 in Brussels, the first world exposition to follow World War II, the Bureau International des Expositions made space for an International Section that hosted the pavilions of the United Nations, the Council of Europe, the European Coal and Steel Community (later to evolve into the administrative authority of the European Commission), and the Hall of World Cooperation.[20] The International Section placed the political proposal for a European parliament within the context of a much bigger project of postwar multilateralism. Architects designing pavilions for the Section were promised a central place on the Expo 58 fairgrounds, with proximity to heavy human traffic and hence an expanded audience, but in the end attractions and other paths stirred the crowds away.[21] Although not a novelty (both the 1937 World Fair in Paris and the 1939–40 New York World's Fair featured international institutions), these pavilions pressed on the idea of liberal internationalism and the presence of global institutions as regulatory mechanisms in a transforming world order.[22] And in this reinforcement, the United Nations Headquarters appeared again as a model. Next to Hugo Van Kuyck's dome for the United Nations, Karl Schwanzer designed the Council of Europe Pavilion to be, as he claimed, the "protective roof of Europe."[23] Schwanzer installed at the center of his pavilion another international platform and invited Finn Juhl, the Danish designer who had arranged the Trusteeship Council Chamber at the UN Headquarters, to design it, including a fully operative council chamber—complete with simultaneous interpretation booths and semicircular tables (Plate 13).

The UN's global interiors caught on in films and TV shows for their capacity to represent international order, but also because they spoke to aspirations and imaginaries for the constitution of a world community. The UN Headquarters represented an operative world community and system of global governance for a wider public to put confidence in. As Glenda Sluga shows, Hollywood producers formed a close partnership with the United Nations, as did national broadcasters.[24] Consider for a moment Alfred Hitchcock's *North by Northwest* (1959) where the UN lobby, with its curvaceous balconies, signals a manhunt of diplomatic significance. The UN officials, particularly the Department of Public Information, initially welcomed this entanglement. These films promoted a view of the

Figure E.4. Photographic still from *The Twilight Zone* episode 89, "To Serve Man," 1962. Courtesy of CBS Broadcasting Inc.

organization as aspirational global governance with the capacity to move beyond national borders to address humanity. Often these films featured the UN's itinerant platforms, whether recreated or real, to mark the presence of an international polity in action. Appropriating the UN's architectural language, these films delineated platforms of global politics, and at times even turned the Headquarters into the mise-en-scène of their plot. Rudolph Maté's science fiction movie *When Worlds Collide* (1951) brings the viewer inside the Security Council, at times looking at it through the interpreters' booth and at times from the floor. There an alarmed Dr. Hendron tries to convince an international body (speaking several foreign languages) to pay attention to calculations showing a planet en route to crash into Earth. The film construes the Security Council as a place of political possibility, concealing its asymmetries and the political impasse that often characterizes its operations.[25] Similarly, in the *Twilight Zone* episode "To Serve Man" (1962), a nine-foot-tall extraterrestrial enters the Security Council to address humanity in a ploy to gain the trust of the UN as the world's governing body (Figure E.4).[26] In Maxwell Shane's drama *The Glass Wall* (1953)—an allusion to the Secretariat Tower's curtain wall, but also a double entendre that signifies transparency and exclusion at

Figure E.5. Photographic still from *The Glass Wall* (1953): Vittorio Gassman pleads with the UN ECOSOC. Copyright 1953, renewed 1981 Columbia Pictures Industries Inc. All rights reserved. Courtesy of Columbia Pictures.

once—a desolate Vittorio Gassman, facing deportation, pleads his case with an empty Economic and Social Council on behalf of all displaced peoples (Figure E.5). In *A Global Affair* (1964), a UN bureaucrat who happens upon a baby in a basket outside his office adjures the General Assembly to help him find a family for the child.[27] These moments of filmic projection established UN interiors and their architectural grammar as part of the syntax of global governance, but also as sites where one could address the world even when (and despite the fact that) governance lay outside the organization's purview and legal authority. Acting as filmic stand-ins for world governance, these physical interiors presented the promise of a democratic global society, with its own organs, platforms, and polities, regardless of its failures to include (ECOSOC is empty, the Security Council does not believe the scientist, and so on), and at times even hesitation to deliver.

But the social and political structures that architecture shaped within the United Nations also traveled outside the space itself, allowing for their use by

organizations and collectivities that at times even criticized the liberal internationalism of the institution itself. At colleges, universities, and schools, Model
UN taught students to be part of this new world society, celebrating the UN
General Assembly as a democratic public sphere where member states bring the
interests of their interiors.[28] Workshops and seminars carried those structures
of internationalism further inside the decolonizing world. The UN reinforced its
image as an organization installing workshops around the world, with illustrations of experts and managers sitting around tables full of paperwork vis-à-vis
photographs of people at work: women operating switchboards, nurses, teachers,
farmers. The idea was that the UN's reports and resolutions did not gather dust
inside file cabinets, but rather translated into action on the ground—actions that,
however, appeared to consistently build a differential and trap the world into two
positionalities: that of a presumably aid-seeking global South and that of a global
North as vector of expertise, progress, and philanthropy. Specialized agencies
such as UNESCO, FAO, and WHO used those itinerant platforms for their outreach efforts, elevating them into techniques of world organization and development. They created international publics; they taught skills; and ultimately they
moved the values of liberal internationalism from one institution to the next.

The UN's physical interiors taught convening bodies how to exist and work
in the space of institutional multilateralism. They even dictated what a space of
multilateralism can be. In this sense, those physical interiors installed modalities
of diplomacy. But, at the same time, these did not go unchallenged. The emerging Non-Aligned Movement, a critical counterpublic inside the United Nations
Headquarters, appropriated those spaces and structures to lobby for an anti-
colonial vision of world organization. The UN General Assembly functioned as
the platform and the medium through which this coalition of member states col-
lectively pushed the body politic to protect the interest of smaller and newer
member states.[29] But from Bandung (1955) to Belgrade (1961) to Lusaka (1970),
this itinerant body of nonaligned member states reimagined the architectures of
assembly for a more equal, anti-colonial vision for world organization, even when
framed within the ideas of liberal representative democracies. Their criticisms of
the UN Security Council as a limiting and excluding organ extended to the architecture. Starting with the meeting in Belgrade, the Non-Aligned Movement challenged and enlarged the structure of the round table to bring on equal footing not
only a limited number of national governments, as was the case at the Security
Council, but all member states joining in (Figure E.6).[30] In more than one way
those physical interiors materialized another imagination of world order and revealed the power politics in effect (especially in the case of the Security Council),
hence challenging them and inviting their critique.

At the end of the day, the UN offered its itinerant platforms as instruments

Figure E.6. First summit of the Non-Aligned Movement in Belgrade, showing the expanded oval table at the center, 1961. Courtesy of the Museum of Yugoslavia.

of representational democracy and ways to bring the world community inside the spaces of international relations and diplomacy. These global interiors, the public front of the diplomatic habitat, worked as stages and platforms for a world elite, a means to produce internationalism on the level of government rather than people, built on a liberal investment in political representation. Inside the United Nations, this imagination produced international bureaucracies as communications and translation machines that extended far beyond their physical limits, often organizing themselves in networks, while holding onto a coherent image of institutional internationalism and world governance at the core. And while seemingly redundant, this image marked the United Nations as an ever-expanding, open-ended infrastructure of communication, rather than a resolute and absolute enforcer of policy.

There are, of course, all the ways that these itinerant interiors also failed. As stages they have often encouraged performative politics and diplomacy for domestic audiences. The transparency these global interiors promise tends to be more representational than literal, with backstage diplomacy in lobbies and lounges many a time determining negotiations and results. Peoples, the vast world community—the majority that the organization enjoys evoking in its published matter and public announcements—exist only as audiences for its circulation of expertise, technique, and know-how. The global interior is designed to speak, but has very limited capacity to listen, and even less so to act. And, of course, the very organizational structure of the United Nations limits the kind of democratic procedures that the global interior enables, with the unwieldy power of the permanent members of the Security Council actively undermining any attempts at a global democracy in the General Assembly. History tells us so. It may be time for a new architecture, one that allows for a democratic organization of society to center on the majority. And to realize this political horizontality on the scale of the world, as something that acts not just on our immediate surroundings but on a planetary level, we need to keep thinking, building, and expanding how we come together, how we assemble. Perhaps we can learn from this twentieth-century experiment in creating a global interior for international organization, reconsider the structural limits of a world ordered by nations tenuously united, and move together toward more just and open structures of assembly.

Acknowledgments

During my junior sabbatical year, reality caught up with me. I was writing my first book on an organization gargantuan in scale and with very little time on my hands. I needed all the help I could get and it arrived in all different forms and shapes. So, this is the space and time to tip my hat with enormous gratitude to all the people who supported me along the way, making the completion of this project possible.

First and foremost, I thank Antoine Picon, who gave me the opportunity of a lifetime when he offered me a place at the doctoral program at Harvard. He encouraged me to develop my own research agenda and historical approach, while offering crucial and sustained feedback throughout the initial phase of my research and writing. He cautioned against causal historical claims, challenging me to pay attention to the multitude of shifting vectors that shaped imaginaries of globality during the twentieth century. And when the time arrived, he gently pushed me out the door. Discussions with K. Michael Hays reconnected me with language and poetics at a moment when the bureaucratic language of the institution started taking over my own voice. A big thank-you also goes to Peter Galison, who not only decidedly changed the direction of my research when he pointed me toward World War II military research on sound and communications but also generously shared his words, thoughts, and criticisms on my work. His suggestion to stay with the United Nations in my historical examination of global spaces proved catalytic for the formation of this book. Mara Mills carefully read and commented on the entirety of my dissertation manuscript. An interdisciplinary scholar, she immediately grasped the crux of my argument, encouraging me to take on the question of global governance as a communications enterprise. Mara, I am eternally thankful.

Courses and lectures by Eve Blau, Margaret Crawford, Arindam Dutta, Mark Jarzombek, and Caroline Jones shaped my thinking on politics, governance, and space. For the opportunity to test my ideas in numerous conferences, panels, and classrooms, I am thankful to Jay Cephas, Aliki Economides, Neta Feniger, Anna

Flach, Dale Gyure, Jack Hartnell, Ayala Levin, Wanda Liebermann, Kevin Lotery, Jacqueline Maurer, Tyler Morgensten, John W. Ott, Sun-Young Park, Vassiliki Petridou, Melissa Renn, Timothy Rohan, Carsten Ruhl, Anooradha Iyer Siddiqi, and Ilkay Tanrisever. At the Buell Dissertation Colloquium at Columbia University, I articulated for the first time the idea of the book before a formidable crew of fellow historians of architecture—Gretta Tritch-Roman, Ginger Nolan, Ana María León, Shiben Banerji, Rafico Ruiz, Michael McCulloch, Moritz Gleich, Sam Dodd, and Catherine Boland Erkkila. The Architecture and Bureaucracy conference that Rika Devos, Fredie Floré, and Ricardo Costa Agarez co-organized motivated me to consider bureaucracy in tandem with the architecture of international organizations. Time at the Max-Planck-Institut für Wissenschaftsgeschichte and Viktoria Tkaczyk's research group Epistemes of Modern Acoustics helped me pin down the role that acoustics and communications played on these global platforms. Panayiota Pyla's invitation to the vibrant academic community at the University of Cyprus gave me time to complete my manuscript next to the UN Buffer Zone in Nicosia. Parts of the argument of this book have been fleshed out in two chapter-length essays in the edited volume *Architecture in Development: Systems and the Emergence of the Global South* (2022) edited by Arindam Dutta, Ateya Khorakiwala, Ayala Levin, Fabiola López-Durán, and Ijlal Muzaffar; and in Sven Sterken's and Dennis Pohl's fantastic special issue *The Architecture of Global Governance for Architectural Theory Review* (2023). The feedback I received during the editorial process was invaluable.

Jonathan Sterne, whose own groundbreaking work is an inspiration and a model of how scholars, in my opinion, should exist in the world, generously engaged me in conversations on the history of acoustic spaces. The late Leo L. Beranek answered questions and shared information on his work at the Psycho-Acoustic and Electro-Acoustic laboratories at Harvard, as well as his research on the acoustic design for the UN Headquarters. The work of Fred Turner, Barry Katz, and Mark Mazower has been in my mind throughout the process. Dr. Theodoros Radisoglou talked to me extensively about the archives of the International Military Tribunal in Nuremberg and sent me valuable secondary sources and brochures.

Quick, but significant for me, exchanges with Ed Eigen, Jacob Gaboury, John Harwood, Timothy Hyde, Daniel Immerwahr, Ben Kafka, Brian Kane, Paula Lupkin, Shannon Mattern, Linda Mulcahy, Dominique Rouillard, and Emily Thompson opened new questions and shifted my thinking on the role of media, art, and law in international bureaucracies. Bernard Dionysius Geoghegan gave crucial positive feedback on my last chapter at a moment of ambivalence about its place. John Durham Peters, who owed me nothing and whose mind operates on a different level altogether, read and commented on chapters 3 and 4. To all of you, I am grateful for your time and insights, but errors remain my own.

Archivists and librarians provided guidance and access to invaluable resources and documents. At the United Nations Archives and Records Management, Jill Annitto, Paola Casini, Wei-wen Chiang, Marvin Cordova, Seymour Edwards, Aleksandr Gelfand, Neshantha Karunanayake, Romain Ledauphin, Kathryn Lee, Amanda Leinberger, Corinne O'Connor, and Cheikh Ndiaye expertly guided me through mountains of documents, going above and beyond to unearth minutes, photographs, and drawings from the UN's collection. At Harvard, Mark Gerstel offered access to the closed library of the Psycho-Acoustic Laboratory; Cristina Prochilo, E. P. Jackson, and Maureen Jennings shared the drawings of the anechoic chamber in the UPO PIRC collection; and Mary Daniels and Inés Zalduendo at the Frances Loeb Library's Special Collections pointed to resources and connections I did not anticipate. Janet Parks and Jason Escalante provided valuable guidance to Max Abramovitz's and Wallace K. Harrison's architectural records and papers at the Avery Architectural and Fine Arts Library. For facilitating in-person visits I also thank Arnaud Dercelles at the Fondation Le Corbusier; the staff at the Rockefeller Archive Center; Lauren Alderton at the RIBA Drawings and Archives Collection; Christine Rosenlund at the Designmuseum Danmark; Frida Melin at ArkDes; Bente Solbakken at the Nasjonalmuseet for kunst, arkitektur og design; John Calhoun at the Billy Rose Theatre Division of the New York Public Library; Jacobine Wieringa at the Carnegie Foundation at The Hague; Cyril Emery at the Documentation Division and Library of the International Court of Justice; and Mary Caldera at the Yale University Manuscripts and Archives.

Gratitude also goes to the archivists who assisted me remotely: staff at the National Archives and Records Administration at College Park and at the New York City Municipal Library and Archives; Marc Brodsky at the Special Collections at Virginia Tech; Rodney Obien at Keene State College; Elisabeth Thomas at the MoMA Archives; librarians at the Special Collections Research Center at the University of Michigan; Randy Sowell at the Harry S. Truman Library; Jacques Oberson and Amanda Howland at the Library Research Center of the United Nations Office at Geneva; Nicole Westerdahl at the Special Collections Research Center at the Syracuse University Libraries; the inimitable Giota Pavlidou at the Constantinos A. Doxiadis Archives; Filine Wagner and Irina Davidovici at gta Archives; Stephen Van Dyk, Elizabeth Broman, and Emily M. Orr at the Cooper Hewitt Museum; Daniel Huws for permission to access and use Jaqueline Tyrwhitt's papers at RIBA; Dawn Stanford at the IBM Corporate Archives; Kristen McDonald at the Yale University Archives; and Brandon E. Barton at the UCLA Library Special Collections. Librarians at Bard saved the day more than once. Betsy Cawley, Billey Albina, and Melanie Mambo, I am in constant awe of your ability to scavenge rare articles and archival resources. The administrative support of Jeanette McDonald, who scanned endless pages of book chapters and articles throughout the years, made everything easy and possible.

A number of small private collections gave me an intimate view of the design work that went into the UN's initial platforms. Laurie Pasler, who is directing the Descendants Media Group, offered snippets into her father's collection; Jill Lundquist opened her home and gave me access to the papers of Oliver Lincoln Lundquist; and Donna Firer, Brian McLaughlin, and Katie Garber, generous hosts, allowed me in their attic during a raging pandemic to consult Donal McLaughlin's invaluable collection of interviews, minutes, and other memorabilia from the San Francisco Conference on International Organization.

In some cases, the building is the archive. Henrike Claussen took me on a backstage tour of Courtroom 600 while I was visiting Nuremberg. I had fascinating and productive conversations while touring the UN Headquarters with Michael Adlerstein, former Assistant Secretary General of the United Nations and executive director of the United Nations Capital Master Plan; Ginni Wiik of the Royal Norwegian Consulate General; and Jonathan Mishal, whose knowledge of the UN Headquarters and all its nooks and crannies is endless and who took me on an intimate and thorough tour that I will remember for years and that makes for a lot of bulletproof insider jokes.

The book was researched, written, and completed with the generous support of the Konstantinos Katseas Foundation; the Alexander S. Onassis Foundation; the Propondis Foundation; a Frederick Sheldon Fellowship; and a CCA Research Grant. The Bard Research Fund supported archival research in Scandinavia and the National Endowment for the Humanities gave me time and space to write the first chapter.

The number of conversations that informed this book are too many to mention, but some stand out. A passing comment by Kostis Kornetis on the history of third worldism sent me to dig deeper into the political history of multilateralism; Andreas Kalpacki introduced me to Paul Otlet's network sensibilities; Niko Vicario probed me to think about tables and the shape of diplomacy; Kahlila Chaar-Pérez pushed me to consider how my work speaks to fields outside architecture; Iris Moon suggested that I look at adaption of theaters for the National Assembly in postrevolutionary France; Isobel Roele, a true inspiration in her own right, pointed me to the structural (and structuring) nature of the distinction between the headquarters and the field; and David Theodore, dear friend and expert provocateur, challenged me to articulate the broadcast studio elements of the UN's designs. Research on acoustics and sound in architecture is growing, but when I started the community was tiny. Carlotta Daró, Shundana Yusaf, and Joseph Clarke made important conversations possible. I owe even more to Sabine von Fischer whose "acoustic argument" has been an inspiration and who brought me to the Max Planck. Sabine, thank you for all the fun our conspiring brought about in panels and special issues.

At the University of Minnesota Press, Pieter Martin expertly shepherded my book to production. His advice, kindness, and perspective have been invaluable.

I am in his debt for obtaining two excellent readers for my manuscript, whose comments greatly molded the form and language of the book. A big thank-you goes to Reinhold Martin, who welcomed this book to his series and offered critical comments on book chapters. At Minnesota, Anne Carter, Shelby Connelly, Rachel Moeller, and Laura Westlund approached my book with attention, care, and utmost professionalism. Jenn Kane masterfully dealt with copyright permissions, a task I dreaded. I would be in the wrong not to mention Jenny Gavacs, who guided me through the development of the manuscript, and Catherine Osborne, for her precise copyediting. Everything I know about prose and writing in English, I owe to the excellent staff at the MIT Writing Center. Marilyn Levine, Elizabeth Fox, and Bob Irwin, thank you!

I am particularly grateful for two writing groups. Katherine Boivin, the gem of a human I call my friend and peer, read every single page of this manuscript more than once. She is a master of structure and flow and one of the most careful readers I could have ever asked for. Maria Sonevytsky, a crucial interlocutor and dear friend, always offered plenty of food for thought, keeping big-picture arguments at the center of her razor-sharp feedback. I am so lucky to keep conversing with you. In a second writing group, Ateya Khorakiwala and Jay Cephas both read final drafts and offered critical feedback on how buildings get to enact politics. Hiba Bou Akar saved the day with sage advice when the book entered production, and Marcia Mihotich lent her design expertise for the book cover.

Teaching at Bard College has also shaped my writing. Special mention should go to my colleagues at the Sound Cluster that Laura Kunreuther organized and ran for years. Alex Benson, Matthew Deady, Danielle Riou, Whitney Slaten, Maria Sonevytsky, and Drew Thompson, I assure you that your comments and work found their way to my book. In the Art History and Visual Culture Program, I thank Susan Aberth, Anne Chen, Laurie Dahlberg, Patricia Karetzky, Alex Kitnick, Susan Merriam, Julia Rosenbaum, Heeryoon Shin, and Tom Wolf. I could not have asked for better colleagues. Nana Adusei-Poku, Myra Armstead, Karen Barkey, Laura Battle, Roger Berkowitz, Maria Sachiko Cecire, Christian Ayne Crouch, Ellen Driscoll, Elias Dueker, Kevin Duong, Jeannette Estruth, Tabetha Ewing, Miriam Felton-Dansky, Jackie Goss, Nora Jacobsen Ben Hammed, Sandi Hillal and Alessandro Petti, Kwame Holmes, Mie Inouye, Tom Keenan, Pinar Kemerli, Peter Klein, Cecile E. Kuznitz, Nicholas Lewis, Pete L'Official, Allison McKim, Leslie Melvin, Alys Moody, Greg Moynahan, Michelle Murray, Dina Ramadan, Jana Schmidt, Nate Shockey, Sophia Stamatopoulou-Robbins, Pelin Tan, Dominique Townsend, Eric Trudel, and Marina van Zuylen, you made Bard a better place. Ross Exo Adams and Ivonne Santoyo-Orozco, who arrived to launch the Architecture Program, created a community around the politics of space that was much needed.

A brilliant cohort of peers made research and writing a more rewarding adventure: Fallon Samuels Aidoo, Alejandra Azuero-Quijano, John R. Blankinger, Alex Bueno, Daniel Cardoso Llach, Peter Christensen, Christina Crawford, John Davis, Aliki Economides, Jacob Emery, Nacho Galan, Rania Ghosn, Matt Gin, Lisa Haber-Thomson, Jeanne Haffner, Max Hirsh, El Hadi Jazairy, Jordan Kaufman, Duks Koschitz, Michael Kubo, Matt Lasner, John Lopez, Jennifer Mack, Diana Martinez, Anna-Maria Meister, Elli Mosayebi, Brian Norwood, Yetunde Olaiya, Sun-Young Park, Petros Phokaides, Andrei Pop, Diana Ramirez, Enrique Ramirez, Rebecca Ross, Ivan Rupnik, Sebastian Schmidt, Peter Sealy, Dubravka Sekulić, Molly Wright Steenson, Irene Sunwoo, Zenovia Toloudi, Rebecca Uchill, Olivier Vallerand, Alla Vronskaya, Tijana Vujosevic, Eldra-Dominique Walker, Delia Duong Ba Wendel, and Mechtild Widrich, thank you for being part of this book's journey. In Cyprus, Popi Iacovou and Giorgos Artopoulos showed me around; in Paris, Sharon Kanach, Dimitris Mavridis, and Nikola Jankovic made my stay less lonely; and in Zurich, Elli Mosayebi, Marcel Bleuler, and Eleana Akrita offered much needed respite from work.

Friendship and camaraderie moved me forward, even when the task ahead seemed mission impossible. The Feminist Art and Architecture Collaborative taught me about friendship and intersectionality—thank you Ana María León, Tessa Paneth-Pollak, and Martina Tanga; and a second collective sustained me during the pandemic: Christina Crawford, Brian Goldstein, Jennifer Hock, Min Kyung Lee, Catalina Mejía Moreno, and Robin Schuldenfrei offered valuable support in the form of meaningful Zoom get-togethers.

Some people are just special. Jilly Traganou, getting to know you helped me make home out of New York; Emilie Lemakis, your lucky charm kept me safe and sound; Jason Nguyen, the "archives" might have moved, but a day has not passed; Stephanie Tuerk, we made stories happen and that was fun and real; Zeynep Oguz, seeing the world with you has been a lifetime adventure; and Theodora Vardouli, your big soft heart, wisdom, and openness, unmatched and unparalleled, helped me see that in this academic world of ours every voice matters, including ours. From the bottom of my heart, I would like to thank Mariana Mogilevich, the voice of logic and good sense, who guided my ignoramus younger self throughout uncharted territories of academic life. And Ateya Khorakiwala, you are my friend, the smartest person I know and a truly beautiful human, with whom I could talk forever.

My friends, my family—Anestis Touloumis, Stavroula Parnassou, and Ellie Touloumis, Evangelia Chatzikonstantinou, Emi Kitsali, Chrisa Kofti, Stella Pantelia, Domna Pardali, Paschalis Samarinis, Eleni Sgouridou, Efi Terzidou and Olga Terzidou—you turned every single trip into a small celebration, reminding me that there is life before and after the book (maybe even during). Eleftheria Zografou, Ourania Tsoukala, and Vana Tentokali, you are special to me.

I finished the writing of the book in the midst of the Covid-19 global pandemic. During that period of isolation, away from my family and friends, Alistair Bevington (1926–2021) and Christine Benglia Bevington (1937–2020) opened their home and accepted me as part of their family. Feeding the pigeons with Alistair and listening to Christine's stories grounded me emotionally and carried me through an otherwise horrendous period of loss.

Last, but not least, I thank Alexander Bevington, my best friend and, in all honesty, the best human I know. Your endless humor (delivered exactly how I like it, extra-dry), your delicious cooking, and your care nurtured me and kept me going. I could not have done this without you. Lucas Wilson-Bevington, you brought a lot of fun, and love, and adventures, although please let your dad beat you at chess from time to time. Our small family grew with Margot, the black half-rottweiler that passes as labrador and whose mischief made for a lot of laughter despite the occasional whining.

I dedicate this book to my parents, Effrosini Touloumi and Konstantinos Touloumis, who accepted and embraced my path regardless of how foreign to them it was. This project would not have been possible without the consistency of their presence, their acceptance, and their love. I hope that in publishing this book I am also returning something to you both.

Notes

Introduction

1. I am thankful to Vjeran Kursar for confirming this translation.

2. Slavenka Drakulić makes the case that Praljak used his directorial background to orchestrate a message for domestic audiences; see "Playing to the Audience: The Televised Suicide of Slobodan Praljak," *Eurozine,* December 12, 2017, https://www.eurozine.com/playing-to-the-audience-the-televised-suicide-of-slobodan-praljak.

3. The spatial presentation of justice as even-handed and uncontaminated was so important to the legitimacy of the proceedings that, according to Judge Lal Chand Vohrah, ICTY had to find a new space for the prosecution outside the Aegon Insurance Building that Courtroom One occupied. See L. C. Vohrah, "Some Insights into the Early Years," *Journal of International Criminal Justice* 2, no. 2 (June 1, 2004): 388–95.

4. Laura Kurgan, "Residues: ICTY Courtroom No. 1 and the Architecture of Justice," *Alphabet City Magazine* 7 (2001): 112–29.

5. Megan A. Black uses the metaphor of the "global interior" to underpin the imperialistic aspirations of the U.S. Department of Interior, particularly in relation to mineral extraction, in the post–World War II periods. See *The Global Interior: Mineral Frontiers and American Power* (Cambridge: Harvard University Press, 2018), 1–15.

6. For an intellectual history of world governance and the transition from empires to international institutions, see Mark Mazower, *Governing the World: The History of an Idea, 1815 to the Present* (New York: Penguin Books, 2013); Or Rosenboim, *The Emergence of Globalism: Visions of World Order in Britain and the United States 1939–1950* (Princeton: Princeton University Press, 2017); Guy Fiti Sinclair, *To Reform the World: International Organizations and the Making of Modern States* (Oxford: Oxford University Press, 2017); Adom Getachew, *Worldmaking after Empire: The Rise and Fall of Self-Determination* (Princeton: Princeton University Press, 2019); Quinn Slobodian, *Globalists: The End of Empire and the Birth of Neoliberalism* (Cambridge: Harvard University Press, 2018).

7. Cornelius Castoriadis, *The Imaginary Institution of Society,* trans. Kathleen Blamey (Cambridge: The MIT Press, 1998), 340–73.

8. Cornelius Castoriadis, "The Imaginary: Creation in the Social Historical Domain," in *World in Fragments: Writings on Politics, Society, Psychoanalysis, and the Imagination,* trans. David Ames Curtis (Stanford: Stanford University Press, 1997), 3–18.

9. "UN Site—Symbol of UN Job," in *United Nations World,* April 1947, Box 3, Folder 104, Avery Architecture and Fine Arts Library, Columbia University, New York City, New York (Avery).

10. Jane C. Loeffler and Ezra Stoller, *The United Nations* (New York: Princeton Architectural Press, 1999); Adam Bartos and Christopher Hitchens, *International Territory: The United Nations, 1945–95* (London: Verso, 1994); Aaron Betsky and Ben Murphy, *The U.N. Building* (London: Thames & Hudson, 2005), 10–28.

11. George A. Dudley, *A Workshop for Peace: Designing the United Nations Headquarters* (Cambridge: The Architectural History Foundation, MIT Press, 1994).

12. Stanislaus von Moos, *Le Corbusier: Elements of a Synthesis* (Cambridge: MIT Press, 1988), 248–51; Styliane Philippou, *Oscar Niemeyer: Curves of Irreverence* (New Haven: Yale University Press, 2008), 137–40; Aliki Economides, "Modern Savoir-Faire: Ernest Cormier, 'Architect and Engineer-Constructor,' and Architecture's Representational Constructions" (PhD diss., Harvard University, 2015), 308–27; Victoria Newhouse, *Wallace K. Harrison, Architect* (New York: Rizzoli, 1989), 104–43.

13. I am including here a selection of recent work and groundbreaking treatises that have informed my own perspective. See Anooradha Iyer Siddiqi and Rachel Lee, "On Margins: Feminist Architectural Histories of Migration," *ABE Journal* 16 (December 31, 2019); Naomi Stead, Janina Gosseye, and Deborah van der Plaat, *Speaking of Buildings: Oral History in Architectural Research* (New York: Princeton Architectural Press, 2019); Hélène Frichot, Catharina Gabrielsson, and Helen Runting, eds., *Architecture and Feminisms: Ecologies, Economies, Technologies* (London: Routledge, 2018); Mary Pepchinski, *Frau Architekt: seit mehr als 100 Jahren: Frauen im Architektenberuf [Over 100 years of women as professional architects]* (Tübingen: Wasmuth, 2017); Feminist Art and Architecture Collaborative, "Counterplanning from the Classroom," *Journal of the Society of Architectural Historians* 76, no. 3 (September 2017): 277–80; Alice T. Friedman, *Women and the Making of the Modern House: A Social and Architectural History* (New York: Harry N. Abrams, 2009); Diana Agrest, Patricia Conway, and Leslie Weisman, *The Sex of Architecture* (New York: Harry N. Abrams, 1996); Dolores Hayden, *The Grand Domestic Revolution: A History of Feminist Designs for American Homes, Neighborhoods, and Cities* (Cambridge: MIT Press, 1981).

14. Henry-Russell Hitchcock and Arthur Drexler, eds., *Built in USA: Post-War Architecture* (New York: Museum of Modern Art, 1952), 22–23.

15. Reyner Banham, *The Architecture of the Well-Tempered Environment* (London: Architectural Press, 1969), 221–23; Alexandra Quantrill, "The Aesthetics of Precision: Environmental Management and Technique in the Architecture of Enclosure, 1946–1986" (PhD diss., Columbia University, 2017), 26–76; Joseph M. Siry, *Air-Conditioning in Modern American Architecture, 1890–1970* (State College: Pennsylvania State University Press, 2021).

16. Rem Koolhaas, *Delirious New York: A Retroactive Manifesto for Manhattan* (New York: Monacelli Press, 1994).

17. Ada Louise Huxtable, *Four Walking Tours of Modern Architecture in New York City* (New York: Museum of Modern Art, 1958), 54–56.

18. William J. R. Curtis, *Modern Architecture since 1900* (London: Phaidon, 1982), 267; Marvin Trachtenberg and Isabelle Hyman, *Architecture: From Prehistory to Postmodernity*, 2nd ed. (Saddle River, N.J.: Prentice Hall, Inc., 2003), 517; Manfredo Tafuri and Francesco Dal Co, *Modern Architecture: History of World Architecture*, trans. Robert Erich Wolf (New York: Electa/Rizzoli, 1986), 2:317; Peter Gössel and Gabriele Leuthäuser, *Architecture in the Twentieth Century* (Köln: Taschen, 2005), 225; Jean-Louis Cohen, *The Future of Architecture, Since 1889* (London: Phaidon, 2012), 338. More recently, Mark Crinson critically

placed the UN and its Headquarters within a larger history of internationalist projects that span from Otto Neurath's visual language to the anti-colonial visions of the Indian *Marg Magazine.* Crinson asks us to consider internationalism as a design imperative that mobilized modern architects across continents and political contexts. See *Rebuilding Babel: Modern Architecture and Internationalism* (London: I. B. Tauris, 2017).

19. Lewis Mumford, "UN Model and Model UN," "A Disoriented Symbol," and "Buildings as Symbols," in *From the Ground Up: Observations On Contemporary Architecture, Housing, Highway Building, And Civic Design* (Orlando: Harcourt Brace Jovanovich, 1956).

20. Giedion's criticism stems from a partisan devotion to Le Corbusier, who enlisted him to convince Harrison to keep him. See Sigfried Giedion, *Space, Time and Architecture: The Growth of a New Tradition,* 5th ed. (Cambridge: Harvard University Press, 1967), 532, 564–65, 685.

21. Samuel Zipp, *Manhattan Projects: The Rise and Fall of Urban Renewal in Cold War New York* (Oxford: Oxford University Press, 2012), 33–72; Robert A. M. Stern, Thomas Mellins, and David Fishman, *New York 1960: Architecture and Urbanism between the Second World War and the Bicentennial* (New York: Monacelli Press, 1997), 601–40; Linda Sue Phipps, "Constructing the United Nations Headquarters: Modern Architecture as Public Diplomacy" (PhD diss., Harvard University, 1998); Charlene Mires, *Capital of the World: The Race to Host the United Nations* (New York: New York University Press, 2015), 194–218; Jessica Field, "United Nations Headquarters, New York: The Cultural-Political Economy of Space and Iconicity," *Journal of History and Cultures* 1 (2012): 19–36.

22. For example, see Samuel Isenstadt, "'Faith in a Better Future': Josep Lluis Sert's American Embassy in Baghdad," *Journal of Architectural Education (1984-)* 50, no. 3 (1997): 172–88; Elizabeth Gill Lui, Keya Keita, and Jane C. Loeffler, *Building Diplomacy* (Los Angeles: Four Stops Press, 2004); Cammie McAtee, "All-over inside-out: Eero Saarinen's United States Embassy in London," in *The Politics of Furniture: Identity, Diplomacy and Persuasion in Post-War Interiors,* ed. Fredie Floré and Cammie McAtee (London: Routledge, 2017).

23. Jane Loeffler has offered a monumental account of the program-building embassies in *The Architecture of Diplomacy: Building America's Embassies* (Princeton: Princeton Architectural Press, 1998). The U.S. Pavilion curators for the 2014 Venice Biennale offer a similar argument through an extensive look at the global outreach of U.S. architectural offices; see Eva Franch i Gilabert, et al., eds., *OfficeUS: Atlas* (Zürich: Lars Müller Publishers, 2015).

24. See Reinhold Martin, *The Organizational Complex: Architecture, Media, and Corporate Space* (Cambridge: MIT Press, 2005); John Harwood, *The Interface: IBM and the Transformation of Corporate Design, 1945–1976* (Minneapolis: University of Minnesota Press, 2011).

25. Lucia Allais, *Designs of Destruction: The Making of Monuments in the Twentieth Century* (Chicago: University of Chicago Press, 2018); Felicity D. Scott, *Outlaw Territories: Environments of Insecurity/Architectures of Counterinsurgency* (Cambridge: Zone Books, 2016); M. Ijlal Muzaffar, "The Periphery Within: Modern Architecture and the Making of the Third World" (PhD diss., Massachusetts Institute of Technology, 2007); Lukasz Stanek, *Architecture in Global Socialism: Eastern Europe, West Africa, and the Middle East in the Cold War* (Princeton: Princeton University Press, 2020); Aggregate (Group), *Architecture in Development: Systems and the Emergence of the Global South* (London: Routledge, 2022).

26. Fredie Floré and Cammie D. McAtee, eds., *The Politics of Furniture: Identity, Diplomacy and Persuasion in Post-War Interiors* (London: Routledge, 2017), 1–11.

27. Most specifically on the kitchen debate, see Greg Castillo, *Cold War on the Home Front: The Soft Power of Midcentury Design* (Minneapolis: University of Minnesota Press, 2010); Beatriz Colomina, "Enclosed by Images: The Eameses' Multimedia Architecture," *Grey Room,* no. 2 (2001): 7–29.

28. Castillo, *Cold War on the Home Front;* Gay McDonald, "Selling the American Dream: MoMA, Industrial Design and Post-War France," *Journal of Design History* 17, no. 4 (2004): 397–412.

29. Iris Moon, *The Architecture of Percier and Fontaine and the Struggle for Sovereignty in Revolutionary France* (London: Routledge, 2016); Joseph Berger, "Still No Place in New York for Qaddafi's Tent," *The New York Times,* September 23, 2009.

30. Iris Moon, "Occupation, Interior Decoration and the Tent at Napoleon's First Official Residence, Malmaison," 33rd Annual NESAH Student Symposium, Cambridge, Massachusetts, January 20, 2011.

31. For a nuanced reading of this conflation of interiority and interiors see Charles Rice, *The Emergence of the Interior: Architecture, Modernity, Domesticity* (London: Routledge, 2007); Beate Söntgen and Ewa Lajer-Burcharth, *Interiors and Interiority* (Berlin: De Gruyter, 2016); Diana Fuss, *Sense of an Interior: Four Rooms and the Writers That Shaped Them* (London: Routledge, 2004).

32. Peter Galison and Emily Ann Thompson, *The Architecture of Science* (Cambridge: MIT Press, 1999); Robin Evans, *The Fabrication of Virtue: English Prison Architecture, 1750–1840* (New York: Cambridge University Press, 1982); Susie McKellar and Penny Sparke, eds., *Interior Design and Identity* (Manchester: Manchester University Press, 2004); Michel Foucault, *The Birth of the Clinic: An Archaeology of Medical Perception,* trans. Alan Sheridan (London: Routledge, 1994); Michel Foucault, *Discipline and Punish. The Birth of the Prison,* trans. Alan Sheridan (New York: Vintage Books, 1977); Mark Pimlott, *The Public Interior as Idea and Project* (Heijningen, Netherlands: Jap Sam Books, 2016), 10–11.

33. Peter Sloterdijk, *In the World Interior of Capital: For a Philosophical Theory of Globalization,* trans. Wieland Hoban (Cambridge: Polity, 2017), 6.

34. To discuss the limitations of democratic models, Sloterdijk points to the National Assembly in revolutionary France, when the representatives of the Third Estate attempted to bring the revolt into spaces of governance, taking over and renaming venues of the ancient regime. He identifies the moment of the Festival of the Federation, the massive celebration of the Storming of the Bastille, as a moment of realization of the tragedy of assembling. See Peter Sloterdijk, *Spheres. Volume 3, Foams: Plural Spherology* (South Pasadena, Calif.: Semiotext(e), 2016), 567–83, 608–9.

35. Paul N. Edwards, *The Closed World* (Cambridge: MIT Press, 1996); Lydia Kallipoliti, *The Architecture of Closed Worlds* (Zürich: Lars Müller, 2018); Andrea Vesentini, *Indoor America: The Interior Landscape of Postwar Suburbia* (Charlottesville: University of Virginia Press, 2018).

36. For a discussion of the focus on the "democratic personality" in cultural production in the United States, see Fred Turner, *The Democratic Surround: Multimedia and American Liberalism from World War II to the Psychedelic Sixties* (Chicago: University of Chicago Press, 2013), 39–76.

37. Hannah Arendt, *The Human Condition* (Chicago: University of Chicago Press, 1958).

38. For a comparative analysis of the Arendt, Habermas, and Rawls conceptualizations of the public sphere see Seyla Benhabib, "The Embattled Public Sphere: Hannah

Arendt, Juergen Habermas and Beyond," *Theoria: A Journal of Social and Political Theory*, no. 90 (1997): 1–24.

39. Nancy Fraser, "Rethinking the Public Sphere: A Contribution to the Critique of Actually Existing Democracy," *Social Text* 25/26 (1990): 56–80.

40. See Alexander John Watson, *Marginal Man: The Dark Vision of Harold Innis* (Toronto: University of Toronto Press, 2006).

41. Harold Adams Innis, *Empire and Communications* (Toronto: Dundurn Press, 2008), 21–32, 138–63; Harold A. Innis, *The Bias of Communication* (Toronto: University of Toronto Press, 1951).

42. Erkki Huhtamo and Jussi Parikka, eds., *Media Archaeology: Approaches, Applications, and Implications* (Berkeley: University of California Press, 2011), 1–21.

43. Dwayne R. Winseck and Robert M. Pike, *Communication and Empire: Media, Markets, and Globalization, 1860–1930* (Durham: Duke University Press, 2007).

44. Nicole Starosielski, *The Undersea Network* (Durham: Duke University Press, 2015).

45. Lisa Parks, *Cultures in Orbit: Satellites and the Televisual* (Durham: Duke University Press, 2005).

46. Karl W. Deutsch, *The Nerves of Government: Models of Political Communication and Control* (New York: Free Press of Glencoe, 1963), 27.

47. I use here Agatha C. Hughes and Thomas P. Hughes, *Systems, Experts, and Computers: The Systems Approach in Management and Engineering, World War II and After* (Cambridge: MIT Press, 2000); Jennifer S. Light, *From Warfare to Welfare* (Baltimore: Johns Hopkins University Press, 2003).

48. W. Boyd Rayward, ed., *European Modernism and the Information Society: Informing the Present, Understanding the Past* (London: Routledge, 2017).

49. Peter Galison, "Aufbau/Bauhaus: Logical Positivism and Architectural Modernism," *Critical Inquiry* 16, no. 4 (Summer 1990): 709–52; Peter Galison and David J. Stump, eds., *The Disunity of Science: Boundaries, Contexts, and Power* (Stanford: Stanford University Press, 2001), 1–36; Mazower, *Governing the World*, 94–115.

50. For some examples see Nader Vossoughian, *Otto Neurath: The Language of the Global Polis* (Rotterdam: NAi, 2011); Markus Krajewski, *World Projects: Global Information before World War I*, trans. Charles Marcrum (Minneapolis: University of Minnesota Press, 2015); William Rankin, *After the Map: Cartography, Navigation, and the Transformation of Territory in the Twentieth Century* (Chicago: University of Chicago Press, 2016).

51. Jonas Brendebach, Martin Herzer, and Heidi J. S. Tworek, eds., *International Organizations and the Media in the Nineteenth and Twentieth Centuries: Exorbitant Expectations* (London: Routledge, 2018), 1–16.

52. Rosenboim, *The Emergence of Globalism*, 45.

53. Susan Buck-Morss, "A Global Public Sphere?," *Radical Philosophy* (blog), February 2002, https://www.radicalphilosophy.com/commentary/a-global-public-sphere; Mary Kaldor, "The Idea of Global Civil Society," *International Affairs (Royal Institute of International Affairs 1944-)* 79, no. 3 (2003): 583–93; Manuel Castells, "The New Public Sphere: Global Civil Society, Communication Networks, and Global Governance," *The Annals of the American Academy of Political and Social Science* 616 (March 2008): 78–93; Ingrid Volkmer, *The Global Public Sphere: Public Communication in the Age of Reflective Interdependence* (Cambridge: Polity, 2014).

54. Castells, "The New Public Sphere: Global Civil Society, Communication Networks, and Global Governance," 91.

55. Danielle Allen, "Reconceiving Public Spheres: The Flow Dynamics Model," in *From Voice to Influence: Understanding Citizenship in a Digital Age,* ed. Danielle S. Allen and Jennifer S. Light (Chicago: University of Chicago Press, 2015), 178–208.

56. Arjun Appadurai, *Modernity At Large: Cultural Dimensions of Globalization* (Minneapolis: University of Minnesota Press, 1996), 32–36.

57. Pierre Bourdieu, *Distinction: A Social Critique of the Judgment of Taste* (Cambridge: Harvard University Press, 1984), 170.

58. Brian R. Jacobson, *Studios Before the System: Architecture, Technology, and the Emergence of Cinematic Space* (New York: Columbia University Press, 2015); Brian R. Jacobson, *In the Studio: Visual Creation and Its Material Environments* (Oakland: University of California Press, 2020); Susan Schmidt Horning, *Chasing Sound: Technology, Culture & the Art of Studio Recording from Edison to the LP* (Baltimore: Johns Hopkins University Press, 2013); Shundana Yusaf, *Broadcasting Buildings: Architecture on the Wireless, 1927–1945* (Cambridge: MIT Press, 2014); Lynn Spigel, *TV by Design: Modern Art and the Rise of Network Television* (Chicago: University of Chicago Press, 2008), 110–43.

59. Kate Lacey, *Listening Publics: The Politics and Experience of Listening in the Media Age* (Cambridge: Polity, 2013), 7.

60. Carolyn Birdsall, *Nazi Soundscapes: Sound, Technology and Urban Space during Nazi Germany* (Amsterdam: Amsterdam University Press, 2012).

61. Turner, *The Democratic Surround,* 2–5, 39–76.

62. Emily Ann Thompson, *The Soundscape of Modernity: Architectural Acoustics and the Culture of Listening in America, 1900–1933* (Cambridge: MIT Press, 2002); Joseph L. Clarke, *Echo's Chambers: Architecture and the Idea of Acoustic Space* (Pittsburgh: University of Pittsburgh Press, 2021).

63. I have previously argued this point in Olga Touloumi, "Sound in Silence: Design and Listening Cultures in the Woodberry Poetry Room," *The Journal of Architecture* 23, no. 6 (2018): 1003–29; and Sabine von Fischer and Olga Touloumi, "Sound Modernities: Histories of Media and Modern Architecture," *The Journal of Architecture* 23, no. 6 (2018): 873–80.

64. Steven Feld, "Acoustemology," in *Keywords in Sound,* ed. David Novak and Matt Sakakeeny (Durham: Duke University Press, 2015), 112–24.

65. Timothy Hyde, "The Building Site, Redux," *Journal of Architectural Education* 75, no. 1 (January 2, 2021): 84–93.

66. Pierre Bourdieu, "Site Effects," in *The Weight of the World: Social Suffering and Impoverishment,* trans. Priscilla Parkhurst Ferguson (Cambridge: Polity Press, 1999), 123–29.

67. See for example Glenda Sluga, *The Invention of International Order: Remaking Europe after Napoleon* (Princeton: Princeton University Press, 2021); Stella Ghervas, *Conquering Peace: From the Enlightenment to the European Union* (Cambridge: Harvard University Press, 2021).

68. Bob Duynstee, et al., *The Building of Peace: A Hundred Years of Work on Peace through Law: The Peace Palace, 1913–2013* (Amsterdam: Carnegie Foundation, 2013), 50–77; Arthur Eyffinger, *The Peace Palace: Residence for Justice, Domicile of Learning* (The Hague: Carnegie Foundation, 1992); Diana Palazova-Lebleu, "La place de Louis-Marie et Louis-Stanislas Cordonnier dans les évolutions architecturales et urbanistiques en Europe septentrionale, 1881–1940" (PhD diss., Lille, Université de Lille 3—Charles de Gaulle, 2009).

69. Shiben Banerji, *Lineages of the Global City: Occult Modernism and the Spiritualization of Democracy* (Austin: University of Texas Press, forthcoming).

70. Sonne, *Representing the State,* 242, citing Otto Antonia Graf, *Die vergessene Wagner-schule* (Vienna, 1969), 31.

71. Sonne, *Representing the State,* 255; Wouter Van Acker and Geert Somsen, "A Tale of Two World Capitals: The Internationalisms of Pieter Eijkman and Paul Otlet," *Revue Belge de Philologie et d'Histoire* 90, no. 4 (2012): 1389–1409.

72. Koos Bosma, "World Centre of Communication 1912," in *Mastering the City: North-European City Planning 1900–2000* (Rotterdam: NAi Publishers, 1998), 176–83.

73. Hendrik Christian Andersen et al., *Creation of a World Centre of Communication* (Paris: Philippe Renouard, 1913), 1: 13–97.

74. Anna Ciotta, *La cultura della comunicazione nel piano del Centro mondiale di Hendrik Ch. Andersen e di Ernest M. Hébrard* (Milan, Italy: FrancoAngeli, 2011).

75. See, for example, Andersen, *Creation of a World Centre of Communication,* 1: 6–9.

76. See also A. E. Richardson, "A Capitol for the League of Nations," *The Architects' Journal* 49 (March 26, 1919): 183–85; and several articles in *The Architectural Review* 46 (December 1919): Patrick Abercrombie, "Planning a City for the League of Nations," 151–54; Major H. Barnes, "Messrs. Andersen and Hébrard's Scheme," 138; Sir Aston Webb, "A World Centre: The Home for the League of Nations: A Suggestion," 135–36; Robert Cecil, "The League of Peace as a Living Organism," 133–34.

77. Society of Beaux-Arts Architects, "Official Notification of Awards, Judgment of November 24, 1919, Final Competition for the 12th Paris Prize of the Society of Beaux-Arts Architects," *The American Architect* 117 (January 28, 1920): 117–20; G.L., "Le Grand Prix de Rome d'architecture," *L'Architecture* 32 (1919): 722–26.

78. Architectural Competition for the Erection of a League of Nations Building at Geneva, Report of the Jury, May 23, 1927, C 239 M 97 1927, R1537, League of Nations Archives, United Nations Office in Geneva (UNOG), Geneva.

79. John Ritter, "World Parliament: The League of Nations Competition, 1926," *Architectural Review* 136 (July 1964): 17–24; Kenneth Frampton, "The League of Nations, the Centrosoyus and the Palace of the Soviets, 1926–31," *Architectural Design* 55, no. 7–8 (n.d.): 41–55; Moos, *Le Corbusier.*

80. Sabine von Fischer, "Debating Volume: Architectural Versus Electrical Amplification in the League of Nations, 1926–28," *The Journal of Architecture* 23, no. 6 (2018): 904–35.

81. F. M. Osswald, "The Acoustics of the Large Assembly Hall of the League of Nations, at Geneva, Switzerland," *The American Architect* 134 (December 20, 1928): 833–42.

82. Hannes Meyer, "The New World (1926)," in *The Weimar Republic Sourcebook,* ed. Anton Kaes, Martin Jay, and Edward Dimendberg (Berkeley: University of California Press, 1994), 446–48.

83. Meyer, "The New World (1926)," 447.

84. Pallas, *Histoire et architecture du Palais des Nations,* 54–60; Kenneth Frampton, "The Humanist v. the Utilitarian Ideal," *Architectural Design* 38 (March 1968): 134–36; Dennis Sharp, "Architectural Competitions: A Watershed between Old and New" and Kenneth Frampton, "Le Corbusier at Geneva: The Debacle of the Société des Nations," both in *Architects in Competition: International Architectural Competitions of the Last 200 Years,* ed. Hilde de Haan and Ids Haagsma (London: Thames and Hudson, 1988), 181–91, 193–203.

85. Pallas, *Histoire et architecture du Palais des Nations,* 89–93.

86. A. Louvet, "Projets de quelques architectes français ayant pris part au concours pour le Palais de La Société des Nations à Genève," *L'Architecture. Revue mensuelle de la corporation des architectes publiée par la société centrale des architectes* 41, no. 11 (November 15, 1928): 359–70; "The British Designs at Geneva," *The Architect & Building News,* December 9, 1927, 881–87.

87. Alex Wright, *Cataloguing the World: Paul Otlet and the Birth of Information Age* (New York: Oxford University Press, 2014); Françoise Levie and Benoît Peeters, *L'homme qui voulait classer le monde. Paul Otlet et le Mundaneum* (Bruxelles: Impressions nouvelles, 2006); Wouter van Acker, "La remédiation de la connaissance encyclopédique," and Charles van den Heuvel, "Paul Otlet et les versions historiques de la genèse du World Wide Web, du web sémantique et du web 2.0," both in *Paul Otlet, Fondateur du Mundaneum (1868–1944): architecte du savoir, artisan de paix,* ed. Jacques Gillen, Stéphanie Manfroid, and Raphaèle Cornille (Brussels: Impressions nouvelles, 2010), 177–198, 159–75.

88. Otlet, *Mundaneum,* 3.

89. Otlet, *Mundaneum,* 30–40.

90. See, for example, P.V., "Le Palais de La Société Des Nations: Architectes Nenot et Flegenheimer, Broggi, Lefevre et J. Vago," *L'Architecture d'aujourd'hui* 10 (May 1939): 3–5.

91. Howard Robertson, "The League of Nations Buildings, Geneva," *The Architect & Building News* 149 (January 22, 1937): 118–21.

92. Robertson, "The League of Nations Buildings," 121.

93. Jean-Louis Cohen, *Architecture in Uniform: Designing and Building for the Second World War* (New Haven: Yale University Press, 2011).

1. Staging the World

1. Sabina Ferhadbegović, Kerstin von Lingen, and Julia Eichenberg, "The United Nations War Crimes Commission (UNWCC), 1943–1948, and the Codification of International Criminal Law: An Introduction to the Special Issue," *Journal of the History of International Law / Revue d'histoire Du Droit International* 24, no. 3 (2022): 305–14, https://doi .org/10.1163/15718050-12340208; Julia Eichenberg, "Crossroads in London on the Road to Nuremberg: The London International Assembly, Exile Governments and War Crimes," *Journal of the History of International Law / Revue d'histoire Du Droit International* 24, no. 3 (2022): 334–53, https://doi.org/10.1163/15718050-bja10071.

2. Letter from Edward Stettinius to General William J. Donovan, January 10, 1945, Oliver Lincoln Lundquist Papers (Lundquist Papers), Bard College, New York.

3. Letter to H. C. Barton Jr and Donal McLaughlin, February 26, 1945, Donal McLaughlin Papers and Estate (McLaughlin Papers), Takoma Park, Maryland.

4. On the beginnings of OSS, see Barry Katz, *Foreign Intelligence: Research and Analysis in the Office of Strategic Services, 1942–1945* (Cambridge: Harvard University Press, 1989), 1–28; Jennifer Davis Heaps, "Tracking Intelligence Information: The Office of Strategic Services," *The American Archivist* 61, no. 2 (1998): 287–308; Bradley F. Smith, *The Shadow Warriors: O.S.S. and the Origins of the C.I.A.* (London: Deutsch, 1983).

5. Letter from Donal McLaughlin to Dorwin Teague, February 12, 1999, McLaughlin Papers.

6. Barry Katz, "The Arts of War: 'Visual Presentation' and National Intelligence," *Design Issues* 12, no. 2 (1996): 3–21.

7. Julia Moszkowicz, "Gestalt and Graphic Design: An Exploration of the Humanistic

and Therapeutic Effects of Visual Organization," *Design Issues* 27, no. 4 (2011): 56–67; Zeynep Çelik Alexander, *Kinaesthetic Knowing: Aesthetics, Epistemology, Modern Design* (Chicago: University of Chicago Press, 2018), 167–202; Frederic J. Schwartz, *The Werkbund: Design Theory and Mass Culture before the First World War* (New Haven: Yale University Press, 1996), 96–105.

8. Nader Vossoughian, *Otto Neurath: The Language of the Global Polis* (Rotterdam: NAi, 2011); Eve Blau, "Isotype and Architecture in Red Vienna: The Modern Projects of Otto Neurath and Josef Frank," *Austrian Studies* 14 (2006): 227–59; Wim Jansen, "Neurath, Arntz and ISOTYPE: The Legacy in Art Design and Statistics," *Journal of Design History* 22, no. 3 (2009): 227–42; Whitney Battle-Baptiste and Britt Rusert, eds., *W. E. B. Du Bois's Data Portraits: Visualizing Black America; The Color Line at the Turn of the Twentieth Century* (Hudson, N.Y.: Princeton Architectural Press, 2018).

9. Mark Corrinet, Interview with Donal McLaughlin, December 11, 1993, McLaughlin Papers.

10. Alger Hiss and Oliver Lundquist, "Conference—Stage Arrangements," March 30, 1945, Jo Mielziner Papers, Box 81, Folder 1, Billy Rose Theatre Division, The New York Public Library for the Performing Arts (NYPL), New York, New York.

11. Oliver Lundquist, "Visual Presentation 1941–1945," September 2004, Lundquist Papers.

12. Carl Marzani, *The Education of a Reluctant Radical: From Pentagon to Penitentiary*, (New York: Topical Books, 1995), 4: 87.

13. Letter from Donal McLaughlin to Carl Marzani, July 14, 1993, McLaughlin Papers.

14. "Brian McLaughlin interviews father, Donal McLaughlin Jr," September 25, 1984, McLaughlin Papers.

15. Autobiographical Notes of Donal McLaughlin, March 23, 1991, McLaughlin Papers.

16. Mark Corrinet, Interview with Donal McLaughlin, December 11, 1993, McLaughlin Papers.

17. United States Congress Senate Committee on the Judiciary, *Activities of United States Citizens Employed by the United Nations: Hearings Before the Subcommittee to Investigate the Administration of the Internal Security Act and Other Internal Security Laws of the Committee on the Judiciary, United States Senate, Eighty-Second Congress, Second Session [Eighty-Third Congress, First-Second Session]* (U.S. Government Printing Office, 1952), 150–51.

18. Letter from Ed Stettinius to Richard Wilson, April 17, 1945, Lundquist Papers.

19. The team also joined Ivan Spear, Jack Becker, David M. Flax, Marty Vaill, and Richard Opfar. See OSS Presentation Branch Production Meetings, 28 March–16 April 1945, McLaughlin Papers.

20. Carl Marzani, manuscript narrative, p. 127, McLaughlin Papers.

21. For a discussion of the memorial complex, see Leta Miller, "Opera as Politics: The Troubled History of San Francisco's War Memorial Opera House," *California History* 92, no. 4 (2015): 4–23.

22. United Nations Conference on International Organization, ed., *Guide: The United Nations Conference on International Organization, San Francisco, 1945* (Washington, D.C.: U.S. Government Printing Office, 1945).

23. OSS Presentation Branch Production Meetings, 28 March–16 April 1945, McLaughlin Papers.

24. Walter Winchell, "In San Francisco," *NY Daily Mirror,* April 25, 1945.

25. Oliver Lundquist, "A Memoir of World War II," September 2004, Lundquist Papers.

26. Mark Corrinet, Interview with Donal McLaughlin, December 11, 1993, McLaughlin Papers.

27. Letter from Oliver Lundquist to William vanden Heuvel, November 5, 2003, Lundquist Papers; James S. Sutterlin, Interview with Oliver Lundquist, Transcript (UN, April 19, 1990), http://digitallibrary.un.org/record/485024.

28. Office of Strategic Services, Dumbarton Oaks Proposal, January 1945, Lundquist Papers.

29. Melva Trevor, "Visual Aid for Delegates: Conference Progress in Charts, Maps," *San Francisco Chronicle,* May 27, 1945.

30. Letter from Oliver Lundquist to William vanden Heuvel, November 15, 2003, Lundquist Papers.

31. The United Nations Conference on International Organization, "Proposed Organization & Functions," April 11, 1945, RG226 S85 Box 17 Folder 300, National Archives and Records Administration (NARA), College Park, Maryland.

32. See, for example, letter from Elizabeth Armstrong to Oliver Lundquist, May 31, 1945, Lundquist Papers.

33. Mark Corrinet, Interview with Donal McLaughlin, December 11, 1993, McLaughlin Papers.

34. Perry Biddiscombe, "Branding the United Nations: The Adoption of the UN Insignia and Flag, 1941–1950," *The International History Review* 42, no. 1 (January 2, 2020): 21–30.

35. Donal McLaughlin, "Design for Peace: Origin of the UN Emblem," *UN Chronicle* 32, no. 3 (September 1995); Donal McLaughlin, *Origin of the Emblem and Other Recollections of the 1945 UN Conference,* ed. Jennifer Truran Rothwell, 1995, 4–6.

36. Mark Corrinet, Interview with Donal McLaughlin, December 11, 1993, McLaughlin Papers.

37. Alger Hiss and Oliver Lundquist, "Conference—Stage Arrangements," March 30, 1945, Jo Mielziner Papers, Box 81, Folder 1, NYPL.

38. Oliver Lundquist, "A Memoir of World War II," September 2004, Lundquist Papers. For a history of Dazian's Theatricals company, see Timothy R. White, "'A Factory for Making Plays': Broadway's Industrial District," in *Blue-Collar Broadway: The Craft and Industry of American Theater* (Philadelphia: University of Pennsylvania Press, 2015), 35–63.

39. Oliver Lundquist, "A Memoir of World War II," September 2004, Lundquist Papers.

40. Lundquist recalls Hu Barton extending an invitation to Jo Mielziner in a letter to Mary Henderson, April 22, 2001, Lundquist Papers. For the appointment contract see Office of Strategic Services, Jo Mielziner Expected Appointment, March 24, 1945, Jo Mielziner Papers, Box 81, Folder 1, NYPL.

41. For Mielziner's work at the camouflage corps and OSS during World War II, see Mary C. Henderson and New York Public Library, *Mielziner: Master of Modern Stage Design* (New York: Back Stage Books, 2001), 132–35, 146–48; Sonja Dümpelmann, *Flights of Imagination: Aviation, Landscape, Design* (Charlottesville: University of Virginia Press, 2014), 153–207; Hanna Rose Shell, *Hide and Seek: Camouflage, Photography, and the Media of Reconnaissance* (Cambridge: MIT Press, 2012), 77–126.

42. Henderson and New York Public Library, *Mielziner,* 147–48.

43. Oliver Lundquist, scrapbook, n.d., Lundquist Papers.

44. Specifications for Covering, April 13, 1945, Jo Mielziner Papers, Box 81, Folder 1, NYPL.

45. Letter from Jo Mielziner to George Gebhardt, April 12, 1945, Jo Mielziner Papers, Box 81, Folder 1, NYPL.

46. Mielziner articulated his modern theater theory during the Ford Foundation workshop The Ideal Theater. See Jo Mielziner, *The Shapes of Our Theatre,* ed. C. Ray Smith (New York: Clarkson N. Potter, 1970), 14–40.

47. Cited in Harry W. Smith, "An Air of the Dream: Jo Mielziner, Innovation, and Influence, 1935–1955," *Journal of American Drama and Theater* 5, no. 3 (Fall 1993): 53.

48. Letter from Marie to Jo Mielziner, July 28, 1945, Jo Mielziner Papers, Box 81, Folder 1, NYPL.

49. McLaughlin, *Origin of the Emblem,* 8.

50. "Liaison Officer's Agenda for Signing Ceremony (To Accompany Floor Plan and Photograph)," Lundquist Papers.

51. Mark Corrinet, Interview with Donal McLaughlin, December 11, 1993, McLaughlin Papers.

52. Robert O'Brien, "San Francisco," n.d., McLaughlin Papers.

53. Lawrence E. Davies, "Nation After Nation Sees Era of Peace in Signing Charter," *The New York Times,* June 27, 1945.

54. Mark Corrinet, Interview with Donal McLaughlin, December 11, 1993, McLaughlin Papers.

55. Letter from Donal McLaughlin, May 2, 1945, McLaughlin Papers.

56. There were hundreds of local papers reporting on the San Francisco Conference, mostly through the Associated Press releases. See, for example, "United Nations Sign Charter," *Life Magazine* 19, no. 2 (July 9, 1945); "World Conference Ends Fruitful Sessions," *The Times and Democrat,* June 27, 1945; Associated Press, "Failure Will Betray Dead, Parley Told," *The Morning News,* June 27, 1945; "Truman Sounds Keynote of Peace as Frisco Conference Ends Work," *The News and Observer,* June 27, 1945; R. H. Shackford, "Nations Sign Security Pact," *The Vancouver Sun,* June 26, 1945.

57. Walter Winchell, "In San Francisco," *NY Daily Mirror,* April 25, 1945.

58. For the role of OSS during the Nuremberg process see Michael Salter, *Nazi War Crimes, US Intelligence and Selective Prosecution at Nuremberg: Controversies Regarding the Role of the Office of Strategic Services* (London: Routledge-Cavendish, 2007), 246–306; Michael Salter, *US Intelligence, the Holocaust and the Nuremberg Trials: Seeking Accountability for Genocide and Cultural Plunder* (Leiden: M. Nijhoff, 2009), 32–43.

59. Whitney R. Harris, *Tyranny on Trial: The Evidence at Nuremberg* (New York: Barnes & Noble, 1995), 4–9; Bradley F. Smith, *The American Road to Nuremberg: The Documentary Record, 1944–1945* (Stanford: Hoover Institution Press, 1982), 138–39; Ferhadbegović, Lingen, and Eichenberg, "The United Nations War Crimes Commission."

60. "Memorandum of Proposals for the Prosecution and Punishment of Certain War Criminals and Other Offenders," April 25–30, 1945, in Smith, *The American Road to Nuremberg,* 169.

61. "Agreement and Charter, August 8, 1945," in Robert H. Jackson, *Report of Robert H. Jackson United States Representative to the International Conference on Military Trials* (Washington, D.C.: Government Printing Office, 1949), 420–28.

62. Salter, *Nazi War Crimes,* 255–56.

63. "Minutes of Conference Session of July 13, 1945," in Jackson, *Report,* 213.

64. The other cities were Berlin, Wiesbaden, Munich, Leipzig, and Luxemburg. See Gordon Dean, "Memorandum for the Chief of Counsel: The Site of the Trial," June 26, 1945, RG 238, Entry PI21–51, Box 39, Folder Nuremberg-Physical Arrangements, NARA.

65. For background on the Justizpalast see Ulrich Grimm, "Kleine Chronik des Baus" and "Gebäude oder Palast für Justitia?," in *Justizpalast Nürnberg: Ein Ort der Weltgeschichte wird 100 Jahre,* ed. Ewald Behrschmidt (Neustadt an der Aisch, Germany: VDS Verlagsdruckerei Schmidt, 2016), 23–44.

66. Stephen Brockmann, *Nuremberg: The Imaginary Capital* (Rochester, N.Y.: Camden House, 2006), 131–75.

67. Carolin Höfler and Matthias Karch, eds., *MARSCHORDNUNGEN. Das Reichsparteitagsgelände in Nürnberg* (Berlin: Stiftung Topographie des Terrors, 2016), 22–24.

68. For more on the labor economy behind the design of the monumental grounds, see Paul B. Jaskot, *The Architecture of Oppression: The SS, Forced Labor and the Nazi Monumental Building Economy* (London: Routledge, 2000), 47–79; Martin Kitchen, *Speer: Hitler's Architect* (New Haven: Yale University Press, 2017), 29–56.

69. "Oeil pour oeil" was initially published in French as Simone de Beauvoir, "Oeil pour oeil," *Les temps modernes* 5 (February 1946), 813–830. The English translation I use is from *Philosophical Writings,* ed. Margaret Simons, Marybeth Timmerman, and Mary Beth Mader (Urbana: University of Illinois Press, 2004), 237–60.

70. For an analysis of de Beauvoir's phenomenology of revenge, see Sonia Kruks, *Simone de Beauvoir and the Politics of Ambiguity* (New York: Oxford University Press, 2012), 151–81.

71. Primo Levi, *The Drowned and the Saved* (New York: Simon & Schuster, 2017), 154.

72. Assistant Secretary of War, "War Crimes Prosecutions: Planning Memorandum," May 17, 1945, RG 226, Entry 85, Box 42, File 687, NARA.

73. Christian Delage, "The Nuremberg Trials: Confronting the Nazis with the Images of Their Crimes," in *Images of Conviction: The Construction of Visual Evidence,* ed. Diane Dufour et al. (Paris: Editions Xavier Barral, 2015), 133–48; Christian Delage, *La verité par l'image: de Nuremberg au procès Milosevic* (Paris: Denoël, 2006), 91–158.

74. On the history of the visual presentations put together for the Nuremberg Trials see Christian Delage, "L'image Comme Preuve: L'expérience Du Procès de Nuremberg," *Vingtième siècle. Revue d'histoire* 72 (December 2001): 63–78; Katz, "The Arts of War," 17–19; Salter, *Nazi War Crimes,* 11–42, 162–64, 513–15.

75. Jennifer L. Mnookin, "The Image of Truth: Photographic Evidence and the Power of Analogy," in Dufour et al., *Images of Conviction,* 14; Susan Schuppli, *Material Witness: Media, Forensics, Evidence* (Cambridge: MIT Press, 2020).

76. Alejandra Azuero-Quijano, "Making the 'World Spectacle Trial': Design as Forensic Practice at the Nuremberg Trials," *Grey Room,* no. 82 (February 1, 2021): 66.

77. My account of his life and work is based on Dan Kiley, *Dan Kiley: the Complete Works of America's Master Landscape Architect* (Boston: Little, Brown and Company, 1999); Dan Kiley, *Dan Kiley in His Own Words: America's Master Landscape Architect* (London: Thames and Hudson, 1999); and Calvin Thomkins, "The Garden Artist," *The New Yorker,* October 16, 1995.

78. Daniel Donovan, "The Hundred Gardens: The Social, Historical, and Design Contexts of Hollin Hills," in *Daniel Urban Kiley: The Early Gardens,* ed. William Saunders (New York: Princeton Architectural Press, 1999), 40.

79. Pearlman argues that the creation of the Graduate School of Design introduced

discussions of "total design" in the U.S. scene. See Jill E. Pearlman, *Inventing American Modernism: Joseph Hudnut, Walter Gropius, and the Bauhaus Legacy at Harvard* (Charlottesville: University of Virginia Press, 2007), 50–84.

80. Garret Eckbo, Dan Kiley, and James C. Rose, "Landscape Design in the Urban Environment," *Architectural Record* 85, no. 5 (May 1939): 74.

81. Eckbo, Kiley, and Rose, "Landscape Design in the Urban Environment," 77.

82. Mark Pendergrast, "Trial and Error: Mark Pendergrast Interviewed Dan Kiley in His Office on a Dirt Road in Charlotte," *North by Northeast,* c. July 1988, McLaughlin Papers.

83. Bruce M. Stave and Michele Palmer, eds., *Witnesses to Nuremberg* (New York: Twayne Publishers, 1998), 20.

84. Daniel Kiley, "Architect of Palace of Justice Renovations," in Stave and Palmer, *Witnesses to Nuremberg,* 15.

85. Costas Douzinas and Lynda Nead, "Introduction," in *Law and the Image: The Authority of Art and the Aesthetics of Law,* ed. Costas Douzinas and Lynda Nead (Chicago: University of Chicago Press, 1999), 1–18; Peter Goodrich, *Legal Emblems and the Art of Law: Obiter Depicta as the Vision of Governance* (Cambridge: Cambridge University Press, 2015), 23–48; Desmond Manderson, *Songs without Music: Aesthetic Dimensions of Law and Justice* (Berkeley: University of California Press, 2000), 40–43.

86. For more on the aesthetic dimensions of law, particularly in relationship to space, see Manderson, *Songs without Music,* 40–43.

87. Piyel Haldar, "In and Out of Court: On Topographies of Law and the Architecture of Court Buildings," *International Journal for the Semiotics of Law/Revue internationale de Semiotique juridique* 7, no. 2 (1994): 185–200.

88. Linda Mulcahy, *Legal Architecture: Justice, Due Process and the Place of Law* (Abingdon, UK: Routledge, 2011), 14–37; Katherine Fischer Taylor, "Geometries of Power: Royal, Revolutionary, and Postrevolutionary French Courtrooms," *Journal of the Society of Architectural Historians* 72, no. 4 (2013): 434–74; Katherine Fischer Taylor, *In the Theater of Criminal Justice: The Palais de Justice in Second Empire Paris* (Princeton: Princeton University Press, 1993).

89. Taylor makes an excellent case with the post-Revolutionary French palace of justice in *In the Theater of Criminal Justice,* xvii–xviii.

90. Katz, "The Arts of War," 18–19; Salter, *US Intelligence, the Holocaust and the Nuremberg Trials,* 253–54; Azuero-Quijano, "Making the 'World Spectacle Trial.'"

91. Cornelia Vismann, *Medien Der Rechtsprechung* (Berlin: Fischer Taschenbuch, 2011), 146–83. On transitional trials and the difference between tribunals and courts, see Kim Christian Priemel, *The Betrayal: The Nuremberg Trials and German Divergence* (Oxford: Oxford University Press, 2016), 1–20.

92. Jean-Louis Cohen, *Architecture in Uniform: Designing and Building for the Second World War* (Montréal: Canadian Centre for Architecture, distributed by Yale University Press, 2011), 386.

93. Beatriz Colomina, "Enclosed by Images: The Eameses' Multimedia Architecture," *Grey Room,* no. 2 (2001): 7–29.

94. Presentation History, January 15, 1945, RG226, Entry 99, Box 98, Folder 7, NARA.

95. Outline Agenda of State Department Meeting on the Presentation Room Proposals, January 30, 1945, RG226, Entry 85, Box 25, Folder 413, NARA.

96. "V. Visual Presentation and Field Photographic: The Rise and Fall of Q-2," RG226,

Entry 99, Box 136, Folder 2, NARA. For a more detailed history of situation rooms, see Katz, "The Arts of War," 5–7; Colomina, "Enclosed by Images"; and Cohen, *Architecture in Uniform,* 322–25.

97. Office of Strategic Services, *Some Facts about the Presentation Room in the Combined Chiefs of Staff Building* (Washington, D.C.: U.S. Government Printing Office, 1943), 4–6.

98. Neither the sketch nor the letter identifies the architect. Examining the detail and drawing technique in comparison to Kiley's sketches, I speculate that the sketch's architect was not Kiley, but somebody with experience on situation rooms. See Gordon Dean, "Memorandum to the Chief of Counsel," July 17, 1945, RG238, Entry PI21–51, Box 39, NARA.

99. William J. Donovan to Chief of Counsel, "Lt. Dean's Memorandum on The Site of the Trial," June 28, 1945, RG 238, Entry PI21–51, Box 39, Folder Nuremberg-Physical Arrangements, NARA.

100. Kiley, "Architect of Palace of Justice Renovations," 21.

101. Robert H. Jackson, "Memorandum to US Chief of Counsel," October 5, 1945, RG 238, Entry PI21–51, Box 39, Folder Nuremberg-Physical Arrangements, NARA.

102. Colonel Robert J. Gill, "Memorandum for the Chief of Counsel: The Site of the Trial," June 26, 1945, RG 238, Entry PI21–51, Box 39, Folder Nuremberg-Physical Arrangements, NARA.

103. The annex initially served as a Jury Court, a briefly active court in the German judicial system.

104. Robert B. Konikow, "The Trials at Nürnberg," unpublished manuscript, McLaughlin Papers.

105. On the systemic presentation of international law in the Nuremberg Trials see Azuero-Quijano, "Making the 'World Spectacle Trial.'"

106. Olga Touloumi, "Building the Case for the Nuremberg Trials [70 Years After Nuremberg]," *Human Rights Archives* (blog), November 18, 2015, https://blogs.lib.uconn .edu/humanrights/2015/11/18/building-the-case-for-the-nuremberg-trials-70-years -after-nuremberg; Olga Touloumi, "Architectures of Global Communication: Psycho-acoustics, Acoustic Space, and the Total Environment, 1941–1970" (PhD diss., Harvard University, 2014), 57–62.

107. Mark Somos, "A New Architecture of Justice: Dan Kiley's Design for the Nuremberg Trials' Courtroom," *MPIL Research Paper Series,* no. 4 (2018): 1–27.

108. Manderson, *Songs without Music,* 43.

109. "Presentation Branch Work on War Crimes Project," June 14, 1945, RG 226, Box 42, Folder 688, NARA.

110. Harris, *Tyranny on Trial,* 26; Stave and Palmer, *Witnesses to Nuremberg,* 1998.

111. Salter, *Nazi War Crimes,* 255–77.

112. See, for example, Vladimír Rýpar and Karel Hájek, *Norimberk: zločin a soud* (Praha: Světa obrazech, s.s.r.o., vydavatelstva ministerstva informací, 1946).

113. *Nuremberg: Its Lesson for Today* (New York: Schulberg Productions and New Day Films, 2014).

114. This is an argument most notably made by James E. K. Parker on the need to address the acoustic component—testimonies, interpretation, oaths, to name a few—within adjudication. See *Acoustic Jurisprudence: Listening to the Trial of Simon Bikindi* (Oxford: Oxford University Press, 2015), 1–44.

115. Mladen Dolar, *A Voice and Nothing More* (Cambridge: MIT Press, 2006), 108–9.

116. Parker, *Acoustic Jurisprudence,* 139–40.

117. Margareta Bowen, "Interpreting at the League of Nations," in *Report of the Thir-teenth Annual Conference of the Center for Research and Documentation on World Language Problems in Cooperation with the Office of Conference Services,* ed. Humphrey Tonkin (Hart-ford: Center for Research and Documentation on World Language Problems, 1996); Margareta Bowen, "Interpreters and the Making of History," in *Translators Through His-tory,* ed. Jean Delisle and Judith Woodsworth (Amsterdam: John Benjamins Publishing Company, 1995), 245–73; Wolfram Wilss, *Translation and Interpretation in the 20th Cen-tury: Focus on German* (Amsterdam: J. Benjamins, 1999), 32–36.

118. Robert Lansing, *The Big Four and Others of the Peace Conference* (Boston: Houghton Mifflin Co., 1921), 106.

119. Arthur Herbert Birse, *Memoirs of an Interpreter* (London: Joseph, 1967), 106.

120. Jean Herbert, "How Conference Interpretation Grew," in *Language Interpretation and Communication,* ed. NATO Symposium on Language Interpretation and Communica-tion et al. (New York: Plenum Press, 1978), 7.

121. Laura Kunreuther, "Earwitnesses and Transparent Conduits of Voice: On the Labor of Field Interpreters for UN Missions," *Humanity: An International Journal of Human Rights, Humanitarianism, and Development* 11, no. 3 (Winter 2020): 298–316.

122. "Rules of Procedure," in *The United Nations Conference on International Organization, San Francisco, California, April 25 to June 26, 1945. Selected Documents* (Washington, D.C.: United States Government Printing Office, 1946), 75–76.

123. Jesús Baigorri-Jalón, *From Paris to Nuremberg: The Birth of Conference Interpreting,* trans. Holly Mikkelson and Barry Slaughter Olsen (Philadelphia: John Benjamins Pub-lishing Company, 2014), 131–64.

124. The first installation of the system, or "the Filene Experiment," as ILO adminis-trators referred to it, kept interpreters in the public eye, close to the speaker's podium. ILO delegates embraced simultaneous interpretation for accelerating their meetings. The enthusiastic reception among ILO delegates encouraged Filene to reach out again to the League of Nations Secretary-General in 1930, offering to finance the installation of his Filene-Finlay Translator inside the Assembly Hall at Palais Wilson, but it was only after 1931 that the League allowed Filene to install his system and wire delegates with tele-phone lines into a single communication network. Filene turned to telecommunications experts at AT&T to build a more extensive and robust version of his system, but after his proposal was turned down, he approached Thomas Watson of IBM, whom he had met in the International Chamber of Commerce. Watson, seeing the Filene-Finlay system as another opportunity to tie his company to the international market, acquired the patent and agreed to develop and install the system at the Palais des Nations, an agreement that lasted up to 1949, when the Filene-Finlay patent expired and IBM dropped Filene's name from the nameplates of the selector switches. See "Le système Filene-Finlay de traduction téléphonique des discours," undated pamphlet, R3427, League of Nations Archives (LON), United Nations Office in Geneva (UNOG), Geneva, Switzerland; letter from Edward Filene to Chairman, League of Nations Council, September 14, 1929. R3427, LON; Bowen, "In-terpreting at the League of Nations"; Egon Ferdinand Ranshofen-Wertheimer, *The Inter-national Secretariat: A Great Experiment in International Administration* (Washington, D.C.: Carnegie Endowment for International Peace, 1945), 139–41; Wilss, *Translation and In-terpretation in the 20th Century,* 30–49; Herbert, "How Conference Interpretation Grew," 5–10; A. C. Holt, "International Understanding: A Tribute to Mr. Thomas J. Watson," 1954, Box 1, Folder 19, IBM Archives. For a short account of the negotiations among the two U.S. businessman and the British engineer that resulted in the creation of the

Filene-Finlay translator see George E. Berkley, *The Filenes* (Boston: International Pocket Library, 1998), 202–5.

125. Ranshofen-Wertheimer, *The International Secretariat*, 140.

126. Baigorri-Jalón, *From Paris to Nuremberg*, 161–62.

127. George Slocombe and Emery Kelen, *A Mirror to Geneva* (London: J. Cape, 1937), 63.

128. Preliminary Notes on Peace Conference—Interpreting & Translating, RG 226, Entry 85, Box 17, Folder 300, NARA.

129. Groff Conklin, "Preliminary Action Report to H. C. Barton, Jr.," April 19, 1944, RG 226, Entry 85, Box 17, Folder 300, NARA.

130. "Le système Filene-Finlay de traduction téléphonique des discours," undated pamphlet, R3427, LON.

131. "THAT ALL MEN MAY UNDERSTAND—Each in His Own Tongue—with the INTERNATIONAL TRANSLATOR SYSTEM," n.d., IBM Documents, Box 2 Folder 6, IBM Archives.

132. This is an argument more distinctly made by Parker, *Acoustic Jurisprudence*, 9.

133. Jonathan Sterne, *The Audible Past: Cultural Origins of Sound Reproduction* (Durham: Duke University Press, 2003), 163–65.

134. I take the term "collectivized isolation" from Jonathan Sterne, "Headset Culture, Audile, Technique, and Sound Space as Private Space," *TMG Journal for Media History* 6, no. 2 (September 17, 2014): 57–82.

135. James Parker, "The Soundscape of Justice," *Griffith Law Review* 20, no. 4 (2011): 973.

136. Joseph Kessel, *L'Heure des châtiments,* as cited in Delage, "The Nuremberg Trials," in Dufour et al., *Images of Conviction*, 133, 148.

137. Rebecca West, "Extraordinary Exile," *The New Yorker*, September 7, 1946.

138. Colonel Robert J. Gill, "Memorandum to US Chief of Counsel," October 5, 1945, RG 238, Entry PI21–51, Box 39, Folder Nuremberg-Physical Arrangements, NARA.

139. Jackson is cited in Gaiba, *The Origins of Simultaneous Interpretation*, 34. Gaiba suggests that Colonel Léon Dostert, who was Eisenhower's interpreter, proposed the use of the IBM system, since Justice Jackson, who was arranging for the trial in Europe, was in communication with Dostert, who was at the time in Washington. For research that attributes to Jackson the import of the IBM system see Leo Kahn, *Nuremberg Trials* (New York: Ballantine, 1972); and Robert E. Conot, *Justice at Nuremberg* (New York: Harper, 1983).

140. "The International Filene Finlay Translator System," 1946, IBM Documents, Box 2, Folder 6, IBM Archives.

141. Kayoko Takeda, *Interpreting the Tokyo War Crimes Trial* (Ottawa: University of Ottawa Press, 2010), 32–38.

142. A. C. Holt, "Memorandum to Mr. L. H. LaMotte: Wireless Translator," November 27, 1953, L. H. LaMotte Papers, Box 40, Folder 3, IBM Archives.

143. A. C. Holt, "International Understanding: A Tribute to Mr. Thomas J. Watson," 1954, Box 1, Folder 19, IBM Archives.

144. Kunreuther makes this argument in "Earwitnesses and Transparent Conduits of Voice."

145. Letter from Edward R. Stettinius Jr. to Bill Donovan, July 24, 1945; letter from Edward R. Stettinius Jr. to Oliver Lundquist, June 6, 1946; and letter from Wallace K. Harrison to Oliver Lundquist, October 22, 1947, Lundquist Papers.

146. Lundquist disagrees with Donal McLaughlin's account, claiming the work to be a collaborative effort. See letter from Oliver Lundquist to Stephen C. Schlesinger, November 23, 2003, Lundquist Papers. For the reference to the Rand McNally map see Donal

McLaughlin, "Origin of the United Nations Seal" Draft, McLaughlin Papers; and Peter Kihas, "New Emblem for UN Drawn—A Global One," *New York Herald Tribune,* November 20, 1946.

147. Harris, *Tyranny on Trial,* 537.

2. Cultures of Assembly

1. Trygve Lie, *In the Cause of Peace: Seven Years with the United Nations* (New York: Macmillan, 1954), 57.

2. For a detailed analysis of the regionalist and globalist imperative in Roosevelt's political geography, see Neil Smith, *American Empire: Roosevelt's Geographer and the Prelude to Globalization* (Berkeley: University of California Press, 2004), 374–415.

3. Sumner Welles, *Where Are We Heading?* (New York: Harper, 1946), 31–32.

4. Robert C. Hilderbrand, *Dumbarton Oaks: The Origins of the United Nations and the Search for Postwar Security* (Chapel Hill: University of North Carolina Press, 2001), 36, 106–7.

5. For example, see letter from Mabel Morris, December 2, 1945, S-0539-0004-16, United Nations Archives and Records Management (UN), New York.

6. The Preparatory Commission announced the "principle of centralisation" in a press release, "Permanent Headquarters of the United Nations: Discussion on Selection of Seat," September 29, 1945, S-0930-0003-02, UN.

7. Committee 10, "A Study of the Recruitments for the Location of the Headquarters of the United Nations and its Specialized Organisations," September 10, 1945, S-0930-0006-02, UN.

8. For a short history of the Royal Institute of International Affairs, see Laurence Martin, "Chatham House at 75: The Past and the Future," *International Affairs (Royal Institute of International Affairs 1944-)* 71, no. 4 (1995): 697–703; Edward Carrington Cabell and Mary Bone, *Chatham House: Its History and Inhabitants* (London: Royal Institute of International Affairs, 2004).

9. James Eric Drummond et al., *The International Secretariat of the Future: Lessons from Experience by a Group of Former Officials of the League of Nations* (London: Royal Institute of International Affairs, 1944), 11–16.

10. Drummond et al., *The International Secretariat of the Future*, 47–49, 61–64.

11. "Former Directors General: Clarence Wilfred Jenks," International Labor Organization, February 8, 2006, http://www.ilo.org/global/about-the-ilo/how-the-ilo-works/ilo-director-general/former-directors-general/WCMS_192713/lang--en/index.htm.

12. C. Wilfred Jenks, *The Headquarters of International Institutions* (London: Royal Institute of International Affairs, 1945).

13. Jenks, *The Headquarters of International Institutions,* 10–11.

14. Jenks, *The Headquarters of International Institutions,* 17.

15. Jenks, *The Headquarters of International Institutions,* 25–27.

16. "Eleventh Meeting of Committee 8 (General Questions) of the Preparatory Commission of the United States," December 13, 1945, S-0931-0004-01, UN.

17. Summary Report of the Sixth Meeting of Committee 10, December 11, 1945, S-0930-0006-02, UN.

18. Summary Report of the Sixth Meeting of Committee 10, December 11, 1945, S-0930-0006-02, UN.

19. Committee 8: General Questions, "Summary Record of Meetings," No. 3, November 30, 1945, S-0532-0001-04, UN.

20. Committee 8: General Questions, "Summary Record of Meetings," No. 11, December 15, 1945, S-0532-0001-04, UN.

21. Committee 8: General Questions, "Summary Record of Meetings," No. 7a, December 11, 1945, S-0532-0001-04, UN.

22. Press Release No. 95, "Second Day of Discussion on Permanent Headquarters of the United Nations, Committee 8: General Questions," December 8, 1945, S-0930-0003-02, UN.

23. Committee 8: General Questions, "Summary Record of Meetings," No. 9, December 12, 1945, S-0532-0001-04, UN.

24. "Twelfth Meeting of Committee 8 (General Purposes) of the Preparatory Commission of the United Nations," December 14, 1945, S-0931-0004-01, UN.

25. The discussion on the procedure started on December 7, 1945. See Committee 8: General Questions, "Summary Record of Meetings," No. 7, December 8, 1945, and No. 20, December 24, 1945, S-0532-0001-04, UN.

26. Committee 8: General Questions, "Summary Record of Meetings," No. 9, December 18, 1945, S-0532-0001-04, UN.

27. Press Release, Technical Advisory Committee on Information, December 8, 1945, S-0930-0003-02, UN.

28. Charlene Mires offers an excellent account of the selection of the UN site and the events leading up to the purchase of the plot on Turtle Bay in *Capital of the World: The Race to Host the United Nations* (New York: New York University Press, 2015).

29. Letter from Ben P. Choate to President Harry S. Truman, October 6, 1945, S-0539-0004-16, UN.

30. The proposal submitted was initially published in the *Periodicum Mundaneum*, No. 50, April 1945. See "Memorandum on Sites Already Formally Proposed for the Headquarters of the United Nations Organisation Submitted by Committee 10," September 12, 1945, S-0930-0006-02, UN.

31. Sub-Committee No. 10—proposed sites for United Nations Headquarters A-L, S-0539-0004-15, UN.

32. Letter from James J. Lyons to Preparatory Commission, December 14, 1945, S-0539-0004-16, UN.

33. Letter from Mildred Webster to United Nations Organization, January 7, 1946, S-0532-0003-11, UN.

34. Resolution adopted by the American Institute of Architects, American Institute of Planners, American Society of Landscape Architects, and American Society of Civil Engineers, March 2, 1946, S-0472-0004-01, UN.

35. "The Capitol of the World," *Interiors* 105 (1946): 76–77; Kenneth Reid, "A Home for the U.N.O.," *Progressive Architecture* 27 (1946): 98–100; Ed Allen, "Capital for the United Nations," *Architectural Record* 99 (March 1946): 82–85; "United Nations Headquarters: New York Site Suggested," *Architects' Journal* 104 (November 14, 1946): 349–50; "Proposed United Nations Center," *Architectural Forum* 82 (August 1945): 98–101; "New York Proposes a World Capitol for the United Nations," *Architectural Forum* 85 (1946): 116–20; "Statement on the Report of the Headquarters Commission by the Joint Advisory Committee on Planning and Development of the United Nations Headquarters," *American Institute of Planners* 12 (October 1946): 27–30; Thomas H. Locraft, "A Capital for the U.N.O.," *Journal of the American Institute of Architects* 5 (April 1946): 178–84; "La casa dei

popoli il concorso dell O.N.U.," *Domus* 207 (March 1946): 2–5; Frederick P. Clark, "Planning a World Headquarters," *American Institute of Planners* 12 (April 1946): 10–15.

36. For a conversation of the British delegation and Australian delegation memorandums in particular, see Mires, *Capital of the World,* 124–30.

37. Memorandum, January 11, 1946, S-0532-0002-03, UN.

38. New York City Mayor's Committee on Plan and Scope, *Plan for Permanent World Capitol at Flushing Meadows Park,* September 1946, Box 04, Ralph Walker Papers (Walker Papers), Syracuse University, Syracuse, New York.

39. The abbreviated version of the lecture "A World Center for the United Nations" was published in *Progressive Architecture* 27 (August 1946): 70–72; *Architects' Journal* 104 (July 25, 1946): 37–39, 70; and *Builder* 171 (July 19, 1946): 57–58. Convinced of the effects that the new global institution would have on the city, Mumford continued his public criticism through his column in the *New Yorker,* well after all committees formed and architects were chosen. Lawrence J. Vale offers an overview of Mumford's reaction and continuous engagement with the construction of the UN in "Designing Global Harmony: Lewis Mumford and the United Nations Headquarters," in *Lewis Mumford: Public Intellectual,* ed. Thomas P. Hughes and Agatha C. Hughes (Oxford: Oxford University Press, 1990), 256–82.

40. Lewis Mumford, "Memorandum on the United Nations Organization Headquarter and Community," n.d., S-0532-0005-07, UN.

41. Mumford, "Memorandum on the United Nations."

42. Mumford, "Memorandum on the United Nations."

43. Mumford, "Memorandum on the United Nations."

44. Letter from R. S. Childs to Lewis Mumford, January 21, 1946, S-0532-0005-07, UN. Some of his Skyline essays critical of the UN building have been republished in Lewis Mumford, *From The Ground Up: Observations on Contemporary Architecture, Housing, Highway Building, and Civic Design* (Orlando: Harcourt Brace Jovanovich, 1956).

45. Verbatim Minutes of the Closing Plenary Session, Opera House, June 26, 1945, S-0537-0074-01, UN.

46. Verbatim Minutes of the Opening Session, Opera House, April 25, 1945, S-0537-0074-01, UN.

47. A. H. Feller, *United Nations and World Community* (Boston: Little, Brown, 1953), 30.

48. For a history of the emergence of corporate form in the late nineteenth-century United States, see Charles Perrow, *Organizing America: Wealth, Power, and the Origins of Corporate Capitalism* (Princeton: Princeton University Press, 2002).

49. Reinhold Martin, *The Organizational Complex: Architecture, Media, and Corporate Space* (Cambridge: MIT Press, 2005), 80–121.

50. "Headquarters, n.," in *OED Online* (Oxford University Press), accessed October 10, 2019, http://www.oed.com/view/Entry/84964.

51. Letter from Le Corbusier to Trygve Lie, July 9, 1946, S-0186-0001-09, UN.

52. Le Corbusier, "Report," June 19, 1946, S-0532-0008-09, UN. Le Corbusier's report was later published as Annex I to the Headquarters Commission's report. See *Report of the Headquarters Commission to the Second Part of the First Session of the General Assembly of the United Nations* (Lake Success, N.Y.: United Nations, 1946), 19–39. Le Corbusier later published the report as a book; see Le Corbusier, *UN Headquarters: Practical Application of a Philosophy of the Domain of Building* (New York: Reinhold Publishing Corporation, 1947).

53. Le Corbusier, "Report."

54. Le Corbusier, "Report."

55. Le Corbusier, "Report."

56. Report by M. Le Corbusier, Observations by Sir Angus Fletcher, August 16, 1946, and Critique of Le Corbusier's June 19th Report, August 13, 1946, S-0532-0008-09, UN.

57. Memorandum from Awni Khalidy to Sir Angus Fletcher, "Meeting of the Negotiations Committee in Washington," June 25, 1946, S-0532-0007-03, UN.

58. Victoria Newhouse, *Wallace K. Harrison, Architect* (New York: Rizzoli, 1989), 3–25.

59. Newhouse, *Wallace K. Harrison.*

60. Committee 8: General Questions, "Summary Record of Meetings," December 22, 1945, S-0532-0001-04, UN.

61. A sample checklist is "Site Check List Assumptions," July 18, 1946, S-0532-0007-08, UN.

62. "Report and Recommendations of the Inspection Group on Selecting the Permanent Site and Interim Facilities for the Headquarters of the United Nations," February 4, 1946, S-0532-0001-07, UN.

63. Draft Resolution—Harrison (White Plains) Site, December 8, 1946, S-0532-0006-05, UN.

64. This argument has most notably been made by Samuel Zipp, who claims that the final selection was motivated by Rockefeller's interest in keeping the headquarters close to his estate. See Samuel Zipp, *Manhattan Projects: The Rise and Fall of Urban Renewal in Cold War New York* (Oxford: Oxford University Press, 2012), 33-72.

65. Lie, *In the Cause of Peace,* 115.

66. Conversations on the Interim Facilities can be found in the minutes of the Inspection Group, S-0532-0002-03, UN.

67. "A Comparison of the Facilities at Hunter College in the Bronx and the Sperry Gyroscope Plant at Lake Success for the Interim Headquarters for the United Nations," April 8, 1946, S-0186-0001-19, UN.

68. Minutes of the Meeting of the Inspection Group, January 25, 1946, S-0532-0002-03, UN.

69. For correspondence on the negotiations around the leasing of Hunter College see Mayor William O'Dwyer Records, Series II, Box 164, Folder 1773, Municipal Archives, New York, New York. The sites at Flushing Meadows and Lake Success were confirmed by mid-April 1946. See letter from Trygve Lie to Mayor O'Dwyer, April 11, 1946, Mayor William O'Dwyer Records, Series II, Box 164, Folder 1774, The New York City Municipal Archives, New York.

70. Jean-Claude Pallas, *Histoire et architecture du Palais des Nations (1924–2001): l'art déco au service des relations internationales* (Geneva: Nations Unies, 2001), 89–113.

71. Correspondence with requests can be found in folder S-0472-0001-12, UN.

72. This was the case with the Swedish nomination, as Ragnar Hjorth was replaced by Sven Markelius, and the Greek one, as Kouremenos was replaced with Le Corbusier's collaborator Stamos Papadakis, who then was replaced by Jean Antoniades. Correspondence with individual member states can be found in S-0472–0003, UN.

73. After correspondence with Secretary-General Trygve Lie, Wallace K. Harrison confirmed that his Board of Design would include Nikolai D. Bassov from the USSR, Gaston Brunfaut from Belgium, Le Corbusier from France, Ernest Cormier from Canada, Liang Ssu-ch'eng (Sicheng) from China, Sven Markelius from Sweden, Oscar Niemeyer

from Brazil, Howard M. Robertson from the United Kingdom, G. A. Soilleux from Australia, and Julio Vilamajó Echaniz from Uruguay, with the addition of collaborators, such as Vladimir Bodiansky, Hugh Ferriss, and Ernest Weissmann, forming a group of special consultants. The board also consulted representatives of three major architecture firms with experience in large-scale construction projects in the United States: Louis Skidmore of Skidmore, Owings & Merrill (SOM), Gilmore D. Clarke of Clarke, Rapuano & Holleran, and Ralph Walker of Voorhees, Walker, Foley & Smith. They also called in consulting engineers for technical questions on mechanical and electrical issues. See Ad Hoc Committee on Headquarters, "Second Meeting: Resume of Remarks Made by the Director of Planning," September 26, 1947, Max Abramovitz Architectural Records and Papers, 1925–1990, Box 15, Folder 5, Avery.

74. George Dudley, Minutes of Meeting, January 8, 1947. Wallace K. Harrison Architectural Drawings and Papers, 1913–1986, Box 8, Folder 4, Avery.

75. Hugh Ferriss, "Designing the United Nations Headquarters," *Royal Architectural Institute of Canada Journal* 25 (1948): 69–80.

76. George A. Dudley, *A Workshop for Peace: Designing the United Nations Headquarters* (Cambridge: The Architectural History Foundation, MIT Press, 1994), 66–67.

77. The list of requirements was based on the guidelines created by the Committee on Requirements and the questionnaire that de Ranitz had put together. After an initially more robust plan for collection of information fell through, the questionnaire was answered with informed "guesses" by Adriaan Pelt, the Assistant Secretary-General for Conferences and General Services, and J. B. Hutson, the Assistant Secretary-General for Administrative and Financial Services. See Annex No. 4 Headquarters Commission, Summary of the Requirements of the United Nations Based on the Replies from the Secretariat to the Questionnaire of the Headquarters Commission, S-0532-0012-01, UN. For the basic requirements see UN Planning Office, "Basic Requirements for U.N. Headquarters," February 17, 1947, UN.

78. Report of the Headquarters Commission to the Second Part of the First Session of the General Assembly of the United Nations, October 1946, S-0532-0012-12, UN.

79. Ralph Walker, "Aesthetics of the U.N. Headquarters," 1947, Box 16, Walker Papers.

80. Using his personal notes as a source, George Dudley offers one of the most thorough accounts we have of the events inside the Board of Design and from the perspective of Wallace K. Harrison in *A Workshop for Peace.*

81. *1946. The Early Days of the U.N. Inspire an International Legacy at Lehman College* (Bronx: Lehman College of Media Relations and Publications, 2008).

82. Design Meeting, March 17, 1947 Box 10, George A. Dudley Papers (Dudley Papers), Yale University, New Haven, Connecticut.

83. Headquarters Planning Office, "Investigation of Space Requirements," July 24, 1947, 001-2011-361 T, Box 2, Ernest Cormier fonds, Canadian Centre for Architecture (CCA), Montreal, Canada.

84. Material Requirements of the United Nations, n.d., S-0186-0001-02, UN.

85. Soilleux, Shortwave Broadcast to Australia—UN Radio, June 4, 1947, S-0542-0043-33, UN.

86. "Ogdensburger's Brother: Helped Change Skyline; Cormier Noted Architect," *Ogdensburg News,* December 21, 1952. 001-2011-361 T, Box 2, Ernest Cormier fonds, CCA.

87. Headquarters Planning Office, Declaration, April 18, 1947, 001-2011-361 T, Box 2, Ernest Cormier fonds, CCA.

88. Design Meeting, February 21, 1947 Box 10, Dudley Papers.

89. Jan Molema provides a full account of the episode from the perspective of the archives in the Netherlands and the Fondation Le Corbusier; see "Unknown History: Le Corbusier in Front of the 'Academism' of Jan de Ranitz in the Preparations for the United Nations Headquarters at New York," *Forma y Construcción En Arquitectura* 8 (May 2013): 18–27.

90. Dudley, *A Workshop for Peace*, 204–6.

91. Ralph Walker, "The Architect and the Post-War World: Paper given at fifty-sixth annual meeting of the Ontario Association of Architects," January 26, 1946, Box 8, Walker Papers.

92. Ralph Walker, "The Architect as a Liberal," February 28, 1940, Box 2, Walker Papers.

93. Gertrude Samuels, "What Kind of Capitol for the U.N.?," *New York Times,* April 20, 1947.

94. Design Meeting, April 18, 1947, Box 10, Dudley Papers.

95. Headquarters of the United Nations, Report of the Ad Hoc Committee on Headquarters, Rapporteur: Alexis Kyrou (Greece), A/485 November 18, 1947, UN.

96. "Ogdensburger's Brother."

97. Ad Hoc Committee on Headquarters, "Second Meeting: Resume of Remarks Made by the Director of Planning," September 26, 1947, Max Abramovic Collection, Box 15, Folder 5, Avery.

98. G. A. Soilleux, "The Planning of the United Nations Headquarters: A Paper Read before the A.A. by Mr. G. A. Soilleux, F.R.A.I.A.," *The Architectural Association Journal* 63 (1948): 198–99.

99. Pencil notes on minutes for Design Meeting, February 24, 1947, Box 10, Dudley Papers.

100. Design Meeting, February 27, 1947, Box 10, Dudley Papers.

101. *Report to the General Assembly of the United Nations on the Permanent Headquarters of the United Nations,* 3.

102. *Report to the General Assembly of the United Nations on the Permanent Headquarters of the United Nations,* 27.

103. Letter from J. D. Fuller to Frank Begley, June 4, 1947, S-0472-0001-14, UN.

104. *Report to the General Assembly of the United Nations on the Permanent Headquarters of the United Nations,* 34.

105. Design Meeting, March 18, 1947, Dudley Papers.

106. Letter to Mrs. Barlow, October 23, 1946, S-0925-0007-09, UN.

107. Here I am alluding to Ella Myers, who introduces the term "worldly things" to propose new models of democratic participation and mobilization around a care for "the world as a world" rather than a care for the self (Foucault) or a care for the Other (Levinas). See in particular *Worldly Ethics: Democratic Politics and Care for the World* (Durham: Duke University Press, 2013), 85–110.

108. Hannah Arendt, *The Human Condition* (Chicago: University of Chicago Press, 1958), 52.

109. See for example: Philosophy and Religion in Their Relation to the Democratic Way of Life Conference on Science et al., eds., *Approaches to World Peace: Fourth Symposium* (New York: Harper, 1944); Philosophy and Religion in Their Relation to the Democratic Way of Life Conference on Science and Lyman Bryson, eds., *Learning and World Peace:*

Eighth Symposium (New York: Conference on Science, Philosophy and Religion in their Relation to the Democratic Way of Life, 1948).

110. UNESCO's Tensions Project is an example: Hadley Cantril, *Tensions That Cause Wars: Common Statement and Individual Papers by a Group of Social Scientists Brought Together by UNESCO* (Urbana: University of Illinois Press, 1950).

111. For a discussion of the "technical turn" and the UNESCO headquarters see Lucia Allais, "Architecture and Mediocracy at UNESCO House," in *Marcel Breuer: Building Global Institutions,* ed. Barry Bergdoll and Jonathan Massey (Zurich: Lars Müller Publishers, 2018), 81–115.

112. George Bernard de Huszar, *Practical Applications of Democracy* (New York: Harper & Brothers Publishers, 1945). On de Huszar see Marguerite De Huszar Allen, "Living Dangerously: George de Huszar," *Chicago Review* 45, no. 3/4 (1999): 136–50.

113. Mark Corrinet, Interview with Donal McLaughlin, December 11, 1993, McLaughlin Papers.

114. Wallace K. Harrison, "Talk Made by W. K. Harrison before the American Society of Landscape Architects, Hotel Baltimore, New York," June 9, 1947. He gave the same talk on November 19, 1947 at the Joint Meeting of Detroit Charter of the AIA and Engineering Society, Detroit; on December 7, 1948 at the Meeting of the Boston Society of Architects, Boston; and at the Joint Meeting of Cleveland Charter of the AIA Cleveland, Ohio, on April 27, 1949, Wallace K. Harrison, Collection II, Box 3, Folder 3, Avery.

115. Jean Ferriss WBOW Broadcast, March 28, 1946. Includes excerpts from interview with Ralph Walker, Box 16, Walker Papers.

116. Design Meeting, February 28, 1947, Box 10, Dudley Papers.

117. Cited in Dudley, *A Workshop for Peace,* 151.

118. Design Meeting, February 26, 1947, Box 10, Dudley Papers.

119. Most prominently in the extensive criticism of the three interiors that Olga Gueft offered in "An Unodious Comparison: The Three Council Chambers of the United Nations," *Interiors* 111 (July 1952): 46–67.

120. Design Meeting, March 18, 1947, Box 10, Dudley Papers.

121. Quote found in Dudley, *A Workshop for Peace,* 138.

122. Barry Katz, "The Arts of War: 'Visual Presentation' and National Intelligence," *Design Issues* 12, no. 2 (1996): 3–21.

123. Design Meeting, April 21, 1947, Box 10, Dudley Papers.

124. On the history of the Security Council and the asymmetries that produced it, see David L. Bosco, *Five to Rule Them All: The UN Security Council and the Making of the Modern World* (Oxford: Oxford University Press, 2009).

125. Dudley, *A Workshop for Peace,* 56, 66.

126. Design Meeting, March 14, 1947, Box 10, Dudley Papers.

127. Isobel Roele, "Around Arendt's Table: Bureaucracy and the Non-Permanent Members of the UN Security Council," *Leiden Journal of International Law* 31, no. 3 (2020).

128. For an in-depth discussion of the Security Council chamber see Bosco, *Five to Rule Them All,* 10–79.

129. Ingeborg Glambek, "The Council Chambers in the UN Building in New York," *Scandinavian Journal of Design History* 15 (2005): 8–39; Alexa Griffith Winton, "A Striking Juxtaposition: Hand-Woven Textiles in the United Nations Conference Building Interiors," *The Journal of Modern Craft* 8, no. 2 (May 4, 2015): 181–93; Lili Blumenau, "Textiles in the United Nations Buildings," *Handweaver & Craftsman* 4 (Winter 1952/53): 10–14.

130. Karsten R. S. Ifversen, Birgit Lyngbye Pedersen, and Finn Juhl, *Finn Juhl at the UN: A Living Legacy* (Copenhagen: Strandberg Publishing, 2013), 73.

131. According to a biographical note, Abel Sorensen arrived in the United States in 1938 and worked for Oscar Stonorov and Louis Kahn, later designing for Knoll. See Acquisition Musee des arts decoratifs de Montréal, Oliver Lincoln Lundquist Papers, Bard College, New York.

132. For example, see letter from Abel R. Sorensen to Jacob Kjaer, July 6, 1950; letter from Abel R. Sorensen to A. Hertogh, July 7, 1950; letter from Abel R. Sorensen to S. Carbonier, July 7, 1950; all in S-0472-0001-12, UN.

133. Letter from Arnstein Arneberg, August 3, 1950, NAMT aar621, Box 1, Folder Korrespondanse 1950, Arnstein Arneberg Papers (Arneberg Papers), Nasjonalmuseet for kunst, arkitektur og design, Oslo, Norway.

134. For a sample letter to member states see: letter from Trygve Lie to the Minister for Foreign Affairs, Royal Swedish Ministry of Foreign Affairs, April 20, 1950, AM 1972–10, Folder UN Manhattan, Markelius Papers, ArkDes, Stockholm, Sweden.

135. Draft letter from Trygve Lie to the Board of Art Advisers, March 1, 1950, S-0472-0044-02, UN. Letters of nomination went out to all three nominees on March 2, 1950.

136. Irwin Edman, "Statement of Some Principles Underlying the Choice of Works of Art for the United Nations Headquarters," n.d., S-0472-0044-05, UN.

137. Report of the Board of Art Advisers to the Secretary-General after its First Session, June 5–9, 1950, S-0472-0044-05, UN.

138. For correspondence about the trip see S-0472-0044-04, UN.

139. Gueft, "An Unodious Comparison," 49.

140. Letter from Sven Markelius to Abel Sorensen, June 25, 1952, S-0472-0030-01, UN.

141. Letter from Finn Juhl to Glenn E. Bennett, August 15, 1950, and letter from Abel Sorensen to Finn Juhl, August 23, 1950, S-0472-0029-16, UN.

142. Edgar Kaufmann Jr., "Finn Juhl on the American Scene," manuscript, 1000:0386, Box 6, Finn Juhl Papers, Archives of Designmuseum Danmark, Copenhagen.

143. Gueft, "An Unodious Comparison."

144. Dudley, A Workshop for Peace, 223 and Newhouse, *Wallace K. Harrison,* 130.

145. "Global Architect: Wallace K. Harrison," *Parade*, Vol. VI, No. 24, June 15, 1947, clipping in Box 2, B01–036.6, Ernest Weissmann Papers (Weissmann Papers), Loeb, Harvard University, Cambridge, Massachusetts.

146. Graham Beckel and Felice Lee, *Workshops for the World: The United Nations Family of Agencies* (New York: Abelard-Schuman, 1954).

3. The Voice of the World

1. *Report to the General Assembly of the United Nations by the Secretary-General on the Permanent Headquarters of the United Nations* (Lake Success, N.Y.: United Nations, 1947), 27.

2. *Report to the General Assembly of the United Nations*, 34.

3. Syska & Hennessy Engineers, Preliminary Report on Mechanical and Electrical Equipment for the United Nations Permanent Headquarters, June 1947, 001-2011-361 T, Box 2, Ernest Cormier fonds, CCA.

4. Sokolsky is cited in Ralph Walker, "The Aesthetics of the U.N. Headquarters," 1948, Box 1, Walker Papers. Victoria Newhouse points to the similarities between the shape of the Hall Auditorium and the UN General Assembly; see *Wallace K. Harrison, Ar-*

chitect (New York: Rizzoli, 1989), 129–30. In his speech to the AA, Soilleux discussed how Harrison, in response to a similar building in South America, changed the elevations from curved to straight. It is unclear to me when the visit to South America took place, but see G. A. Soilleux, "The Planning of the United Nations Headquarters: A Paper Read before the A.A. by Mr. G. A. Soilleux, F.R.A.I.A.," *The Architectural Association Journal* 63 (1948): 199.

5. "Summary Record of the First Meeting of the Executive Committee of the United Nations," August 16, 1945, S-0930-0003-03, UN.

6. Letter from Groff Conklin to H. C. Barton Jr., April 19, 1944, Records of the Office of Strategic Services, RG226 S85, Box 17, Folder 300, NARA.

7. "Preliminary Notes on Peace Conference: The Press," February 10, 1944, Records of the Office of Strategic Services, RG226 S85, Box 17, Folder, 300, NARA.

8. Rules of Procedure, May 9, 1945, S-0537-0074-02, UN.

9. "Memorandum of the United Nations," November 13, 1945, S-0930-0005-02, UN.

10. Preparatory Commission of the United Nations, "Revisions of the Report to the Executive Committee from Committee 10 on the Selection of a Seat for Headquarters of the United Nations," October 2, 1945, S-0924-0002-04, UN.

11. Technical Advisory Committee on Information, "Publicity of Meetings of the Principal Organs. Extracts from the Provisional Rules of Procedure as Adopted by the Executive Committee Prepared by the Secretariat for the Use of Members of the Technical Advisory Committee of Information," December 9, 1945, S-0930-0002-01, UN.

12. "Summary of Meeting Held to Discuss Photographic and Motion Picture Facilities for the Preparatory Commission and the General Assembly Held at Church House, Westminster," November 14, 1945, S-0925-0002-13, UN.

13. "Summary of Meeting."

14. Minutes of a Meeting Held in Central Hall, December 7, 1945, S-0925-0002-13, UN.

15. James B. Reston, "Fifty-One Nations in Search of Unity: Here Is a Picture of UNO at Work," *New York Times,* January 27, 1946.

16. Mladen Dolar, *A Voice and Nothing More* (Cambridge: MIT Press, 2006), 109–10.

17. J. L. Austin, *How to Do Things with Words: The William James Lectures Delivered at Harvard University in 1955* (Oxford: Oxford University Press, 1962).

18. Notes on Meeting between Mr. Herman and Mr. Monk, December 18, 1945, S-0925-0002-13, UN.

19. Memorandum on the Adaptations to be made in the Central Hall, Westminster, for the First Meeting of the Assembly of the United Nations, S-0925-0002-13, UN.

20. Minutes of Meeting Held in Central Hall, December 22, 1945, S-0925-0002-13, UN.

21. Central Hall: Sound-proofing of Broadcasting Studios, December 12, 1945, S-0925-0002-13, UN.

22. Memorandum of the Meeting in Central Hall, November 30, 1945, S-0925-0002-13, UN.

23. Preparations for the Meeting of the Preparatory Commission, November 8, 1945, S-0539-0002-01, UN.

24. "Conference Planning. Accommodation Requirements for the General Assembly of the United Nations." April 18, 1946, Box 1, Dudley Papers.

25. Natalie de Blois interviewed by Detlef Mertins, June 17, 2004, Chicago, Natalie

de Blois Architectural Collection, Special Collections and University Archives, Virginia Polytechnic Institute, Blacksburg, Virginia.

26. Letter from Lloyd B. Herman to Byron F. Wood, June 7, 1946, S-0186-0001-02, UN.

27. Today a lottery to decide which national delegation occupies the front row takes place at the beginning of each session. See Preparatory Commission of the United Nations, Memorandum by the Executive Secretary on Seating Arrangements for the General Assembly, December 17, 1945, S-0924-0004-06, UN.

28. "New World Stage: AS THE U.N. MEETS ON FLUSHING MEADOW," *New York Times*, October 27, 1946.

29. Cornelia Epping-Jäger, "Voice Politics: Establishing the 'Loud/Speaker' in the Political Communication of National Socialism," in *Media, Culture, and Mediality: New Insights into the Current State of Research*, ed. Ludwig Jäger, Erika Linz, and Imela Schneider, trans. Brigitte Pichon and Dorian Rudnytsky (Bielefeld, Germany: Verlag, 2010), 161–85.

30. Cornelia Epping-Jäger, "Hitler's Voice: The Loudspeaker under National Socialism," trans. Caroline Bem, *Intermédialités: Histoire et théorie des arts, des lettres et des techniques / Intermediality: History and Theory of the Arts, Literature and Technologies* 17 (2011): 83–104.

31. Memorandum on the Adaptations to be made in the Central Hall, Westminster, for the First Meeting of the Assembly of the United Nations, S-0925-0002-13, UN.

32. Letter from C. J. Brackenbury to Captain Herman, November 17, 1945, S-0925-0002-13, UN.

33. See Lawrence W. Levine and Cornelia R. Levine, *The Fireside Conversations: America Responds to FDR during the Great Depression* (Berkeley: University of California Press, 2010); "The Fireside Chats: Roosevelt's Radio Talks," WHHA (en-US), accessed July 9, 2020, https://www.whitehousehistory.org/the-fireside-chats-roosevelts-radio-talks.

34. For a critical discussion of the X-City project within Zeckendorf's real estate practices during the period see Sara Stevens, *Developing Expertise: Architecture and Real Estate in Metropolitan America* (New Haven: Yale University Press, 2016), 187–205. For an account of the incident, see George A. Dudley, *A Workshop for Peace: Designing the United Nations Headquarters* (Cambridge: MIT Press, 1994), 21; William Zeckendorf and Edward A. McCreary, *Zeckendorf: The Autobiography of William Zeckendorf* (New York: Holt, Rinehart and Winston, 1970), 68.

35. See Carlotta Darò, "Lines for Listening: On Gustave Lyon's Geometrical Approach to Acoustics," *The Journal of Architecture* 23, no. 6 (2018): 881–902

36. For a thorough examination of the debates around acoustics at the League of Nations competition, see Sabine von Fischer, "Debating Volume: Architectural Versus Electrical Amplification in the League of Nations, 1926–28," *The Journal of Architecture* 23, no. 6 (2018): 904–35.

37. George Dudley, Design Meeting, March 19, 1947, Box 10, Dudley Papers.

38. George Dudley, Design Meeting, March 24, 1947, Box 10, Dudley Papers; and Max Abramovitz, Meeting Minutes, April 25, 1947, Box 15, Folder 6, Max Abramovitz Papers, Avery.

39. Conference Planning, "Accommodation Requirements for the General Assembly of the United Nations," April 18, 1946, Box 1, Dudley Papers.

40. Letter from Guy R. Fountain to Joe Lopez, July 19, 1951, S-0441-0138-11, UN.

41. "House of Commons Sound System: Low-Intensity Reinforcing Installation in the New Chamber," Reprint from Wireless World (Overseas Section), April 1951, S-0441-0138-11, UN.

42. "House of Commons Sound System."

43. "Sound Reinforcement: New Tannoy Installation at Church House, Westminster, Gives Comprehensive Facilities, Including Foreign Language Interpretation," reprint from *The Wireless & Electrical Trader,* November 23, 1950, S-0441-0138-11, UN.

44. Dominic Pettman, *Sonic Intimacy: Voice, Species, Technics (or, How to Listen to the World)* (Stanford: Stanford University Press, 2017), 79–84.

45. Letter from Ernest Weissmann to Wallace K. Harrison, February 11, 1947, Box 02, B01–036.1, Weissmann Papers.

46. Le Corbusier, Le Carnet de Poche de l'O.N.U, Fondation Le Corbusier, Paris: "It is important that the Councils take their decision before the eyes of public opinion." See Design Meeting, February 28, 1947, Box 10, Dudley Papers.

47. "The Eyes of the World. Paramount News Reel Cameraman in Every Country," *Northern Territory Times,* December 18, 1928.

48. Design Meeting, February 26, 1947, Box 10, Dudley Papers.

49. Meeting Official Communication Requirements and Space for Radio, Sound Control, Films and Television, June 14, 1948, S-0542–0045-Meetings Sound Control, UN.

50. United Nations Headquarters Planning Office, Meeting, Department of Public Information, July 20, 1948, S-0542–0045-Meetings Sound Control, UN.

51. Le Corbusier, "Tic-Tac á l'horloge des Nations Unies," n.d., D1-20-137-151, Fondation Le Corbusier.

52. "IBM World Service," *The Binghamton Sun,* September 18, 1947, Box 2, Folder 1, IBM Archives.

53. Minutes of Meeting #6, October 27, 1949, S-0542–0045-Meetings Electronic Installations, Telecommunications, UN.

54. A. C. Holt to G. S. Blackwell, "IBM Simultaneous Interpretation Equipment," August 8, 1961, United Nations, Box 1, Folder 11, IBM Archives.

55. D.D.J., "Notes," May 23, 1951, S-0441-0138-11, UN.

56. For his acceptance of the offer see letter from Vern O. Knudsen to Harmon H. Goldstone, February 23, 1948, Box 53, Folder 7, Vern O. Knudsen Papers (Knudsen Papers), University of California, Los Angeles.

57. Vern O. Knudsen, interview by Leo Delsasso and W. J. King, May 18, 1964, https://www.aip.org/history-programs/niels-bohr-library/oral-histories/4713; Vern O. Knudsen, "The Hearing of Speech in Auditoriums," *The Journal of the Acoustical Society of America* 1, no. 1 (1929): 56–82.

58. Letter from Vern O. Knudsen to Glenn E. Bennett, January 10, 1949, Box 53, Folder 7, Knudsen Papers.

59. On the decision to hire Richard Bolt and have Knudsen serve as an external consultant, see letter from Vern O. Knudsen to Wallace K. Harrison, May 21, 1948, Box 53, Folder 7, Knudsen Papers. In his autobiography, Beranek claims that Knudsen's bid was higher than Bolt's, resulting in Bolt winning the commission. See Leo L. Beranek, *Riding the Waves: A Life in Sound, Science, and Industry* (Cambridge: MIT Press, 2008), 105.

60. President's Report, *Massachusetts Institute of Technology Bulletin* 83, No. 1 (October 1947): 153; and Beranek, *Riding the Waves,* 75–78.

61. Leo L. Beranek, interview by Jack Purcell, February 26, 1989, https://www.aip.org/history-programs/niels-bohr-library/oral-histories/5191, Niels Bohr Library & Archives, American Institute of Physics, College Park, Maryland.

62. Leo L. Beranek, "BBN's Earliest Days: Founding a Culture of Engineering Creativity," *IEEE Annals of the History of Computing* 27, no. 2 (2005): 6–14.

63. For The Committee on Soundproofing Aircrafts see letter from Thomas K. Sherwood to Dr. Karl T. Compton, October 1, 1940, Papers of Stanley Smith Stevens (Stevens Papers) 1906–1973, HUGFP 2.14, Box 1, Harvard University Archives, Cambridge, Massachusetts. See also Irvin Stewart, *Organizing Scientific Research for War: The Administrative History of the Office of Scientific Research and Development* (Boston: Little, Brown & Co., 1948), 12.

64. See Beranek's 1960 compilation of correspondence in letter from Leo L. Beranek to S. S. Stevens, December 5, 1960, HUGFP 2.14, Box 1, Stevens Papers. See also official accounts: Stewart, *Organizing Scientific Research*, 6, 54–57; James Phinney Baxter, *Scientists Against Time* (Boston: Little, Brown, 1947), 188–89; Office of Scientific Research and Development, *Sciences in World War II: Applied Physics, Electronics, Optics, Metallurgy*, ed. Guy Suits et al. (Boston: Little Brown, 1948), 277–89.

65. Geraldine Stone and Harvard University Psycho-Acoustic Laboratory, *Final Report* (Cambridge: Psycho-Acoustic Laboratory Harvard University, 1961); and Paul N. Edwards, *The Closed World* (Cambridge: MIT Press, 1996), 209–37.

66. Letter from Philip M. Morse to Vannevar Bush, December 11, 1940, UAV 713.9021. Box 2, [17.3 c-5 Sound Sources], Records of the Psycho-Acoustic Laboratory, 1940-1972, Harvard University Archives. For a story of NDRC and OSRD see Daniel Jo Kevles, *The Physicists: The History of a Scientific Community in Modern America* (Cambridge: Harvard University Press, 1995), 302–23; David Dickson, *The New Politics of Science* (Chicago: University of Chicago Press, 1988), 107–62.

67. Psycho-Acoustic Laboratory and S. S. Stevens, "Project II: The Effects of Noise and Vibration on Psychomotor Efficiency, Report on Present Status," March 31, 1941, 885.95.5, Box 34, OSRD No. 274, Harvard University Archives.

68. NRC Committee on Sound Control and S. S. Stevens, "Report on 1. The Effects of Noise on Psychomotor Efficiency, II. Noise Reduction in Aircraft as Related to Communication, Annoyance and Aural Injury," December 1, 1941, UAV 885.95.5, Box 34, OSRD No. 274, Harvard University Archives.

69. Henning Schmidgen, "*Camera Silenta:* Time Experiments, Media Networks, and the Experience of Organlessness," in *Music, Sound, and the Laboratory from 1750–1980*, ed. Alexandra Hui, Julia Kursell, and Myles W. Jackson, special issue, *Osiris* 28 (2013): 162–88.

70. Leo L. Beranek and Harvey P. Sleeper, "The Design and Construction of Anechoic Sound Chambers," *The Journal of the Acoustical Society of America* 18, no. 1 (July 1946): 140–50.

71. E. H. Bedell, "Some Data on a Room Designed for Free Field Measurements," *The Journal of the Acoustical Society of America* 8, no. 2 (October 1936): 118–25.

72. OSRD and NDRC, "The Design and Construction of Anechoic Sound Chambers," Report of October 15, 1945, p. 4, World War II Government Contract Records: Contracts, Technical Reports, and Other Records, 1941-1947, UAV 885.95.5, Box 43, OSRD No. 4190, Harvard University Archives.

73. Beranek and Sleeper, "The Design and Construction of Anechoic Sound Chambers."

74. Gilbert Houle, "Acoustic Shock Not Unknown to Humans, Say Professors, Who Cite People Knocked Cold by Loud Clicking of Phone," *Boston Sunday Post*, September 15, 1946.

75. Beranek and Sleeper, "The Design and Construction of Anechoic Sound Chambers."

76. Richard Bolt, "Outline of Acoustics Problems for United Nations Headquarters,"

May 19, 1948, S-0472-0032-02, UN; and Richard Bolt, "Memorandum," July 26, 1948, S-0472-0032-02, UN.

77. Richard H. Bolt and Hamon H. Goldstone, Meeting on Acoustical Problems, May 10, 1948, S-0542–0045-Meetings Acoustics, UN.

78. Interview with Dr. Leo Beranek by Jack Purcell, Los Angeles, California, February 26, 1989, Niels Bohr Library & Archives.

79. Interview with Dr. Leo Beranek.

80. Joseph M. Siry, *Air-Conditioning in Modern American Architecture, 1890–1970* (University Park: Pennsylvania State University Press, 2021), 71–80.

81. Bolt and Beranek, "Acoustics Memorandum for the United Nations Headquarters Planning Office: Noise Measurements on Caldwell and Associates Air Conditioning System in General Motors Laboratories Mock-up, Detroit," September 26, 1949, S-0472-0032-01, UN; Bolt and Beranek, "Acoustics Memorandum for the United Nations Headquarters Planning Office: Noise Measurements on Caldwell and Associates Ventilating System Sears Roebuck and Company, Union City, New Jersey," October 18, 1949, S-0472-0032-01, UN.

82. Letter from Paul Bohanon to Richard H. Bolt, December 1, 1950, S-0472-0032-03, UN; Bolt and Beranek, "Acoustics Memorandum for the United Nations Headquarters: Ventilating Problems, General Assembly," December 18, 1950, S-0472-0032-01, UN.

83. Bolt and Beranek, "Acoustics Memorandum for the United Nations Headquarters," January 29, 1951, S-0472-0032-01, UN.

84. Bolt and Beranek, "Acoustics Memorandum for the United Nations Headquarters," June 23, 1949; and "Acoustics Memorandum for the United Nations Headquarters: Recommendations and Comments on," June 23, 1950, S-0472-0032-01, UN; and letter from Michael H. Harris to Richard H. Bolt, June 16, 1950, S-0472-0032-03, UN.

85. Letter from Michael H. Harris to Richard H. Bolt, June 16, 1950, S-0472-0032-03, UN.

86. Richard H. Bolt, Leo L. Beranek, and Robert B. Newman, "Acoustics Recommendations for the United Nations Permanent Headquarters," October 15, 1948, Box 53, Folder 7, Knudsen Papers.

87. Richard H. Bolt, Leo L. Beranek, and Robert B. Newman, "Acoustics Recommendations for the United Nations Permanent Headquarters," October 15, 1948, Box 53, Folder 7, Knudsen Papers.

88. Letter from V. Glicher (Syska & Hennessy) to H. A. VanName, October 18, 1949, S-0472-0030-07, UN.

89. Memorandum, June 23, 1950, S-0472-0032-03, UN.

90. Bolt and Beranek, "Acoustics Memorandum for the United Nations Headquarters: Public Address System for the General Assembly," November 21, 1950, S-0472-0032-01, UN.

91. Letter from Bolt, Beranek and Newman to Paul Bohanon, December 19, 1951, S-0472-0032-01, UN.

92. Among the different spellings of the name (Adrian, Adriaan, Adrianus), I will be using Adriaan. For a schematic overview of his career at the League, see "Adrianus Pelt," LONSEA—League of Nations Search Engine, accessed July 29, 2020, http://www.lonsea .de/pub/person/4968.

93. "Suggestions by A. Pelt for the Organization of a Secretariat Information Section," in James Eric Drummond et al., *The International Secretariat of the Future: Lessons from*

Experience by a Group of Former Officials of the League of Nations (London: Royal Institute of International Affairs, 1944), 61–64.

94. "Annex I. Recommendations of the Technical Advisory Committee on Information concerning the Policies, Functions and Organization of the Department of Public Information," adopted in A/64, Resolutions Adopted by the General Assembly during the First Part of its First Session from 10 January to 14 February, 1946, UN, https://digitallibrary.un.org/record/209582.

95. Barbara Crossette, "Media," in *The Oxford Handbook on the United Nations,* ed. Thomas G. Weiss and Sam Daws (Oxford: Oxford University Press, 2018), 370–80.

96. Robert H. Cory, "Forging a Public Information Policy for the United Nations," *International Organization* 7, no. 2 (May 1953): 232.

97. Benjamin Cohen, "The U.N.'s Department of Public Information," *The Public Opinion Quarterly* 10, no. 2 (1946): 151.

98. Cohen, "The U.N.'s Department of Public Information," 145–55.

99. Information centers were established at the host country's invitation. See Marcial Tamayo, "The United Nations: A Rich Source of Information," in *The Diplomatic Persuaders: New Role of the Mass Media in International Relations,* ed. John Lee (New York: Wiley, 1968), 190–91.

100. Milan Zivanovic, "United Nations Broadcasting: Its Origins, Principles, and Their Implementation" (PhD diss., University of Wisconsin, 1972), 87.

101. Cohen, "The U.N.'s Department of Public Information," 148.

102. "Gijsbert Frans van Dissel," LONSEA—League of Nations Search Engine, accessed July 27, 2020, http://www.lonsea.de/pub/person/5449.

103. Draft of Van Dissel, "Possible Sites for the Future Radio Stations of the United Nations," August 20, 1946, S-0532-0009-11, UN. For his role within the Headquarters Commission see "Staff of the Headquarters Commission," S-0532-0012-01, UN.

104. Committee to assist the Secretary-General in negotiations with the United States Government regarding the arrangements necessary as a result of the establishment of the seat of the United Nations in the United States of America, Seventh Meeting, May 24, 1946. D1–17, Fondation Le Corbusier.

105. Zivanovic, "United Nations Broadcasting," 20–21.

106. Telecommunications Coordinating Committee, Minutes of Tenth Meeting of Telecommunications Coordinating Committee, June 19, 1946. D1–16, 271–280, Fondation Le Corbusier.

107. Premiere séance du comite interdepartemental charge d'etudier les besoins des Nations Unies en radio-communications, Septembre 6, 1946, S-0916-0002-15, UN.

108. Broadcasting Arrangements for Meetings of the Preparatory Commission and General Assembly of the United Nations, November 19, 1945, S-0539-0008-35, UN.

109. For the growth of the BBC World Service, see Alban Webb, *London Calling: Britain, the BBC World Service, and the Cold War* (London: Bloomsbury Academic, 2015), 13–25.

110. For an examination of the development of the BBC World Service and its ties to the Empire Broadcast Service see Marie Gillespie and Alban Webb, "Corporate Cosmopolitanism: Diasporas and Diplomacy at the BBC World Service, 1932–2012," in *Diasporas and Diplomacy: Cosmopolitan Contact Zones at the BBC World Service (1932–2012),* ed. Marie Gillespie and Alban Webb (London: Routledge, 2013), 1–20; Gordon Johnston and Emma Robertson, *BBC World Service: Overseas Broadcasting, 1932–2018* (London: Palgrave MacMillan, 2019), 1–22.

111. Broadcasting Arrangements for Meetings of the Preparatory Commission and General Assembly of the United Nations, November 19, 1945, S-0539-0008-35, UN.

112. For an argument that international media experienced a post–World War II expansion see Jonas Brendebach, Martin Herzer, and Heidi Tworek, "Introduction," in *International Organizations and the Media in the Nineteenth and Twentieth Centuries: Exorbitant Expectations,* ed. Jonas Brendebach, Martin Herzer, and Heidi J. S. Tworek (London: Routledge, 2018), 1–16.

113. Glenda Sluga, "Hollywood, the United Nations, and the Long History of Film Communicating Internationalism," in Brendebach, Herzer, and Tworek, *International Organizations and the Media in the Nineteenth and Twentieth Centuries,* 138–57.

114. Meyer Berger, "EVERYTHING READY FOR TODAY'S EVENT: Engineers Solve a 'Dead Spot' Problem—Clean-Up Squad Harvests Toadstools," *New York Times,* October 23, 1946.

115. Doron Galili, *Seeing by Electricity: The Emergence of Television, 1878–1939* (Durham: Duke University Press, 2020), 105–44.

116. Overseas Services Section, "Activities of the Department of Public Information from 23rd to the 27th of September, Weekly News Letter to Field Information Offices Overseas," from Mr. Hanson to Mr. Sharpley, S-0925-0001-08, UN.

117. See, for example, Walter Goodesmith, "Broadcasting House: Technical Design," *The Architectural Review* (1932): 73–78; V. H. Goldsmith, "The Studio Interiors," *The Architectural Review* (1932): 53–64; Leo L. Beranek, "Developments in Studio Design," *Proceedings of the IRE* 38, no. 5 (May 1950): 470–44; Carson & Lundin Architects, "Broacasting Studio: A Novel Acoustical Treatment Developed for NBC," *The Architectural Forum* (February 1946): 98–100; Robert M. Morris and George Nixon, "NBC Studio Design," JASA 8, no. 2 (1936): 81–90; and A. Warren Canney, "Sound Control and Air Conditioning in the N.B.C. Radio City Broadcasting Studios," *Architectural Record* 75, no. 1 (January 1934): 73–92.

118. Shundana Yusaf, *Broadcasting Buildings: Architecture on the Wireless, 1927–1945* (Cambridge: MIT Press, 2014).

119. Canney, "Sound Control and Air Conditioning in the N.B.C. Radio City Broadcasting Studios"; Robert M. Morris and George M. Nixon, "NBC Studio Design," *The Journal of the Acoustical Society of America* 8, no. 1 (1936): 68–69.

120. Emily Ann Thompson, *The Soundscape of Modernity: Architectural Acoustics and the Culture of Listening in America, 1900–1933* (Cambridge: MIT Press, 2002), 263–93, 301–6.

121. From V. J. Gilcher to E. A. Van Name, March 22, 1949, S-0472-0030-03, UN.

122. Overseas Services Section, "Activities of the Department of Public Information from the 6th to the 12th September, Weekly News Letter to Information Offices Overseas," from Mr. Tanser to Mr. Sharpley, S-0925-0001-08, UN.

123. Preliminary Summary of Considerations Affecting Planning of United Nations Headquarters, March 28, 1947, 001-2011-361 T, Ernest Cormier fonds, CCA.

124. Headquarters Planning Office, "Investigation of Space Requirements," July 24, 1947. 001-2011-361 T, Box 2, Ernest Cormier fonds, CCA.

125. For an in-depth discussion of the architecture and technology of film studios, see Brian R. Jacobson, *Studios Before the System: Architecture, Technology, and the Emergence of Cinematic Space* (New York: Columbia University Press, 2015), 23–55.

126. Cory, "Forging a Public Information Policy for the United Nations."

127. Richard N. Swift, "The United Nations and Its Public," *International Organization* 14, no. 1 (1960): 73–74.

128. Especially in relationship to the television question, they recommended that the UN continue to study the creation of new television and studio infrastructure. See Swift, "The United Nations and Its Public," 71.

129. Tamayo, "The United Nations," 189.

130. United Nations Department of Public Information, *Your United Nations* (New York: Department of Public Information, 1952), 9.

131. Walter J. Duschinsky, *TV Stations: A Guide for Architects, Engineers, and Management* (New York: Reinhold, 1954), 7.

132. Duschinsky, *TV Stations*, 11 and 27.

133. Karl W. Deutsch, *The Nerves of Government: Models of Political Communication and Control* (New York: Free Press of Glencoe, 1963), 182.

134. Deutsch, *The Nerves of Government*, 75–76.

4. The Headquarters and the Field

1. Ayala Levin, *Architecture and Development: Israeli Construction in Sub-Saharan Africa and the Settler Colonial Imagination, 1958–1973* (Durham: Duke University Press, 2022), 91–94.

2. Important books that articulate this connection between design and development include Aggregate Architectural History Collaborative, *Architecture in Development: Systems and the Emergence of the Global South* (London: Routledge, 2022); Levin, *Architecture and Development*.

3. Lucia Allais, "Architecture and Mediocracy at UNESCO House," in *Marcel Breuer: Building Global Institutions,* ed. Barry Bergdoll and Jonathan Massey (Zurich: Lars Müller Publishers, 2018), 80–115.

4. Mark Mazower, *Governing the World: The History of an Idea, 1815 to the Present* (New York: Penguin, 2013), 94–115. My understanding of scientific internationalism was greatly shaped by the conference "The Science of Information, 1870–1945: The Universalization of Knowledge in a Utopian Age," University of Pennsylvania, February 23–25, 2017. For an examination of the ways that nineteenth-century movements such as the Saint-Simonians imagined this new world order with engineers at its core and how this technopolitics played out in infrastructural projects they undertook, see Antoine Picon, *Les Saint-simoniens. Raison, imaginaire et utopie* (Paris: Belin, 2002). The scholarship on the unification of sciences in the twentieth century is a rather large field, but for a thorough grasp of the early twentieth-century discourse and practices see Peter Galison, "The Americanization of Unity," *Daedalus* 127, no. 1 (1998): 45–71; and Peter Galison and David J. Stump, eds., *The Disunity of Science: Boundaries, Contexts, and Power* (Stanford: Stanford University Press, 2001).

5. "Resolutions," in International Technical Congress, ed., *Proceedings of the International Technical Congress, Paris 16–21 September 1946* (Paris: World Engineering Conference, 1946), 1: 9–11.

6. In 1950, CIAM initiated an application for consultive status at ECOSOC. Correspondence is available in S-0442-0060-12, UN.

7. Arturo Escobar, *Encountering Development: The Making and Unmaking of the Third World* (Princeton: Princeton University Press, 1995).

8. Katherine Rossy and Samantha Knapton, eds., *Relief and Rehabilitation for a Postwar World?: Humanitarian Intervention and the UNRRA* (London: Bloomsbury Academic, 2021).

9. Letter from F. Chalmers Wright to Sir Raphael Cilento, June 8, 1947, S-0921-0005-06, UN. For an overview of Jacob Crane's advisory role at the UN after 1952 see A. Scott Henderson, *Housing and the Democratic Ideal: The Life and Thought of Charles Abrams* (New York: Columbia University Press, 2000), 173–92.

10. Jacob Crane, "Preliminary Report on A Program of International Cooperation in Housing and Urbanism," December 20, 1946, S-0921-0005-06, UN.

11. See S-0441-0285-21780, UN.

12. For some examples, see the valuable map in Allison Cavanagh, *Sociology in the Age of the Internet* (New Delhi: Tata McGraw-Hill, 2010), 23–47. For a discussion of network analysis in international institutions, see Emilie M. Hafner-Burton, Miles Kahler, and Alexander H. Montgomery, "Network Analysis for International Relations," *International Organization* 63, no. 3 (2009): 559–92.

13. Manuel Castells, *The Rise of the Network Society* (Malden, Mass.: Wiley-Blackwell, 2010), 408–9, 442–45.

14. Michael Hardt and Antonio Negri, *Empire* (Cambridge: Harvard University Press, 2001), 32–33.

15. Hugh L. Keenleyside, *International Aid: A Summary, with Special Reference to the Programmes of the United Nations* (New York: James H. Heineman, 1966), 202–48.

16. Richard I. Miller, "Technical Assistance and the UN," *The Clearing House* 33, no. 4 (1958): 198–201; Philip M. Glick, "The Choice of Instruments for Technical Co-Operation," *The Annals of the American Academy of Political and Social Science* 323 (1959): 59–67.

17. This categorization of problem areas exists in Crane's reports. See, for example, Jacob Crane, "Papers on Housing and Town Planning," April 23, 1947, SA/340/202, UN.

18. Letter from Hugh Keenleyside, Director General, Technical Assistance Administration, to John H. E. Fried, January 15, 1952, S-0441-0285-21782, UN.

19. Hugh L. Keenleyside, "U.N. Technical Assistance Programme," *Pakistan Horizon* 5, no. 1 (1952): 33–38.

20. Peter Mandler, "One World, Many Cultures: Margaret Mead and the Limits to Cold War Anthropology," *History Workshop Journal*, no. 68 (2009): 149–72.

21. Henry W. Holmes et al., eds., *Fundamental Education: Common Ground for All Peoples. Report of a Special Committee to the Preparatory Commission of the United Nations Educational, Scientific and Cultural Organization* (New York: The Macmillan Company, 1947), 12; and Ronald R. Kline, *The Cybernetics Moment: Or Why We Call Our Age the Information Age* (Baltimore: John Hopkins University Press, 2015), 37–50.

22. Here I am referring to Said's definition of orientalism as a discourse fundamental to European epistemologies. See Edward W. Said, *Orientalism* (New York: Pantheon Books, 1978), 1–3. For a discussion of orientalism in architecture, see Mark Crinson, *Empire Building: Orientalism and Victorian Architecture* (London: Routledge, 1996).

23. Margaret Mead, "Fundamental Education and Cultural Values" in Holmes et al., eds., *Fundamental Education,* 132–55.

24. Tibor Mende, "Report on Patzcuaro: One of the World's Most Unusual Social Experiments," *Courier* V, no. 2 (February 1952): 3–4.

25. Graham Beckel and Felice Lee, *Workshops for the World: The United Nations Family of Agencies* (New York: Abelard-Schuman, 1954), 93–103.

26. This is an argument most recently put together by Stephen Legg et al., eds., *Placing Internationalism: International Conferences and the Making of the Modern World* (London:

Bloomsbury Academic, 2022), 1–10. Conferences also make a frequent appearance in Karen Gram-Skjoldager, Haakon A. Ikonomou, and Torsten Kahlert, eds., *Organizing the 20th-Century World: International Organizations and the Emergence of International Public Administration, 1920–1960s* (London: Bloomsbury Academic, 2022). For an example of the role they played see one essay in this volume: Amy L. Sayward, "Food and Nutrition: Expertise Across International Epistemic Communities and Organizations, 1919–1963," 109–25.

27. "The Greatest Housing Problem of the World: Survey of Housing Conditions in South and South East Asia," *UN Bulletin*, July 1, 1951.

28. Partha Chatterjee, *Empire and Nation: Selected Essays,* ed. Nivedita Menon (New York: Columbia University Press, 2016), 241–46, 249; Nikhil Menon, *Planning Democracy: Modern India's Quest for Development* (Cambridge: Cambridge University Press, 2022), 119–64.

29. Gyan Prakash, *Another Reason: Science and the Imagination of Modern India* (Princeton: Princeton University Press, 1999), 168–98.

30. Ateya Khorakiwala, "The Well-Fed Subject: Modern Architecture in the Quantitative State, India (1943–1984)" (PhD diss., Harvard University, 2017).

31. Letter from H. K. Sang to P. S. Lokanathan, January 31, 1949, S-0932-0010-07, UN; and Memorandum from Jaqueline Tyrwhitt to N. P. Dube, June 23, 1953, TyJ/31/9, Royal Institute of British Architects (RIBA).

32. The Supplementary Agreement notes that the Basic Agreement was signed on April 2, 1952. See Supplementary Agreement No. 7 to the Basic Agreement concerning Technical Assistance between the United Nations and the Government of India, October 30, 1953, TyJ/31/9, RIBA. For a discussion of the event within the context of India and development, see Peter Scriver and Amit Srivastava, *India* (London: Reaktion Books, 2015); for an examination of the exhibition within Tyrwhitt's larger planning research, see Ellen Shoshkes, *Jaqueline Tyrwhitt: A Transnational Life in Urban Planning and Design* (London: Ashgate, 2013), 165–78; and, for a close look at the seminar and exhibition within the project of low-cost housing and austerity see Farhan Karim, *Of Greater Dignity than Riches: Austerity and Housing Design in Postcolonial India* (Pittsburgh: University of Pittsburgh, 2019), 121–68.

33. Ernest Weissmann, "E. Weissmann: Professional Life," Box 38, Weissmann Papers. Tamara Bjazic Klarin offers a thorough study of Weissmann's early career prior to his arrival in the United States in *Ernest Weissmann: društveno angažirana arhitektura, 1926–1939 [Socially engaged architecture, 1926–1939]* (Zagreb: Hrvatska akademija znanosti i umjetnosti, 2015).

34. M. Ijlal Muzaffar, "Boundary Games: Ecochard, Doxiadis, and the Refugee Housing Projects under Military Rule in Pakistan, 1953–1959," in *Governing by Design*, ed. Aggregate (Pittsburgh: University of Pittsburgh Press, 2012), 169.

35. Regional Seminars on Social Welfare, February 23, 1950, S-0921-0029-01, UN. For more on the place of the workshop in secondary and professional education see A. S. Barr, "Every School a Workshop," *The Journal of Educational Research* 34, no. 8 (1941): 613–15; K. W. Heaton et al., *Professional Education for Experienced Teachers: The Program of the Summer Workshop* (Chicago: University of Chicago Press, 1941).

36. Chapter IV—Social Welfare Seminars, February 11, 1952, S-0921-0046-06, UN.

37. Regional Seminars on Social Welfare, February 23, 1950, S-0921-0029-01, UN.

38. J. Guiton, "Studying Together in International Seminars: Short History of Inter-

national Seminars," September 15, 1949, Regional Seminars on Social Welfare, February 23, 1950, S-0921-0029-01, UN. For more on the place of workshop in secondary and professional education see A. S. Barr, "Every School a Workshop," *The Journal of Educational Research* 34, no. 8 (1941): 613–15; K. W. Heaton et al., *Professional Education for Experienced Teachers: The Program of the Summer Workshop* (Chicago: University of Chicago Press, 1941).

39. Regional Seminars on Social Welfare, February 23, 1950, S-0921-0029-01, UN.

40. Mark Wigley remarks on Tyrwhitt's networking capacities in "Network Fever," *Grey Room,* no. 4 (Summer 2001): 83–122.

41. Shoshkes's thorough account of Jaqueline Tyrwhitt's life and work demonstrates the important role she played in the post–World War II planning community. See Shoshkes, *Jaqueline Tyrwhitt;* Ellen Shoshkes, "Jaqueline Tyrwhitt and the Internationalization of Planning Education," in *Urban Planning Education: Beginnings, Global Movement and Future Prospects,* ed. Andrea I. Frank and Christopher Silver (Berlin: Springer, 2018), 65–80. For more details of the war correspondence course, see Ines Maria Zalduendo, "Jaqueline Tyrwhitt's Correspondence Courses: Town Planning in the Trenches," 2005, https://dash.harvard.edu/handle/1/13442987.

42. The seminar and exhibition involved Bodiansky, Candilis, Ecochard, and Honegger representing CIAM, while Abrams, Weissmann, Milhaud, and Reiner represented the UN. See "TA Project/Morocco: Study and Training Group on Cooperative and Aided Self-help Housing and Community Improvement, September 22, 1952," 42-JT-12–399/404, gta Archives, ETH.

43. Letter from W. Gurney to Jaqueline Tyrwhitt, August 15, 1952, TyJ/48/2, RIBA.

44. Shoshkes, *Jaqueline Tyrwhitt*, 102–4.

45. Letter from Eleanor Hinder to Dr. Steinig, May 14, 1953, TyJ/31/9, RIBA.

46. United Nations, "The Delhi Seminar on Housing & Planning for South East Asia, 1954, Parts II and III," *Housing & Town Planning Bulletin* 9, December 9, 1954, 2, TyJ/29/2, RIBA.

47. For example, the TAA asked her to include Manila in her trip so as to attract the government of the Philippines. See letter from Marcel Schwob to Jaqueline Tyrwhitt, August 26, 1953, TyJ/31/9, RIBA.

48. Some correspondence includes: letter from Eleanor Emery to Jaqueline Tyrwhitt, August 31, 1953, TyJ/31/8, RIBA; Plane Madras/Bangalore, November 21, 1953, TyJ/31/4, RIBA; and letter from N. P. Dube to Dr. Steinig, July 1, 1953, TyJ/31/9, RIBA.

49. Letter from Minnette de Silva to Jaqueline Tyrwhitt, November 16, 1953, 42-JT-18–04, gta Archives, ETH. For more on *Marg,* see Rachel Lee and Kathleen James-Chakraborty, "*Marg* Magazine: A Tryst with Architectural Modernity; Modern Architecture as Seen from an Independent India," *ABE Journal. Architecture beyond Europe* 1 (May 1, 2012), http://journals.openedition.org/abe/623.

50. John P. Humphrey, director of the UN Division of Human Rights, used this description while advocating for a human rights program targeting decolonized countries. He first presented his proposal at the Society for Ethical Culture on December 10, 1952 (copy in S-0917-0009-03, UN). See John P. Humphrey, *Human Rights & the United Nations: A Great Adventure* (Dobbs Ferry, N.Y.: Transnational Publishers, 1984), 204.

51. C. A. Doxiadis, "Manual of Instructions," United Nations, P.3389U, 34705, Constantinos A. Doxiadis Archives, Athens, Greece.

52. Letter from Jaqueline Tyrwhitt to Eleanor Hinder, June 19, 1953, TyJ/31/9, RIBA.

53. Housing and Town and Country Planning Section, Department of Social Affairs, United Nations, United Nations Regional Seminar on Housing and Community Improvement, New Delhi, India, 20 January–17 February 1954, TyJ/28/3, RIBA.

54. Letter to Eleanor Hinder, June 19, 1953, TyJ/31/9, RIBA; letter from Jaqueline Tyrwhitt, July 14, 1953; and letter from Eleanor Hinder to Jaqueline Tyrwhitt, November 13, 1953, TyJ/31/9, RIBA.

55. Jaqueline Tyrwhitt, "History of UN Seminar on Housing & Community Improvement," May 3, 1954, TyJ/32/1, RIBA.

56. Letter from Jaqueline Tyrwhitt to Mr. Ebrahim al Kazi, September 4, 1953, Tyj/31/3, RIBA; and letter from H. L. Keenleyside to Indian Minister of Foreign Affairs, June 16, 1953, TyJ/31/9, RIBA.

57. The set is here: 43-5-6-10–4-F1; 43-5-6-10–4-F3, and 43-5-6-10–4-F4, gta Archives, ETH.

58. Untitled document, May 19, 1953, TyJ/31/9, RIBA.

59. United Nations, *Social Progress through Community Development* (New York: United Nations Bureau of Social Affairs), 37–39. For a comprehensive history of the United States' community development projects initiatives, see Daniel Immerwahr, *Thinking Small: The United States and the Lure of Community Development* (Cambridge: Harvard University Press, 2015).

60. Leonardo Zuccaro Marchi, "CIAM 8—The Heart of the City as the Symbolical Resilience of the City," in *International Planning History Society Proceedings,* ed. Carola Hein (Delft: TU Delft, 2016), 2:135.

61. Eric Paul Mumford, *The CIAM Discourse on Urbanism, 1928–1960* (Cambridge: MIT Press, 2000), 201–14.

62. Historian Gregor Paulsson proposed a genealogy of cores that went back to archetypal spaces of the history of the West. Giedion also mobilized a similar set of Western spaces in his "Historical Background to the Core." See Gregor Paulsson, "The Past and the Present," and Sigfried Giedion, "Historical Background to the Core," in *CIAM 8: The Heart of the City: Towards the Humanisation of Urban Life,* ed. Jaqueline Tyrwhitt, Josep Lluís Sert, and Ernesto N. Rogers (London: Lund Humphries, 1952), 17–29.

63. Sigfried Giedion, "The Need for a New Monumentality," in *New Architecture and City Planning: A Symposium,* ed. Paul Zucker (New York: Philosophical Library, 1944). Daniel M. Abramson has argued for this in "Fairgrounds, Civic Centers, and Citizenship," Department of Art History and Program for Urban Design and Architecture, New York University, April 19, 2021.

64. Sert is cited in Mumford, *The CIAM Discourse on Urbanism,* 206–7.

65. Tyrwhitt, Sert, and Rogers, *CIAM [8],* 8.

66. Jaqueline Tyrwhitt, "Cores with the Urban Constellation," in Tyrwhitt, Sert, and Rogers, *CIAM [8],* 103.

67. Letter from Jaqueline Tyrwhitt to Eleanor Hinder, November 9, 1953; and letter from Eleanor Hinder to Jaqueline Tyrwhitt, December 23, 1953, TyJ/31/9, RIBA.

68. Technical Assistance Programme, United Nations Seminar on Housing and Community Improvement in Asia and the Far East, New Delhi, India, January 21–February 1954, December 1, 1954, TyJ/28/3, RIBA.

69. Memorandum from Jaqueline Tyrwhitt to N. P. Dube, June 23, 1953, TyJ/31/9, RIBA.

70. Jaqueline Tyrwhitt, "Many Problems in the Evolution of the Ideal Village," *The Stateman Engineering Feature,* n.d., TyJ/39/2, RIBA

71. I borrow the term from Richard G. Fox, who has spoken in length about Gandhi's and his disciples' critique of Western focus on industrialization and progress as a utopian project. See *Gandhian Utopia: Experiments with Culture* (Boston: Beacon Press, 1989), 37–39.

72. Mohandas Gandhi, *Village Swaraj* (Ahmedabad, India: Navajivan Publishing House, 1962), 30–32.

73. Ateya Khorakiwala, *The Well-Tempered Environment: Modern Architecture in the Quantitative State, India (1943–1984)* (PhD diss., Harvard University, 2016).

74. This is an argument advanced most prominently by Partha Chatterjee in his criticism of Sarvepalli Gopal's biography of Nehru. See *A Possible India: Essays in Political Criticism* (Delhi: Oxford University Press, 1998), 31–34, 40–50. See also M. S. Swaminathan, "Jawaharlal Nehru and Agriculture in Independent India," *Current Science* 59, no. 6 (1990): 303–7.

75. Alice Thorner, "Nehru, Albert Mayer, and Origins of Community Projects," *Economic and Political Weekly* 16, no. 4 (1981): 117–20; and Nicole Sackley, "Village Models: Etawah, India, and the Making and Remaking of Development in the Early Cold War," *Diplomatic History* 37, no. 4 (September 2013): 749–78.

76. For a historical examination of the project see Sackley, "Village Models"; and Nick Cullather, *The Hungry World: America's Cold War Battle Against Poverty in Asia* (Cambridge: Harvard University Press, 2013), 80–94.

77. Albert Mayer, *Pilot Project, India: The Story of Rural Development at Etawah, Uttar Pradesh* (Berkeley: University of California Press, 1958), 12–29.

78. Karim offers a thorough analysis of the role that the exhibition played in the production of postcolonial Indian modernity, particularly in relationship to low-cost housing, in *Of Greater Dignity than Riches,* 121–68.

79. See especially Jaqueline Tyrwhitt and Patrick Geddes, *Patrick Geddes in India* (London: Lund Humphries, 1947), 57, 62, 64, 84–85.

80. Letter from Eleanor Hinder to P. S. Lokanathan, June 3, 1953, TyJ/31/9, RIBA.

81. Memorandum from Jaqueline Tyrwhitt to N. P. Dube, June 23, 1953, TyJ/31/9, RIBA.

82. Jaqueline Tyrwhitt, "Creation of the Village Centre (Delhi)," *Ekistics* 52, no. 314/315 (1985): 431.

83. Jaqueline Tyrwhitt, "Many Problems in the Evolution of the Ideal Village," *The Statesman Engineering Feature,* n.d., TyJ/39/2, RIBA

84. Memorandum from Jaqueline Tyrwhitt to N. P. Dube, June 23, 1953, TyJ/31/9, RIBA.

85. Letter from Jaqueline Tyrwhitt to Eleanor Hinder, June 10, 1953, TyJ/31/9, RIBA.

86. R. B. Gupta, "Housing and Community Improvement Programmes," in *UN Housing & Community Improvement Seminar,* New Delhi, 1954, Box 36030, Doxiadis Archives.

87. N. Krishnaswami, "Housing in India & 5 Year Plan," in *UN Housing & Community Improvement Seminar,* New Delhi, 1954, Box 36030, Doxiadis Archives.

88. N. Krishnaswami, "Housing in India & 5 Year Plan."

89. Joseph M. Neufeld, "Community Core," in *UN Housing & Community Improvement Seminar,* New Delhi, 1954, Box 36030, Doxiadis Archives.

90. Much of this documentation has been hard to unearth at the UN archives for a multitude of reasons: archiving systems kept changing; when offices closed, files were lost in the transfer; finding aids were designed to construct departmental histories and not document events.

91. Jaqueline Tyrwhitt Notes, July 14, 1953, TyJ/31/9, RIBA.

92. United Nations Housing & Community Improvement, Memorandum, February 2, 1954, TyJ/29/3, RIBA.

93. Letter from Eleanor Hinder to Jaqueline Tyrwhitt, January 29, 1954. TyJ/31/9, RIBA.

94. Marshall McLuhan, *The Gutenberg Galaxy* (Toronto: University of Toronto Press, 1962). Ginger Nolan offers a critique in *The Neocolonialism of the Global Village* (Minneapolis: University of Minnesota Press, 2018). For the historical connections between McLuhan's "global village" and Tyrwhitt's "village center," see Olga Touloumi, "Globalizing the Village: Development Media, Jaqueline Tyrwhitt, and the United Nations in India," in *Architecture in Development: Systems and the Emergence of the Global South,* ed. Aggregate (London: Routledge, 2022), 259–77.

95. See *Tropical Housing & Planning Monthly Bulletin* 3 (October 1955), Doxiadis Archives.

96. United Nations Regional Seminar on Housing and Community Improvement, Final Draft of Conclusions. TyJ/28/3, RIBA.

97. Margaret Mead and Paul Byers, *The Small Conference: An Innovation in Communication* (The Hague: Mouton, 1968), v.

98. Mead and Byers, *The Small Conference,* vi.

99. Mead and Byers, *The Small Conference,* 4.

100. Mead and Byers, *The Small Conference,* 5.

Epilogue

1. Johnson cited in Christopher E. M. Pearson, *Designing UNESCO: Art, Architecture and International Politics at Mid-Century* (London: Routledge, 2010), 220n62.

2. The International Council at the Museum of Modern Art, Press Release, "Design for US Room at UNESCO Headquarters Described by Architects," August 5, 1958, MoMA Archives; Helen M. Franc, "The Early Years of the International Program and Council," in *The Museum of Modern Art at Mid-Century: At Home and Abroad,* ed. John Elderfield (New York: The Museum of Modern Art, 1994), 131–32; Pearson, *Designing UNESCO,* 213.

3. "Gifts from 19 Nations," *The UNESCO Courier: A Window Open to the World* XI, no. 11 (November 1958): 28; "Ultra-Modern Meeting Place," *The UNESCO Courier: A Window Open to the World* XI, no. 11 (November 1958): 25.

4. Pearson, *Designing UNESCO,* 113–223; Lucia Allais, "Architecture and Mediocracy at UNESCO House," in *Marcel Breuer: Building Global Institutions,* ed. Barry Bergdoll and Jonathan Massey (Zurich: Lars Müller Publishers, 2018), 81–115.

5. Joëlle Kuntz, *Genève internationale: 100 ans d'architecture* (Geneva: Editions Slatkine, 2017), 91–93.

6. Kuntz, *Genève internationale,* 104–12.

7. Kuntz, *Genève internationale,* 119–28.

8. The World Intellectual Property Organization (1978), the World Meteorological Organization (1999), the European Organization for Nuclear Research (2002), and the Maison de la paix (2014).

9. In 1984 ECLA changed its name to Economic Commission for Latin America and the Caribbean (ECLAC).

10. Emilio Duhart, "United Nations Building, Santiago, Chile," *Architectural Design* 37 (January 1967): 33–37.

11. Duhart, "United Nations Building, Santiago, Chile," 36.

12. Letter from Edgar Kaufmann Jr. to Max Abramovitz, May 10, 1950, S-0472-0001-13, UN.

13. Letter from George R. Collins to Glenn Bennett, July 31, 1950, S-0472-0001-13, UN.

14. Letter from Lemuel C. Dillenback to Michael M. Harris, October 23, 1950, S-0472-0001-13, UN.

15. Letter from Lee Clemmer to Glenn Bennett, January 13, 1951, S-0472-0001-13, UN.

16. A French, Norwegian, and Japanese delegation toured the headquarters as early as 1951. See S-0472-0001-13, UN.

17. Correspondence between the Rockefellers and Chase Manhattan Bank can be found in SIII-2Q Box 28, Folder 242, The Rockefeller Archive Center, Sleepy Hollow, New York.

18. Arthur Drexler, *Buildings for Business and Government. Exhibition: February 25–April 28, 1957* (New York: Museum of Modern Art, 1957), 6, https://www.moma.org/documents/moma_catalogue_3349_300190165.pdf.

19. Marcial Tamayo, "The United Nations: A Rich Source of Information," in *The Diplomatic Persuaders: New Role of the Mass Media in International Relations,* ed. John Lee (New York: Wiley, 1968), 194–95; Dexter Fergie, "Stewards of Internationalism: United Nations Tour Guides, Gender, and Public Diplomacy, 1952–1977," *Diplomatic History,* forthcoming.

20. Anastasia Remes, "Europe at the Expo: The Pavilions of the European Community in Universal Expositions" (PhD diss., European University Institute, 2022); Anastasia Remes, "Exhibiting European Integration at Expo 58: The European Coal and Steel Community Pavilion," in *World Fairs and the Global Moulding of National Identities: International Exhibitions as Cultural Platforms, 1851–1958,* ed. Joep Leerssen and Eric Storm (Leiden: Brill, 2021), 375–403; Rika Devos, Mil De Kooning, and Geert Bekaert, eds., *L'architecture moderne à l'Expo 58: pour un monde plus humain* (Brussels: Dexia/Fonds Mercator, 2006).

21. Remes, "Exhibiting European Integration," 396.

22. This is an argument made by Nathalie Tousignant, "Geopolitics and Spatiality at Expo 58: The International, Foreign and Belgian Colonial Sections," in *Expo 58: Between Utopia and Reality,* ed. Gonzague Pluvinage (Brussels: Editions Racine, 2008), 95–118. See David Allen, "International Exhibitionism: The League of Nations at the New York World's Fair," in *International Organizations and the Media in the Nineteenth and Twentieth Centuries: Exorbitant Expectations,* ed. Jonas Brendebach, Martin Herzer, and Heidi J. S. Tworek (London: Routledge, 2018), 91–116; Jonathan Voges, "The International Institute for Intellectual Co-Operation at the World Fair 1937 in Paris: Profiling Internationalism in a 'Hyper-Nationalistic' Context?," in Leerssen and Storm, *World Fairs,* 357–74; Jonathan Voges, "Scientific Internationalism in a Time of Crisis: The Month of Intellectual Cooperation at the 1937 Paris World Fair," in *Placing Internationalism: International Conferences and the Making of the Modern World,* ed. Stephen Legg et al. (London: Bloomsbury Academic, 2022), 104–17.

23. Quote found in Tousignant, "Geopolitics and Spatiality at Expo 58," 103.

24. Glenda Sluga, "Hollywood, the United Nations, and the Long History of Film Communicating Internationalism," in Brendebach, Herzer, and Tworek, *International Organizations,* 138–57.

25. Sluga, "Hollywood, the United Nations," 138–57.

26. Nico Israel, "Serving Man: The United Nations Art Collection, Mid-Century Modernisms, and the Apparition of Universality," *Modernism / Modernity* 4, no. 4 (2020), https://modernismmodernity.org/articles/israel-serving-man.

27. Mark D. Alleyne, *Global Lies?: Propaganda, the UN and World Order* (London: Palgrave MacMillan, 2003), 78–86.

28. "History of National Model United Nations," n.d., https://www.nmun.org/assets/documents/about-nmun/mission-and-history/nmun-history.pdf.

29. Seth Center argues that the UN General Assembly facilitated advocacy for non-aligned member states. See "Supranational Public Diplomacy: The Evolution of the UN Department of Public Information and the Rise of Third World Advocacy," in *The United States and Public Diplomacy: New Directions in Cultural and International History,* ed. Kenneth A. Osgood and Brian C. Etheridge (Leiden: Martinus Nijhoff, 2010), 135–64.

30. Dubravka Sekulić, "Non-Aligned (Round) Table and Its Discontents" (Rijeka, 2021).

Index

Page numbers in italics refer to figures.

Olga Touloumi is associate professor of architectural history at Bard College. She is coeditor of *Computer Architectures: Constructing the Common Ground*.